NARCOMEDIA

Latinx: The Future Is Now
A series edited by Lorgia García-Peña and Nicole Guidotti-Hernández

BOOKS IN THE SERIES

Rebeca L. Hey-Colón, *Channeling Knowledges: Water and Afro-Diasporic Spirits in Latinx and Caribbean Worlds*

Tatiana Reinoza, *Reclaiming the Americas: Latinx Art and the Politics of Territory*

Kristy L. Ulibarri, *Visible Borders, Invisible Economies: Living Death in Latinx Narratives*

Marisel C. Moreno, *Crossing Waters: Undocumented Migration in Hispanophone Caribbean and Latinx Literature and Art*

Yajaira M. Padilla, *From Threatening Guerrillas to Forever Illegals: US Central Americans and the Politics of Non-Belonging*

Francisco J. Galarte, *Brown Trans Figurations: Rethinking Race, Gender, and Sexuality in Chicanx/Latinx Studies*

NARCOMEDIA
Latinidad, Popular Culture, and America's War on Drugs

Jason Ruiz

University of Texas Press Austin

Copyright © 2023 by the University of Texas Press
All rights reserved
Printed in the United States of America
First edition, 2023

Requests for permission to reproduce material from this work should be sent to:
Permissions
University of Texas Press
P.O. Box 7819
Austin, TX 78713-7819
utpress.utexas.edu

♾ The paper used in this book meets the minimum requirements of ANSI/NISO Z39.48-1992 (R1997) (Permanence of Paper).

Library of Congress Cataloging-in-Publication Data

Names: Ruiz, Jason, author.
Title: Narcomedia : latinidad, popular culture, and America's War on Drugs / Jason Ruiz.
Description: First edition. | Austin : University of Texas Press, 2023. | Series: Latinx: the future is now | Includes bibliographical references and index.
 Identifiers: LCCN 2022062255 (print)
LCCN 2022062256 (ebook)
ISBN 978-1-4773-2818-7 (hardcover)
ISBN 978-1-4773-2819-4 (paperback)
ISBN 978-1-4773-2820-0 (PDF)
ISBN 978-1-4773-2821-7 (ePub)
Subjects: LCSH: Latin Americans in motion pictures. | Drug traffic in motion pictures. | Drug control—United States. | Latin America—In motion pictures. | Latin America—On television. | Latin America—In popular culture.
Classification: LCC PN1995.9.L37 R85 2023 (print) | LCC PN1995.9.L37 (ebook) | DDC 791.43/628—dc23/eng/2023/eng/20230413
LC record available at https://lccn.loc.gov/2022062255
LC ebook record available at https://lccn.loc.gov/2022062256

doi:10.7560/328187

For Juangui

CONTENTS

Introduction 1

CHAPTER 1. **"SAY GOODNIGHT TO THE BAD GUY"**
South Florida, Cocaine, and the Many Faces of Scarface *15*

CHAPTER 2. **MIAMI VICES**
Whiteness and Otherness in Representing the Criminalized City 45

CHAPTER 3. **"THE MOST ALIVE DEAD MAN IN THE WORLD"**
Plotting the Death of Pablo Escobar 75

CHAPTER 4. **DANCING TOWARD REVENGE**
Queer Representation and What It Means to Be Seen in Narcomedia 101

CHAPTER 5. **DARK MATTERS**
Breaking Bad and the Suburban Crime Drama 125

CHAPTER 6. **BAD HOMBRES**
Narcomedia at the US-Mexico Border 147

CHAPTER 7. **FROM PUBLIC ENEMY TO GLOBAL MEDIA COMMODITY**
Pablo Escobar Transformed 173

EPILOGUE. **"IT'S TIME FOR A WHITE MAN TO LEAVE THE BUILDING"**
Centering Latinidad in Narcomedia 199

Acknowledgments 205

Notes 209

Select Filmography 232

Bibliography 234

Index 242

NARCOMEDIA

INTRODUCTION

For a big portion of my childhood in the 1980s, I slept in front of the television. I would typically click on the TV after school, leave it blaring through my homework and dinner, fall asleep in the TV room, and continue with the morning shows when I woke up. It was there, in front of the always-on television, that I learned a lot of what I know about drugs. In retrospect, I doubt that I tuned in to any of Ronald or Nancy Reagan's televised talks about the dangers of drug use or to George H. W. Bush's telecast declaring war on crack in 1989, but I do remember seeing dozens of *After School Specials* and "very special episodes" of my favorite sitcoms and cartoons that repeated Mrs. Reagan's message: If you're ever offered drugs, just say no. Like many people my age who grew up in the United States, I heard this message reinforced in my elementary and middle schools, including with visits from a local police officer charged with conveying the D.A.R.E. (Drug Abuse Resistance Education) curriculum.

But despite these efforts, television is really how I internalized a resolve to Just Say No. Mrs. Reagan's campaign, conceived by ad executives, launched in 1982, when I was five, and included crossover appearances and targeted messages in shows aimed at kids like me for years to come. I listened carefully when G.I. Joe or He-Man warned about the dangers of ever trying drugs in their post-episode lectures to kids, and I learned alongside Punky Brewster and Arnold Jackson when people in their worlds succumbed to the lure of drugs. I fretted over scrambling my brains on drugs because of a public service announcement from the Partnership for a Drug-Free America that seemed to air during every commercial break for a chunk of the late eighties. When I watched more adult fare alongside my parents, like *Hill Street Blues* or *Cagney & Lacey*, the lessons became less didactic but remained cautionary. In the rare instances in which I could sneak viewings of grittier TV movies, the lessons were harder to follow, but drugs still seemed scary—and, if I'm honest, I am still nervous around hard drugs in part because of movie and TV depictions I saw as a kid. It was lost on me then that, as a Latinx kid growing up in an inner city, I more closely resembled the bad guys than the innocent victims of drug addiction and violence in these TV narratives.

In more recent years, as an academic, I have remained an omnivorous consumer of television (if not narcotics) and have marveled as I saw the medium transform from something that many of my grad school peers and I binged as a secret stress reliever to a marker of good taste at faculty cocktail parties. In my experience, this started with *The Wire*, an early iteration of "prestige TV" that was a darling of the academic set and allowed habitual watchers like me to come clean about how much TV we were watching. Drugs also happened to have an important role in the series. TV shows have grown far more narratively complex over the past few decades, but drugs have remained a staple of TV programming in the prestige television and streaming eras. In fact, recent TV has seen an explosion of shows that depict the drug trade and those who take part in it, with series set in a vast array of different milieus. Unsurprisingly to anyone interested in race and pop culture, the narratives and settings have changed, but the bad guys look and sound the same. I noticed this first as a fan of several series, and now, as a scholar, I want to know how things got this way and what it means that we continuously frame Latinxs and Latin Americans as our enemies in the War on Drugs.

DEFINING NARCOMEDIA

This book brings together and analyzes a large body of cultural texts that I call "narcomedia." Anthropologist Paul K. Eiss has used this term to refer to communication forms that emerge from drug trafficking. These include, as Eiss posits, *narcomensajes* (narcomessages), *narcomantas* (narcosheets, used to convey messages terrorizing one's enemies), *narcovideos*, and other modes of threats or retribution from drug cartels to their enemies, the press, or the general public.[1] Inspired by Eiss, but also as a gentle challenge, I want to suggest that we can extend the term to refer beyond the modes of communication *within* the world of narcotrafficking to those *about* that demimonde. This book argues that narcomedia should be used more expansively and that it can more broadly refer to a wide variety of cultural forms that circulate in popular culture: crime thriller movies, investigative journalism, tell-all confessional memoirs, telenovelas, so-called prestige television series, *corridos* and pop songs, big-budget Hollywood movies and low-budget art house films, memes and gifs, and others. As media forms, these sometimes have little in common, but narcomedia serves as a cultural location—a body of cultural texts—at which they intersect. Thus, I see narcomedia as a category for critical analysis more than a unified cultural or artistic movement.[2] Most importantly, I understand narcomedia texts as weapons in shaping public opinion about the War on Drugs and those implicated in the drug trade.

I want to stress that I do not take the "narco" in narcomedia lightly. Across Latin America, the term is a powerful signifier. The labeling of some countries as "narco states" at various points in their recent histories, for example, is a devastating way to describe a political collapse to the point that cartels and drug lords do the actual governing (something not limited to Latin America). And adding "narco" to another word in Spanish is a common practice to make that word sound more dangerous or threatening or tacky. (My Colombian in-laws call a certain model of the car brand a *narcotoyota*, which probably connotes all three.) By attaching "narco" to "media," I do not intend to imply that the word is an abstraction or a media creation. I do so to signal that various media forms are where societies and cultures unpack what it means to call something or someone "narco," with all the baggage that comes from doing so. I hope, in fact, that this book will be useful to those interested in the realpolitik of drugs and crime, helping them see that media narratives connect in startling and direct ways to how we police and punish "offenders" in our ongoing War on Drugs.

THE WAR ON DRUGS AND POPULAR CULTURE

The US War on Drugs has cost the US government more than $1 trillion over the past five decades, but no one can make a convincing case for its efficacy.[3] It has always been characterized by zero tolerance policies and overzealous policing and sentencing. As economist Diane Coyle put it, "there is no chance of a zero-tolerance policy working when so many citizens of our countries use illegal drugs. A law that more than one in five people (almost one in three Americans over the age of twelve) breaks at some point in their lives, and none of their friends will ever report them for, is a failing law."[4] Furthermore, as just about every serious-minded policy analysis has shown, prohibition leads to increased profits because criminal organizations control the market worldwide. This, in turn, always leads to more violence. The extremity of US prohibition has undermined itself in this way since drugs began to be criminalized in the early twentieth century. Regardless of the faulty logic of draconian drug policies, it is inarguable that the narcotics trade has only increased in the past half-century.

According to many sources, illegal drugs are the world's largest industry. Firm numbers are notoriously difficult to come by, but most governmental and non-governmental organizations estimate that drug trafficking has an annual value in the hundreds of billions of dollars.[5]

The spectacular failures of the War on Drugs hardly need repeating here. Instead, I am interested in how popular culture has narrated the drug trade and attempts at interdiction—and most especially in how those narratives intersect with dominant views of Latinos and latinidad. In this sense, I am following scholars such as Curtis Marez, who has argued that "mass media representations of drug traffic and enforcement have helped to generate powerful ideas about state power, foreign policy, and transnational capitalism" and that "drug-war literature, music, television, and films have become privileged cultural forms for reflecting upon larger political-economic power relations in the Americas."[6] Marez's *Drug Wars* is an invaluable predecessor to this book, but in *Narcomedia*, I aim to explore more specifically how popular culture has connected drugs with latinidad since the early 1980s. I see media representations as serving as a cultural arm of the War on Drugs.

I am not alone in this, of course. In fact, the US government has engaged extensively in both partnership and conflict with various media industries all through the course of the War on Drugs. In 1985, when I was addicted to *Punky Brewster* and *Diff'rent Strokes*, the Senate was investigating the role of the entertainment industry in "deglamorizing" drug use. A hearing on March 20 of that year included testimony from Gerald McRaney, who was then starring on CBS's *Simon & Simon*, as well as various medical and legal professionals.[7] This was one of several instances, starting in the 1970s, in which the federal government investigated whether it could and should work with the entertainment industry to influence how Americans understood drugs.

My aim in this book is not to pound yet another nail in the coffin of the War on Drugs. I start from a position that the War on Drugs has been alternately misguided, ineffectual, and imperialistic, so I do not debate its philosophies or tactics. Instead, I aim to explore how popular culture has both reflected and shaped the policies and practices, however problematic, of the War on Drugs. I am not arguing for a direct cause-effect relationship between pop culture texts and the War on Drugs (e.g., I am not attempting to prove that, say, *Miami Vice* caused Plan Colombia, the bilateral agreement between the United States and Colombia that militarized the War on Drugs in South America). Rather, I suggest that systems of knowledge about what drugs are, how we should prevent their use, and who is responsible for America's drug problems are all interconnected and that a major point of intersection for these knowledge systems is to be found in popular culture.

It is obvious by now that television is a particularly important medium to the cultural history I construct in this book. There are several reasons why TV, specifically scripted television, is so central to my argument. First, there is simply a lot of TV with which to work. Over the course of the War on Drugs, the means of making and receiving televisual narratives changed dramatically, but since the 1970s, the makers of television have remained consistently interested in what drugs are and what they mean. From news footage focused on drug busts to syrupy made-for-TV movies to prestige television that now streams across the globe, TV functions as a primary location for narcomedia. More than movies and other media, TV has explored what narcotics mean from a diverse array of perspectives, all the way up the supply chain from producer to trafficker to dealer to user to survivor. Complex, sprawling series like David Simon's *The Wire* (2002–2008), for example, narrate the drug trade from multiple perspectives over dozens of hours.

It is important to distinguish here between scripted and unscripted TV. Television has been airing or streaming news coverage and documentaries about drugs, as well as unscripted (or supposedly so) reality shows, for decades, but what interests me is scripted programming. Even so, as with so many of the media forms analyzed in *Narcomedia*, the relationships between "real" and "fictional" drug narratives are complicated. For example, the documentary *Cocaine Cowboys* (2006) gained a following when it aired on Showtime in 2007 and gained an even wider audience when it was subsequently picked up for streaming for free via Amazon Prime. The doc takes a somewhat nostalgic look back at the "bad old days" of the 1980s Miami drug wars. Several of its interviewees later became characters in scripted series. In several interviews promoting her Lifetime movie based on the life of Griselda Blanco, Catherine Zeta-Jones told entertainment reporters that she became interested in Blanco's story after watching *Cocaine Cowboys*. Although I do not engage very deeply with documentaries like *Cocaine Cowboys*, its two sequels, and similar documentaries in the chapters that follow, many of the scripted series and made-for-TV movies I analyze undeniably draw inspirations from them. Thus, all these texts work together to produce a bigger narrative of Blanco and her cohort of cocaine importers in Miami.

I'm interested first and foremost in TV, but it would be a mistake to limit this study to televisual iterations of narcomedia. This is because the drug narratives found in shows like *Miami Vice* (1984–1990) or *Narcos* (2015–2017) overlap so profoundly with those in other media. One of the following chapters will show, for example, that Latinx stereotypes in *Breaking Bad* (2008–2013) and *Ozark* (2017–2022), both of which have been hailed as breakthroughs in televisual storytelling, would not exist without movies like *Scarface* (1983), which cemented the trope of the Latinx kingpin (sometimes modified to be a queenpin) in the popular imaginary. So in this book I move between mediums freely, just as narco narratives do, but I give the majority of my attention to television.

Although not a main source material for this book, true crime writing is especially relevant as source material for television and other media because many narratives dramatized in film and television actually begin to circulate in the true crime genre. For example, whether they credit it or not, many of the narratives depicting the life and death of Pablo Escobar are clearly derived from Mark Bowden's *Killing Pablo: The Hunt for the World's Greatest Outlaw* (2001). Bowden is a journalist, but books in this genre have been written, ghostwritten, or doctored by former narcotraffickers, their family members, their lawyers, and their hitmen, as well as by the Drug Enforcement Agency and other federal agents. These works have helped construct the broader narrative of the drug trade and directly influence how other media creators understand the facts and narratives, so many of the texts I analyze in *Narcomedia* owe a debt of gratitude to their true crime predecessors, which they sometimes credit but often do not. When I visited the writers' room of *Narcos*, for example, several crime books were spread across the room and had clearly influenced the "show bible" that one of the production assistants showed me. Where appropriate in the chapters that follow, I read TV and film texts in relation to their true crime sources.

True crime might be dominant in literary narcomedia, but drug trafficking has also influenced fiction writing, from pulpy romances to higher-end literary fiction. The latter has started to take notice of the transnational drug trade as a setting. Ingrid Rojas Contreras's *Fruit of the Drunken Tree* (2018), for example, grappled with growing up in cartel-era Medellín and represented a literary effort at portraying themes that have appeared schlocky elsewhere. It received almost universal praise from critics. In contrast, Janine Cummins's *American Dirt* caused a sensation when it was published in early 2020, inspiring accusations that the author, who identifies as white, had appropriated the migrant experience to position herself as a literary darling. This anger was amplified by frustrations with the publishing industry, which frequently marginalizes writers of color while awarding Cummins a seven-figure advance. This was exacerbated by the fact that Cummins's book had a backdrop of cartel violence, a trope that many critics were quick to describe as cliched and offensive. According to one study cited by the *Los Angeles Times*, Latinos made up only 6 percent of the publishing industry at the time that *American Dirt* launched.[8] The fact that Cummins also borrowed some of the standard tropes of narcomedia, including cinematic shootouts and a Latin lover kingpin, garnered less attention. These literary representations do mean something to the story I am telling in *Narcomedia*, but my work does not center on them. I hope scholars of literature will take note of the tropes and themes deployed in literary representations that are more high-minded than those that I examine in this book.. They have a deep well of literary texts from which to draw.

Many of the most iconic and influential texts that I examine in this book—movies like *Scarface*, television series like *Miami Vice*, *Breaking Bad*, and *Narcos*—center male experiences. They tend to treat women as either brainless, pretty ornaments or worried, one-dimensional wives and mothers to male protagonists. To put it bluntly, narcomedia is depressingly full of misogyny. There are a few important exceptions to this, such as depictions of real-life narco Griselda Blanco and a couple of fictional parts played by Selma Hayek, the sprawling *novela La Reina del Sur* (and its US adaption *Queen of the South*), and a family boss that emerges at the end of *Ozark*. However, narcomedia texts are, for the most part, overwhelmingly and exhaustingly male. As a result, the chapters that follow lean toward being male-centric. By focusing on texts that center men, my intention is not to reinforce male-centeredness but to highlight and analyze the misogynistic messages embedded in narcomedia. In part, I want to ask how feminist media analysis might help us draw new and innovative readings from these texts. After researching this book for years, I am reluctant to embrace the image of the queenpin as an adequate feminist response to the misogyny of narcomedia.

COMPLICATING LATINIDAD

Throughout this book I am first and foremost interested in how ideas about latinidad—roughly translated as "Latino-ness" or "Latinity"—circulate in narcomedia. I do so with a bit of trepidation since, in recent years, scholars and activists have begun to question the usefulness of latinidad as a conceptual and political category. Some, such as Tatiana Flores, have convincingly argued that the very concept of latinidad hinges on the European construction of "Latin America" as a geographic and cultural space that excludes "spaces where the majority populations are Black."[9] Flores is in conversation with other scholars, such as Walter Mignolo, who have argued that Latin America and latinidad are rooted in colonialist ways of organizing the world that both center relations to Europe and whiteness and homogenize diverse populations. What is more, the terms do not upend the problems with previously favored terms such as "Hispanic." As Flores puts it, the "terms Latino, Latina, and Latinx are considered more progressive than Hispanic, even though they replicate similar colonialist constructs."[10] This creates a conundrum for the scholar of Latinx studies, a field that continues to operate under the organizing concept of latinidad. How do we proceed with the work of Latino/a/x studies when we cannot agree on whether "latinidad" is the right unifying concept?

I agree with Flores and others who insist that latinidad needs complicating. Even so, I focus on the term throughout this book because, for better or worse, it carries cultural baggage that demands our unpacking. My exploration is not intended to reify any boundaries around what does or does not constitute latinidad but rather to ask how pop culture serves as something of a cultural archive for understanding the construction of latinidad. Therefore, the term is crucial for this book.

However, anyone who draws on an idea as huge and slippery as latinidad must also decide the definition that works for them. I conceptualize latinidad similarly to how Herman Gray sees Blackness in *Watching Race*, his now-classic study of Blackness on network television during the Reagan era. For Gray, Blackness is "a cultural signifier that, although operating on the basis of specific histories, dynamics, and relations to power, nevertheless remains open to multiple and competing claims" and "the constellation of productions, histories, images, representations, and meanings associated with the black presence in the United States."[11] Gray writes about race and "Latinx" is an ethnic category, but his mode of understanding Blackness as a specter that is rooted in lived experiences and relations to power but always open to interpretation has helped to guide *Narcomedia*. I like how Arlene Dávila puts it when she writes that "no person . . . from [a] Latin American background is born Latinx; they become Latinized by being racialized into, or socialized or acculturated into US racial frameworks and by developing articulating identifications with larger Latinx communities."[12] Dávila succinctly captures the sense that latinidad is not a tangible, given *thing* but a process. It is more verb than noun. I also appreciate how Esteban del Río approaches latinidad as a set of contradictory and contestable concepts that are "a structure of feeling and a box to be checked, a site of both subaltern and hegemonic politics, a contested category, a cultural geography, a racial imaginary, a global market, and a terrain of solidarity."[13] Or, even more succinctly in the words of Ramón Rivera-Severa, we might approach latinidad as "an identity-in-process" rather than a fixed or complete mode of identification.[14] For Dávila, del Río, and Rivera-Severa, along with others who challenge its discreteness or knowability—and I place myself in that camp—latinidad is a fraught category of analysis but one that cannot be abandoned.

Regardless of form or genre, most of the narratives that I examine in this book rely to some extent on Latinx stereotypes. I assume that readers will already have some of them in mind by now: the mustachioed kingpin, the sexy narco moll, the violent gang member, and so on. Since at least the 1990s, Latinx media studies have traced the creation and circulation of stereotypes in film and television, including in works by Charles Ramírez Berg, Rosa Linda Fregoso, Isabel Molina-Guzmán, Clara Rodriguez, Angharad Valdivia, and others mentioned in the following chapters. Brian Herrera provides an excellent summation of the history and discourse of the Latinx stereotype (and stereotypes in general) in his book *Latin Numbers*, in which he posits that "stereotypes have remained insidious scene stealers, pulling focus in nearly every critical discussion of race and ethnicity in US popular performance."[15] Herrera and other scholars mentioned here have both catalogued the various modes of stereotyping and shown how pop culture has shaped ideas about latinidad through stereotypes. *Narcomedia* draws on their groundbreaking work but places the question of stereotype (and resistance and everything else that comes along with filmic stereotyping) within a more specific body of texts.

APPROACHING NARCOMEDIA TEXTS

This book focuses mostly, but not entirely, on US-made texts that narrate the drug trade and the War on Drugs in relation to Latinos and latinidad. In dealing with representations of Pablo Escobar, as I do in chapters 3 and 7, I analyze US-made texts like the film *Escobar: Paradise Lost* (2014) in relation to Colombian-made texts like the telenovela *Pablo Escobar: El Patrón del Mal* (2012).

However, I use the phrase "US-made" with some reservations. In the 1970s and 1980s, it would have been more logical to use a term like "US film and television" than it is today. It would be safe to call, say, *Miami Vice* a "US television series" or *Scarface* a "Hollywood film." But the national boundaries around media texts are no longer so clear, as Angharad Valdivia and other scholars examining the transnational Latinx/Latin American media have argued.[16] The Netflix series *Narcos* provides an excellent example of the transnational dimensions of contemporary media production. The show was written in Los Angeles—as will be clear from some of the interviews I conducted with its creators in Detroit and L.A.—but relies heavily on Latin American acting and directing talent. It streams on a global platform but also airs on Spanish-language cable television in the United States with English subtitles. It also shares some of its sprawling cast with *El Patrón del Mal* and other Colombian and Mexican film and TV texts. All of this complicates the potential for calling *Narcos* a "US television series." This is, in fact, by design, as Netflix acknowledged that the show was created in part to expand the hemispheric audience for its original programming. Doug Miro, the show's co-creator, confirmed this in an interview with me that I cite in chapter 7.

Despite my interest in the intertextuality between US and Latin American pop culture, I mostly use Spanish-language texts made in Latin America for comparisons and contrasts, not as the primary texts for analysis. This includes telenovelas, like *Pablo Escobar: El Patrón del Mal* mentioned above, as well as literary works like Fernando Vallejo's *La Virgen de los Sicarios*, which factors into chapter 4. Gesturing to these works helps me emphasize the transnational flow of narratives and representational patterns across borders. Although I am interested in Latin American cultural production, I really focus in this book on US-made texts that coincide with the country's War on Drugs. When it comes to Colombian representations of Pablo Escobar, I would rather leave the analysis to Aldona Bialowas Pobutsky, who has written insightfully about what Escobar, as a cultural figure, has meant to recent Colombian popular culture. Pobutsky's work, especially her excellent book *Pablo Escobar and Colombian Narcoculture*, is an invaluable resource for my study of narcomedia, but it is also more squarely focused on Colombian cultural production and reception, so it looks at a different set of texts that focus more specifically on Escobar from a distinctly Colombian perspective. (The last chapter of *Narcomedia* does address Escobar as a global brand.)

I have employed multiple methodologies to explore questions about narcotics, ethnicity, nationality, and representation. This book takes two main approaches: a cultural history of drugs and media that seeks to understand how and why these narratives are constructed *and* a critical reading of narcomedia texts. It draws upon both the texts themselves and archival materials related to the creation and reception of those texts, ranging from hundreds of articles that I surveyed at the Cuban Heritage Collection at the University of Miami to original screenplays, scripts, and memoirs published by screenwriters, actors, and directors. Rarely, but whenever possible, I spoke personally to those who make or are represented in some of the key texts examined throughout the book, including the writers' room of *Narcos* in 2019, as well as reporters, politicians, screenwriters, and performers. I also interviewed other figures, such as Federico Gutiérrez, the former mayor of Medellín who was an outspoken critic of musicians and other artists who heroified Pablo Escobar in their works and actions (and who went on to be a major presidential candidate in Colombia shortly after we spent an afternoon together).

A NOTE ON TERMINOLOGY AND NAMING CONVENTIONS

When it comes to the terminology around those of us who negotiate latinidad, I use the term "Latinx" as a default in this book, but deploy "Latina" or "Latino" whenever the gender of a person I am referencing is significant. In my view, Latinx is not a perfect solution to the gendered nature of the original term and will probably appear dated in the near future, but I am satisfied to use it as a placeholder for now—as, I guess, terminology-in-process.

This book addresses both real-life historical persons and fictional characters, with much overlap and gray area between these categories. When describing a real person, I use the last name, but when referring to their representation in a cultural text, I use the first name of the character based on the real person. For example, in the case of Pablo Escobar, I use "Escobar" to refer to the facts of his life and "Pablo" when he is represented in films like *Loving Pablo* (2017) or TV series like *Narcos*. Several of the following chapters examine fictionalized representations of real people, and I use this style of in-text reference in order to differentiate between real people and how they are represented in media texts. I do so with the caveat that the lines of fact and fiction are often blurry, especially in the cases of real-life narcos who were well aware of the power of self-mythologizing.

When real-life figures are better known by a nickname, alias, or nom de guerre, such as in the case of Joaquín "El Chapo" Guzmán, I use that alternative name when referring to their media image. I honor this convention in regard to fictional characters as well, even when those nicknames are racially or otherwise offensive, as they frequently are in both the real and fictional worlds of narcomedia. I also default to personal nicknames when they are part of a person's public image, such as when I refer to Francisco Hélmer "Pacho" Herrera as simply "Pacho Herrera" (or "Pacho," when referring to the fictionalized character based on the real person). Furthermore, I follow Latin American naming conventions, in which one's surname comes after given name(s), whenever it is appropriate. Therefore, I refer to Griselda Blanco Restrepo as "Griselda Blanco" and Carlos Lehder Rivas as "Carlos Lehder." Finally, I use the terms "drugs" and "narcotics" interchangeably with the caveat that, pharmacologically, "narcotic" refers to the psychoactive agent that induces sleep and not, generically, any mind-altering substance. In this sense, cocaine and other stimulants are not technically narcotics. However, colloquially and legally, the words are treated as synonyms, so that is how I use them in this book.

CHANGING THE CHANNEL

The seven chapters in this book traverse national borders, media forms, and four decades. Chapters 1 and 2 focus on the city of Miami as a flashpoint in the War on Drugs of the early 1980s and address the creation and meanings of two texts that set the stages for subsequent forms of narcomedia representation: Brian De Palma's iconic "drug opera" *Scarface* and the long-running NBC series *Miami Vice*. Chapters 3 and 4 do not look at specific texts but at themes that are crucial to understanding narcomedia: death and queerness, respectively. Chapter 5 examines a crucial turn in televisual storytelling—the prestige era—and asks how shows like *Breaking Bad* and others that I place in a genre that I call the "suburban crime drama" portray Mexicans and Mexican Americans as threats to white central characters. Chapter 6 approaches similar terrain, but focuses especially on how narcomedia texts represent the US-Mexico border. The final chapter argues that more recent narcomedia fare such as Netflix's *Narcos* has turned Pablo Escobar into a surprising media sensation and global commodity. This is followed by a brief epilogue that considers the potential for pop culture made by and for Latinxs to reshape the established narratives examined in the book's seven chapters.

    I wrote the majority of this book while living in Cali, Colombia, on a sabbatical year that brought to my doorstep civil unrest and a global pandemic. Over the course of fourteen months in Cali, I spoke with hundreds of locals, tourists, friends, and family members about the time period in which a narco cartel ran the city. This was not part of research for the book you are reading, but an inevitable part of living in Colombia as a foreigner involves listening to locals' views on the War on Drugs and how the cartels shaped twentieth-century Colombian history, along with their memories of how drug violence personally affected them. Caleños reminded me that the 1980s and 1990s left long-standing legacies of violence and trauma that continue to shape how they think of themselves, their communities, and their country. This was obvious everywhere, from the frightening stories of kidnappings and gunfire that my mother-in-law would sometimes tell me over a glass of wine to the surprising number of "narco mansions" that lie in ruins all over the city. Film, television, and popular culture are places that Caleños turned to time and again in narrating how they were making sense of their recent past, whether it was in the form of telenovelas or cheap pulpy paperbacks available for sale on the street. I was constantly surprised by how many locals had questions for me about *Narcos* or *Breaking Bad* when I told them about my work and by how clearly they saw the connections between foreign TV shows and their own lived histories.

When my sabbatical was over, I left Cali even more convinced that representational practices are an important part of the "memory work" that is an essential component of peace building and that pop culture might help a country process its past. As I have mentioned, this book is not a direct political intervention and does not present many real-world solutions to the problems it identifies. It does, however, provide some ways to think beyond the patterns of representation that have inextricably bound together latinidad and drugs in the popular imagination. The media narratives that frame Latinxs as the bad guys in the War on Drugs are pervasive but not permanent. They can and should be challenged and, eventually, undone. This book is an attempt to wake up and change the channel.

CHAPTER 1

"SAY GOODNIGHT TO THE BAD GUY"
South Florida, Cocaine, and the Many Faces of Scarface

The glossy cover of the November 23, 1981, edition of *Time* magazine captured an emerging view of Florida at the time. The northern half of the state is colored deep green, with yellow around the coasts to emphasize the state's famous beaches. The southern half of the state, however, is bright red and bordered not by the golden coasts but with a white haze. A cartoonish sun wears sunglasses and a deep frown. The provocative headline asks, "Paradise Lost?" and the words "South Florida" cover much of the bottom half of the state. Within the vintage postcard-style lettering of these latter words appear photographs of a young man, presumably a detained Marielito, angrily screaming behind a chain-link fence; a white man snorting cocaine and tensely returning the camera's gaze; a white police officer investigating the bloody body of a dead Black man; what appears to be a Haitian boat person scrambling to the shore; and a heavily armed vessel patrolling the waters.

The *Time* cover was not an outlier in media representations of South Florida in the early 1980s. In fact, Miami became a pressure point in the War on Drugs for the entire decade: It served as the example that politicians, news outlets, and popular culture used to exemplify America's seemingly out-of-control drug problem. The *Time* cover story, "South Florida: Trouble in Paradise," itself made headlines, and many media outlets reported on it and then produced their own stories about the chaos in South Florida. This chapter turns to cultural representations of Miami in order to understand the hysteria over cocaine and the Latinization of American cities that appeared in US popular culture in the early 1980s. These cultural texts, including reportage found in mainstream news platforms

1.1. *Time* magazine's framing of South Florida as "Paradise Lost" set the tone for many 1980s representations of Miami as a nexus of the drug trade.

like *Time*, tended to pair the importation of dangerous substances with human migration from the Caribbean and Latin America, creating a representational system that inextricably connected drugs to immigrants and, more specifically, white cocaine with brown bodies. As I will illustrate in this chapter and the next, popular culture quickly translated this viewpoint into movies, television series, pulp novels, and other media. I focus here on one text in particular that undertook this mode of representation: *Scarface*. The surprisingly enduring film reflected deeper cultural anxieties about drugs—cocaine in particular—and latinidad that intersected in cultural representations of South Florida. But in order to understand how images of Miami circulated in US popular culture in the early 1980s, it is first necessary to provide a brief history of the substance that irrevocably shaped the city's history.

COCAINE IN THE UNITED STATES: A VERY BRIEF HISTORY

Indigenous peoples of the Andes have used the coca leaf as a stimulant, medicine, and appetite suppressant for more than a thousand years. Early Spanish conquistadores noted the importance of coca to the Andean populations they encountered and wrote about them in unflattering, pathologizing terms. This racist view of coca use persisted, seemingly unchanged, for centuries. One 1940 US health textbook aimed at high school and college students put it this way: "The use of coca plus food deficiency and lack of sanitary measures produce physical and mental degeneracy among the Andean Indians. In intelligence, they are close to brute level. In physique, they are slight, weak, and emaciated. Their working efficiency is of the lowest type, and their life span is brief."[1]

In the mid-nineteenth century, European and North American scientists began to notice that coca might have unstudied health benefits, and some began to look at the chemistry behind coca in order to harness its medicinal properties. German chemists, struggling against the fact that coca leaves did not ship well to Europe, isolated the narcotic alkaloid in 1855. Five years later, Albert Niemann, a PhD student at the University of Göttingen, perfected the refining process and named the strong narcotic that resulted "cocaine." He, along with scientists and doctors the world over, promoted its seemingly miraculous medical and anesthetic uses, and by the mid-1880s, it became well known as a "panacea" and "miracle drug" in the United States, with uses ranging from an anesthetic that made early eye surgeries possible to a curative for sinusitis and hay fever.[2] Coca and cocaine also subsequently became the active ingredients in over-the-counter tonics in the United States and Europe. Coca-Cola did not remove cocaine from its secret recipe until 1906. The soft drink, which still uses "decocainized" coca in its top-secret mixture of natural flavorings, is the longest-standing remnant from a late-nineteenth century craze for coca- and cocaine-infused wines and tinctures.

Cocaine was also a surprisingly common presence onscreen during the silent film era, as film archivist Cary O'Dell has observed.³ The drug figures prominently in a number of films from the 1910s and early 1920s, from cautionary tales to light-hearted comedies. In one example from the latter category, a spoof of Sherlock Holmes titled *The Mystery of the Leaping Fish* (1916), Douglas Fairbanks portrays a detective named Coke Ennyday who snorts and injects cocaine with abandon. Many well-known silent film performers, including Fatty Arbuckle, Mabel Normand, and Norma Talmadge, are known to have battled addictions to the drug. Even into the 1930s, exploitation films with titles like *The Cocaine Fiends* (1935) ostensibly warned audiences about the dangers of the drug but also titillated with lurid plots and characters.

The heyday of legal cocaine would be brief. As early as the 1890s, physicians, government officials, and prohibitionists began to vilify the drug, often in popular media that relied on racist and nativist representations of non-white "cocaine fiends."[4] Popular opinion shifted away from the idea that cocaine could be a panacea for any variety of ills and toward a vision of the drug as a distinctly racialized social ill. In his classic history of drug control, David F. Musto notes that "fear of the cocainized black coincided with the peak of lynchings, legal segregation, and voting laws all designed to remove social and political power from him. . . . So far, evidence does not suggest that cocaine caused a crime wave but rather that anticipation of black rebellion inspired white alarm."[5] Musto goes on to point out the cultural myths that circulated at the time that claimed cocaine gave Black people seemingly superhuman strength but that medical evidence shows that African Americans used cocaine at a very low rate in this era. Thus, the figure of the Black cocaine fiend emerged during this prohibitionist era as a figment of racist cultural imagination. The federal government began to severely regulate cocaine in the 1910s, culminating in a federal prohibition through the Jones-Miller Act of 1922. Unlike other banned substances, the prohibition of cocaine was quite successful. The drug appeared in only negligible numbers in the United States during the middle third of the twentieth century.[6]

But, starting in the early 1970s, cocaine reentered the American drug scene, this time as an elite party drug. Newspaper stories, magazine articles, and television reports marveled at what they called "the drug of the seventies" and the "champagne of drugs," focusing on Hollywood parties and sophisticated discotheques as places where cocaine flowed freely.[7] Rarely seen on big screens for decades, cocaine again became a common presence in 1970s cinema, where the drug came to be associated with wealth, good times, and, for many, creative output. This onscreen glamor helped to make cocaine the party drug of choice for the disco era.

For much of the seventies, the federal government was unconcerned about cocaine. As Paul Gootenberg notes in *Andean Cocaine*, his definitive history of the drug, a 1975 government white paper "awarded cocaine a 'low priority'—below every other drug except the then-tolerated marijuana—because, it averred, "cocaine does not result in serious consequences such as crime, hospital emergency room admissions, or death." Apparently, the medical, governmental, and popular narratives that constructed cocaine as threatening to the body politic had been forgotten. Heroin and acid had been the defining drugs of the hippie generation, and the former was especially worrisome to parents and the government as the nation reeled from the wave of addiction that followed soldiers returning from the Vietnam War. In Gootenberg's assessment, US Americans of the disco era perceived cocaine to be a "soft drug of elites" rather than a widespread threat to the nation.[8] This sensibility was reinforced in much of the press coverage and popular culture of the seventies.

By the 1980s, as if decades-old memories of cocaine fiends had been recovered, the federal government and popular culture again vilified cocaine. The US Congress Select Committee on Narcotics Abuse and Control focused on cocaine as its "primary target" in late 1979, around the same time that drug violence in Miami started to make national news. Despite the fact that much of the expert testimony at the committee's hearings that year claimed that cocaine did not pose a serious threat to the user, members of the committee described cocaine use as a "pandemic."[9] The members of Congress present in the hearings were especially concerned that the "media helped to glamorize cocaine as an exclusive drug, one whose use was prevalent among the elite and the intellectual classes."[10] As a result of these concerns about the drug's portrayal in popular culture, government agencies and political figures—including most famously, Nancy Reagan—would attempt to harness media influence in their anti-cocaine messaging throughout the eighties.

Anxieties over cocaine intensified when "crack," a smokable and more addictive form of the drug, appeared on the American scene later in the decade. Crack provides a brief but powerful high because of how it enters the human nervous system. After it appeared on the US street drug market, crack was rapidly constructed by the popular press as an "epidemic" afflicting African American communities.[11] Congress declared October 1986 "Crack/Cocaine Awareness Month," and various governmental bodies produced pamphlets and other materials aimed at deterring Americans from crack.[12] Two medical doctors published a handbook on crack addiction and treatment in 1991, advancing a War on Drugs narrative that came to characterize mainstream rhetoric about the drug: "A war threatens the normal existence of the Western Hemisphere, especially from Peru to the United States and Canada. The enemy in the war is freebase ('crack') cocaine and the forces promoting the drug are so ruthless and powerful as to make the Sicilian Mafia appear gentle and weak by comparison."[13]

As the United States redoubled its efforts to eradicate cocaine in the 1980s and 1990s, a challenge compounded by a dramatic drop in the price of cocaine and crack, the government focused not on domestic addiction treatment but on the supply chain through foreign interdiction. (Plan Colombia, signed into law by Clinton in 2000, was the culmination of almost two decades of US government focus on Colombia as the primary enemy in the War on Drugs.) In other words, the war metaphor espoused by the doctor-authors of *Crack: The Broken Promise* became US foreign policy.

Popular culture both instigated and echoed this externalization of North America's cocaine problem. Earlier representations from the 1890s to the 1930s fixated on the threat of domestic addicts, but the early 1980s saw a spate of cocaine-themed books, television, and films that positioned Latin Americans as the progenitors of the more recent craze for the drug. When representations of cocaine depicted middle-class white US Americans in several made-for-TV movies throughout the decade, those characters tended to appear as unwitting victims who become ensnared in addiction, as in *Cocaine: One Man's Seduction* (1983). When it came to cocaine use among white Americans, pop culture tended to represent the user as either innocent victim or unbothered indulger, with cocaine adding to their glamor.[14] But Latinos and Latin Americans, along with African Americans, fared differently.

Pop culture representations also zeroed in on the US city that served as the entry point for most of the cocaine that reached the US consumer market: Miami. Joan Didion even produced a book of essays focused on Miami as a metaphor for the United States in the eighties. Didion described Miami as illusory, a figment of the collective American imagination as seen through popular culture and the news as a "wicked pastel boomtown" that was ultimately not what it seemed. Didion's portrait of the city does not focus on drug violence like the *Time* story and countless other representations of the mid-eighties, but it does tap into the same narrative as the "Paradise Lost?" article in *Time*, at least from an economic perspective:

> Miami seemed, at the time I began spending time there, rather spectacularly depressed. . . . There were new condominiums largely unsold. There were new office towers largely unleased. There were certain signs of cutting and running among those investors who had

misread the constant cash coming in and out of Miami as the kind of reliable American money they understood, and been left holding the notes.[15]

This estimation of the place, while not focused on the lurid details of drug violence, renders Miami as a dangerous, and not entirely American, city. Miami's almost-but-not-quite Americanness is, in fact, a recurring theme in the era's media coverage. *Time*'s publisher John A. Meyers, for example, opened his note to readers in the "Paradise Lost?" issue by observing that Miami had recently been selected as the site for the magazine's Caribbean bureau, its first-ever and only "foreign bureau within the US."[16] For Didion, and for many others captivated by the seedy glamor of Miami, this domestic foreignness was central to the city's allure. For others, it was part of its danger. As scholar Juan León has put it, "Miami forces us to confront our relations to Haiti, Cuba, the Caribbean, and Latin America."[17]

MIAMI AS CRISIS ZONE

The "Paradise Lost?" issue was actually the second time that Florida graced the *Time* cover. A generation previously, in 1955, the magazine featured a portrait of Governor LeRoy Collins in front of a colorful drawing of the state. In this earlier cover, Florida is depicted not through menacing images of social upheaval but as bucolic and booming. It is overflowing with ripe oranges that serve as a background to a head of cattle, a smoking factory, and a buxom, bikini-clad white woman. The Democratic governor's head, well-groomed and bearing a friendly smile, is almost as big as the state. The accompanying article, titled "A Place in the Sun" (the Elizabeth Taylor movie with the same name, which explored the high price of the good life, had premiered in 1951), is the exact opposite of how *Time* described South Florida in the early 1980s. The 1955 article depicts South Florida as a booming place for agriculture, industry, and tourism and its leaders as tireless boosters of Florida's endless potential. The only mention of migration is to note that 60 percent of Floridians were born outside the state.[18] And despite the fact that Florida had well-developed ethnic enclaves of long standing, the author of "A Place in the Sun" makes no mention of the state's racial dynamics in the fifties.

This narrative of endless potential had changed dramatically by the time the magazine published the 1981 "South Florida: Trouble in Paradise" article. In the eight-page essay (quite long for *Time*), Miami-based staff writer

James Kelly tells a story of South Florida as an out-of-control region, one that might serve an ominous bellwether for America's relationships to drugs, crime, and migration.[19] "An epidemic of violent crime, a plague of illicit drugs, and a tidal wave of refugees have slammed into South Florida with the destructive force of a hurricane," Kelly writes. "Those three forces, along with a number of lesser ills, threaten to turn one of the nation's most prosperous, congenial and naturally gorgeous regions into a paradise lost."[20] The title that appears on the cover of the edition includes a question mark, implying that it was up to the reader to decide whether Miami was facing its demise, but the article itself makes it difficult to conclude otherwise. Kelly's message is stark but hardly an outlier among the conclusions drawn by reporters in the first years of the eighties.

Many of the early Cuban refugees and their descendants had established themselves as a stable economic and political force in South Florida, an image cultivated by leaders in the exile community who emphasized stability, upward mobility, and good citizenship. A sidebar of Kelly's article focuses on generational differences in the Marquez Sterling family, headed by a college professor patriarch who had "helped write his country's constitution in 1940" and who then lived in Miami with his wife, daughter, son-in-law, and granddaughters.[21] The profile takes a somewhat lighthearted approach by contrasting the grandparents' views on dating and other social norms with those of the younger family members, closing with a description of the third generation as acknowledging their Cuban roots but living on the cusp of being thoroughly Americanized. The accompanying photo shows a well-heeled multigenerational family posing in front of their art collection. By depicting a white and highly educated family as the only members of the exile community to be quoted in the article, the sidebar provides a portrait in miniature of the respectability that many in the Cuban community craved. But clear demographic shifts contradicted any sense that Miami could remain a majority white city with an easily assimilable Cuban American minority.

In the main article, Kelly focuses as much on racial strife as he does on drugs to explain how Miami came to represent a paradise lost, providing a racial and ethnic taxonomy of the region and suggesting that the growing presence of racial minorities will lead the established white community to abandon Miami altogether. He quotes one white life-long Miamian who had recently moved to Kansas City: "I was going to be damned if I had to learn a foreign language to get a job in a city where I had lived for all my life."[22] The photographs accompanying the article underscore the theme of Miami's squandered potential and immigrant threats. Two full-color photographs open the article: On the left, a string of high-rise hotels "hug the shore in Miami Beach." The beach in front of the hotels is perfectly manicured and the water temptingly aquamarine. On the right, several Black Miamians line a sidewalk along Grand Avenue in Coconut Grove, where heaps of trash have gone uncollected for what looks like weeks or even longer, given the degree of disarray and decomposition on the street.

This latter image foretells the tone in which the article addresses Black populations in the city, especially Haitian immigrants. Kelly describes the Haitians as an especially needy population, implying that they are likely to become wards of the state (in implied contrast to the Marquez Sterling family and other upwardly mobile Cubans). The human subjects in the image take little note of the unnamed photographer, except for one young man who leans back in his folding chair and returns his or her—and the viewer's—gaze. It is tempting to read a trace of defiance in his eyes. Others mostly go about their business, seemingly engaged in conversation. One woman pushes a small baby in a swing. The photograph is open to interpretation as, of course, all images are, but its surroundings—the text and images that provide its context—do not imply that the piled trash in the picture is a metaphor for the city's racial inequities or failure to serve its entire population. Instead, as the reader soon learns, the article implies that the people and the trash are both symptoms of a city that is spiraling out of control.

This provocative juxtaposition of images contrasts sharply with the two black-and-white photographs of almost the same proportions that open the 1955 feature on Florida: a herd of fat Brahmin cattle on the left and, to the right, the world's largest nylon factory. These images, though not exactly picturesque, connote the industriousness of the "New Florida" promoted throughout the long article. A quartet of images from the 1981 article shows just how dramatically the story had shifted a quarter-century later. They include a DEA agent sorting through a big bag of seized contraband, a group of elderly "sunshine boys" gathered on benches and lawn chairs, a Black woman and a dog walking past a huge graffito declaring "ASYLUM FOR HAITIANS," and a white woman practicing her shot at a Dade County gun range. Kelly includes the story of a Christian pastor who takes up arms: "Even the Rev. Mac Vittie has purchased a revolver to keep in his home. 'That is one hell of a way to live,' he says."[23]

The 1981 *Time* article prefigured a wave of national media coverage presenting the narrative of Miami in crisis. Academics also picked up on this and began to study Miami as a contact and crisis zone. Alejandro Portes and Alex Stepick published their now-classic 1993 study of Miami, *City on the Edge*, which was more sympathetic to the city than the news coverage.[24] The ultimate symbol of Miami as the epicenter for drug crime in the United

States came the same year, when multiple national news outlets reported that the Dade County medical examiner's office had rented a refrigerated truck to ease overcrowding in the morgue.[25] An August 1983 episode of the ABC news magazine *Closeup* referred to cocaine as the "national vice of the eighties" and focused equally on Medellín and Miami as cities that were undergoing dramatic transformations because of cocaine money and violence.[26] One segment of the episode focused on real estate in Miami, specifically the problem of Colombian drug lords paying for homes in cash (a reality that actually still reverberates in Miami real estate). In 1987, a *New York Times* headline in a big, bold font asked: "Can Miami Save Itself?"[27] Pop culture, as it often does, took its cues from the news media and began to represent Miami as the epicenter of the nation's cocaine crisis.[28]

Partially because of negative media attention, in early 1982, President Reagan convened a special task force to combat drug trafficking in Miami. Vice President George H. W. Bush headed a staff of more than nine hundred personnel, mostly borrowed from other federal agencies, that focused almost entirely on interdiction.[29] By November of that year—nearly one year after the *Time* cover article—the same magazine reported that the task force was so successful that New England, the Gulf Coast, and the West Coast were seeing record-setting narcotics busts as drug traffickers rerouted away from Florida.[30] Even so, the cocaine business was not about to leave Miami. Dozens of busts were meant to demonstrate the efficacy of the task force and related efforts but, to keener observers, it revealed just how much cocaine was traveling through the city. Governmental fixation on Miami and South Florida both responded to and created pop cultural representations of the city, which only increased after the advent of the task force.

SCARFACE ORIGINS

It was out of these cultural and political contexts that Hollywood produced one of its most iconic images of the drug trade: Brian De Palma's epic 1983 remake of the 1932 classic gangster film *Scarface*. De Palma's film reimagined *Scarface* for the eighties by relocating the action to Miami and changing the contraband substance smuggled by the titular character from alcohol to cocaine. These changes are not surprising, given the national coverage of the drug trade in Miami, and several of the film's creators described the ripped-from-the-headlines nature of their inspiration. Famously, screenwriter Oliver Stone entered treatment for addiction to cocaine shortly after submitting his final draft of the script.

De Palma's *Scarface* borrows its basic structure from its pre-Code predecessor, which had helped to define the genre of the gangster movie. In the original, based on a 1929 novel by Armitage Trail (pen name of pulp fiction writer Maurice R. Coons), Paul Muni plays Tony Camonte, whose rise and fall as a bootlegger and mob boss is based on the life of Al Capone. Though both took many liberties with the facts of Capone's life, the book and movie were two of the first dramatizations of his story, which has inspired several subsequent works of film, television, and literature, including *The Untouchables* (1957 novel, 1959–1963 and 1993–1994 tv series, and 1987 film); *Al Capone* (1959 film); and *Capone* (1975 film, 2020 film).

The 1932 version of *Scarface*, funded by Howard Hughes, adapted by Ben Hecht from the novel, and directed by Howard Hawks, was set mostly on the South Side of Chicago in the 1920s. In Hawks's film, Tony starts out as an ambitious mob lieutenant at odds with his disapproving immigrant mother (Inez Palange) and fast-living sister Cesca (Ann Dvorak), of whom he is so overprotective that their relationship has incestuous undertones. Tony goes against the order of his boss Johnny Lovo (Osgood Perkins) when he takes on the Irish gangs of the city's North Side to expand his bootlegging operations. He also works against Johnny by pursuing the boss's girlfriend, a hardened but beautiful blonde named Poppy (Karen Morley). Tony builds up a crime empire of his own but, true to the gangster film genre of the thirties, he meets a grisly end, shot down by the police in the last beats of the film. As Tony dies on the street, the camera pans upward to an advertisement for Cook's Tours, a sign that he had pointed out to Poppy twice previously. An apt metaphor for Tony's ambition and hubris, the ad flashes "The World Is Yours."

The first movie version of *Scarface* tapped into a national fixation on Al Capone. At least six other films released within a year before or after Hawks's film featured characters loosely or closely based on the crime lord.[31] This cinematic cycle included two similar films that are now considered defining texts of the "gangster canon": *Little Caesar* (1931) and *The Public Enemy* (1931). Along with *Scarface*, these films, both of which are also set in Chicago, coded organized crime as ethnic and immigrant social problems. In *The Public Enemy*, James Cagney plays an Irish American youth who works his way up from petty crime to bootlegging kingpin. *Scarface* and *Little Caesar* both framed the children of Italian immigrants as particularly susceptible to the gangster life—and to disappointing their mothers. They feature heavily accented Italian immigrant mothers who disapprove of their sons' misdeeds. Decades later, one of the first prestige television series, *The Sopranos*, self-consciously referenced these early gangster movies; in one famous scene, mafia boss Tony Soprano is brought to tears as he watches the memorable ending of *The Public Enemy* on TV.[32]

Scarface's boundaries-pushing violence caused a sensation even before its premiere in April 1932. Film historian and critic J. E. Smyth describes it as "one of the most highly censored films in Hollywood history."[33] Its release was delayed by almost a year because of a protracted battle between Hughes and Hawks and the Hays Office, which demanded changes that would downplay the movie's glamorization of organized crime and guns, as well as with various state and city censorship boards that banned screenings.[34] Film scholar Chris Yogerst has noted the "postproduction hell" in which the film languished after it was shot, as Hawks and Hughes tried to figure out a way to get the picture released.[35] Partly to mollify censors, the filmmakers inserted a foreword to the film that portrays the movie as a cautionary tale and a call for viewers to demand government accountability over the problem of organized crime.[36] Despite these obstacles, *Scarface* became a box office success and a classic of pre-Code Hollywood cinema. When the censorship board of Chicago finally allowed the movie to be screened in that city in 1941, audiences came in droves, breaking box office records.[37] The Library of Congress added the movie to the National Film Registry in 1994, an indication that the film had fully gone from racy to revered.

SCARFACE IN MIAMI

According to many tellings, Al Pacino became interested in remaking *Scarface* when he saw the classic gangster movie in revival at the Tiffany Theater in Los Angeles. Pacino told his manager, Martin Bregman, also a major film producer, his idea and Bregman agreed to fund the project as a vehicle for his high-profile client. As Pacino has told the story, Bregman had recently seen and enjoyed the classic film on television.[38] Sidney Lumet, originally attached to the film as its director, and playwright/screenwriter David Rabe developed the idea of relocating the action to Miami and making Tony a Marielito, one of the approximately 125,000 Cubans who left the island via the Mariel Boatlift in 1980. This would make the movie, like its predecessor, a timely representation of a contemporary social problem.

However, any attempt to position it as a social justice film is complicated by the fact that the 1983 film repeats misinformation about the Marielitos that had been circulating throughout the early 1980s in the news media.[39] Contrary to Castro's claims and US media coverage at the time, the Marielitos were not overwhelmingly criminal, as decades of research has shown. Nonetheless, the news media created and reinforced a perception—and stigma—among the public that the Marielitos were the result of Castro emptying prisons and asylums, sending the country's most dangerous and deviant Cubans abroad.⁴⁰ According to historian Jillian Marie Jacklin, "*Scarface* reinforced national media characterizations of Cuban refugee criminality following the Mariel boatlift, and its plot helped to shape one of the dominant images of the Marielitos in popular culture and the US national imagination."⁴¹ Lumet left the project over creative differences, but Stone and De Palma continued with the idea to make Tony a Marielito. Universal also sanctioned a novelization of the screenplay, written by Paul Monette, that was published in early 1983 and reprinted in December of that year to coincide with the release of the film.⁴²

Like the original film, this version of *Scarface* begins with a written prologue that scrolls up the screen. The 1932 movie challenged viewers to demand government action against organized crime (a common feature of exploitation films), but the newer prologue provides political context for how Tony, a Cuban émigré, gets to the United States. It opens by explaining that in May 1980 Castro opened the Mariel harbor "with the apparent intention of letting some of his people join their relatives in the United States," but then claims that "[i]t soon became evident that Castro was forcing the boat owners to carry back with them not only their relatives, but the dregs of his jails. Of the 125,000 refugees that landed in Florida, an estimated 25,000 had criminal records." This cuts to footage of the real Fidel Castro, boat crossings, and the refugee camps in Miami, all of which is interspersed with the opening credits. With the prologue, De Palma unequivocally positions the film as a statement about Miami, the Marielitos, and the social upheavals created by Cuban migration to South Florida. However, the scrolling prologue that appeared in the final film left out one important sentence from the screenplay. In Stone's script, the last line of the prologue reads: "This is the story of that minority—those they call 'Los Bandidos.'"⁴³ This omission is small, but it also changes the overall tone of the movie. Without Stone's qualification, it is easy to interpret the film as representing all Marielitos.

When Tony appears, he is under interrogation by INS officials. It is 1980. The very first shot of Tony is a close-up highlighting, as cinematographer John A. Alonzo put it in the DVD commentary, "this Latin machismo coming out of a man with a scar on his face."⁴⁴ After mouthing off to the agents and making the first of several impassioned speeches over the course of the film, Tony is sent to the Freedom Town refugee camp under a Miami highway, where he is reunited with his friend Manny (Steven Bauer). Tony and Manny team up on their first mission: Kill a former Cuban general in exchange for green cards. From there, they work their way up the ladder of a drug trafficking enterprise run by kingpin Frank Lopez (Robert Loggia). However, Tony, never satisfied, jockeys for control over the entire South Florida drug trade. He also romances and marries Frank's romantic partner, the beautiful but icy Elvira (Michelle Pfeiffer), who, like Poppy in the original film, initially dismisses Tony as a rube. When Tony challenges her that she should be nice to him because he is just trying to be friendly, she rebuffs him, "God, I've got enough friends. I don't need another one. Especially one who just got off a banana boat." Later, when he tries to kiss her, she refuses by saying that she does not "fuck around with the help." But as Tony moves up in the Miami cocaine trade, his ruthlessness grows along with his ambitions: He kills Lopez and takes his place at the top of the Miami cocaine trade. He also gains Elvira's companionship, although she seems fonder of his product than of him.

At Tony and Elvira's wedding, the groom shows off a tiger that he is keeping chained on the grounds of the lavish mansion where he now lives. The tiger roars loudly as some of their guests nervously marvel at the animal. According to Manny earlier in the film, when Tony was still a small-time crook, he would visit the zoo and dream of owning one of the big cats. So the tiger represents the fulfillment of his American Dream—with a touch of exoticism still intact. Of course, the tiger also symbolizes the mercilessness that it took to get there. Stone's screenplay also makes several references to Tony *as* a tiger, so the symbolism is quite intentional.[45] Most of Stone's references did not make it into the final film, but the fleeting mention and then image of the cat nonetheless appears in the film as a metaphor for Tony's excesses and his animalistic behavior.

Tony is so taken with a message that he sees on a blimp—"The World Is Yours," another reference to the original film, only this time it is an ad for Pan American Airlines instead of a travel agency sign—that he makes it the motto of his own shell corporation, Montana Enterprises. However, as it does in all versions of the story, Tony's hubris must catch up with him. In the film's memorable final sequence, all hell breaks loose as Tony snorts a mountain of cocaine. Having found that Manny and Tony's beloved sister Gina (Mary Elizabeth Mastrantonio) are living together in a luxurious Coral Gables house, he kills Manny in cold blood. Gina, stricken with grief, is spirited away to Tony's mansion, where she makes the incestuous subtext of their relationship explicit. Meanwhile, a Bolivian drug kingpin, Alejandro Sosa (Paul Shenar), sends an army of killers to Tony's house to settle a score. Tony, coked out of his mind and horrified that Gina has been killed by one of the assassins, aims a grenade launcher and his famous line, "Say hello to my little friend," at this horde of invaders. Finally, although he has appeared invincible over the course of the long movie, Tony is shot in the back with a sawed-off shotgun by one of Sosa's killers. He falls from his balcony into a shallow pool in the foyer. As blood mixes with water, the camera pans up to reveal a neon sign with the now-ironic message, "The World Is Yours."

Like its predecessor, the 1983 *Scarface* was designed, in part, to push the boundaries of what was acceptable in a mainstream Hollywood film. Reminiscent of Hawks and Hughes's fight with the Hays Office, De Palma battled with the Motion Picture Association of America to get the film an R rating rather than the X that the MPAA assigned.[46] De Palma has boasted in many interviews that he switched the final cut between when the MPAA finally approved the film as an R and when it was released, effectively duping the ratings board.[47] Upon its release, many critics expressed discomfort with the movie's brutality. Some, aware of De Palma's battle with the MPAA, also wondered what it would mean for the ratings system that the hyperviolent movie got by the board with an R. Others took umbrage with the profane language and drug use in the film. According to one reviewer's conservative estimate, characters use the word "fuck" 181 times over the course of the film.[48]

It makes a certain sense that this new version would be relocated to Miami. In the 1930s, Chicago represented, to many Americans, the worst of urban vice; a half-century later, as we have seen and will see in the following chapter, South Florida came to inhabit that place in the popular imagination. Stone's screenplay directly references public perceptions of the city: At one point in the film, an outwardly respectable banker who has been laundering money for Tony tells him that "the IRS is coming down heavy on South Florida. There was a *Time* magazine cover story that didn't help." Like their predecessors, who borrowed the *Scarface* story from recent headlines, the creators of the new *Scarface* saw themselves as tapping into the American zeitgeist. "*Scarface* is not just simply homage," De Palma told the *New York Times* a few weeks after the film was released. "We're dealing with a parallel milieu that's as compelling today as it was in 1932 in Capone's Chicago. Both Hawks's film and my own are about pugnacious immigrants hungry for success."[49]

REMAKING *SCARFACE*: THE KINGPIN, CUBANNESS, AND LATINIDAD

A little-known episode in Miami politics explains why, despite the fact that *Scarface* is perhaps the most famous filmic representation of Miami, little of the movie was actually shot on location in South Florida. In summer 1982, producers Martin Bregman and Lou Stoller began to publicize their plans to shoot *Scarface* on location. Stoller told the *Miami Herald* that the movie would be shot entirely in Miami, which would bring, according to the county film and television coordinator, at least $10 million to the local economy.⁵⁰ Stoller and Bregman also touted the fact that Cuba-born and Miami-raised actor Rocky Echevarría, who had performed on the groundbreaking bilingual PBS series ¿Qué Pasa, USA?, had been cast in the key role of Manny. Echevarría, apparently in an attempt to appear less "ethnic," had recently changed his name to Steven Bauer.

However, some members of Miami's Cuban American community grew nervous about the fact that the main character in Scarface had been reimagined as a Marielito. Several members of the Cuban American business and intellectual elite belonged to a group called the Spanish American League Against Discrimination—or SALAD—that organized a task force to deal with the "tarnished" reputation of Cubans in the media.⁵¹ Chief among the Scarface critics was outspoken City Commissioner Demetrio Pérez Jr. Pérez had arrived in Miami in 1962 when, at the age of sixteen, he emigrated from Cuba as part of Operation Pedro Pan, the mass evacuation of at least fourteen thousand Cuban youths from the island between 1960 and 1962. By the start of the eighties, he was among the most powerful Cuban Americans in the city and an outspoken, self-appointed protector of that community's public image. In 1981, he was elected to the City Commission.

Pérez lodged his first complaints against Scarface in the pages of the Cuban American press; prolific in the 1980s, much of its output is now meticulously archived at the University of Miami's Cuban Heritage Collection. El Imparcial, along with other newspapers, printed an open letter that Pérez sent to the producers, in which he outlines seven steps to "save the credibility of free Cubans." Pérez's demands, paraphrased from Spanish, included:

- The main character should be a pro-Castro infiltrator, reflecting the significant participation of pro-Castro communists in the drug trade;
- The movie should not include a favorable representation of communism;
- An approximate 20 percent of the movie should go to anti-Castro activities and the contributions of Cubans to the enlargement of South Florida;
- The movie should use local talents, especially Cuban artists to portray characters of Cuban origin;
- Minority companies should be used as subcontractors in the filming of the movie;
- The community should have the opportunity to see the final

version of the script in order to dispel rumors of its pro-communist and anti-Cuban leanings;
- The movie must premiere in Miami with proceeds dedicated to helping children who arrived via Mariel and drug rehabilitation programs in the city.[52]

Pérez, apparently unversed in Hollywood moviemaking, thought *Scarface* should amplify his anti-Castro message. As far-fetched as some of these demands appear, Pérez was persistent in making them, repeating variations in several interviews published in Cuban American newspapers and magazines.

Although Pérez had a platform for his views in the Spanish-language press, he also inspired detractors among Cuban American cultural workers. Lifestyle magazine *Réplica* published a long, excoriating essay by journalist Nicolás Ríos claiming that, despite his intentions, Pérez actually damaged the Cuban American community.[53] Like others in the Cuban community, Ríos could not help but note the irony: Pérez, a harsh critic of cultural suppression under the Castro regime, was himself attempting to silence a creative endeavor. "We are part of a community that abandoned its homeland fundamentally for reasons that have to do with the desire for freedom that has proven natural to the human animal," wrote Ríos. "I think our municipal commissioner suffers from basic problems that have to do with an absence of education. If he had it, he would know that what he wants to impose is precisely what is done in Cuba."[54]

Serious conflict between Pérez, other Cuban Americans critical of the production, and the producers played out in the pages of the *Miami Herald* in late August and early September 1982. Bregman, whose temper was infamous in Hollywood, went to the newspaper after he received word about Pérez's demands regarding the movie project.[55] "It's obvious to me that they are afraid I am going to depict the Cuban community as a bunch of animals," Bregman told the *Herald*, as part of a threat that the city would lose tax money if the criticism continued. "That's not the type of movie I make. If they don't want us there, we'll move."[56] Pérez, unabashed, continued to warn the producers to revise their negative portrayal of the Marielitos or they would be banned from filming in the city. In response, Bregman sounded off to reporters for the *Herald* and other news outlets, threatening to relocate production away from Miami and to publicly humiliate Pérez for costing Dade County millions in taxes and expenses. "We'll do it nationally and make an idiot out of this man," he told *Herald* reporter Jay Ducassi.[57]

Other local and state officials attempted to control the damage wrought by Pérez's public denouncements of the *Scarface* project. Maurice Ferré, the Puerto Rico–born mayor of Miami, vigorously campaigned the producers, making calls and sending telegrams, to film on location in the city. Governor Bob Graham told the *Herald* that he understood the "sensitivity" of the Cuban American community to negative portrayals but that "artistic liberties should not be infringed upon by the government."[58] Several Anglo columnists in Miami supported Ferré and Graham's attempts to placate the producers, accusing Pérez of attempting to censor a script that he had not even read. After an emergency meeting with Universal Studios executives, which took into consideration a meeting between producers and Cuban American community leaders, as well as calls and telegrams from Governor Graham and the Greater Miami Chamber of Commerce, Bregman announced that filming would take place in South Florida after all.[59] Mayor Ferré held a press conference assuring Miamians that Hollywood would not stand in for their city.[60]

Bregman was already peeved at Pérez, but two *Herald* columnists pushed him over the edge. On August 27, a few days after the producers announced that filming would indeed take place in Miami and the same day that Pérez announced that he would seek a public referendum on banning the filming of movies that are "detrimental to the image of the city," Guillermo Martinez published a carefully worded essay in the paper's editorial section.[61] "The image of the Mariel refugee as a criminal—whether accurate or not—has been set in our minds," wrote Martinez, who was not himself a Marielito. Like many in the Cuban American community, Martinez lamented the stigmatization of Marielitos and did not feel he could remain silent when a film that was sure to draw a large audience seemed poised to exploit a stereotype. "It is not easy to ignore. It is so prevalent that when Hollywood decided to recast the gangster film classic, *Scarface*, there was never a doubt that the protagonist, the villain, had to be a Mariel refugee. Hollywood is reacting to the stereotype. In turn, it is helping to perpetuate the image."[62]

Martinez's colleague Roberto Fabricio, the editor of the paper's Spanish edition, went a bit further in the next day's edition. After criticizing Pérez's tactics as "irresponsible overkill," Fabricio had some harsh words for Bregman:

> The chief culprit [in the fracas] is executive producer Martin Bregman, who proved to be quite an idiot himself when he began calling Perez an "idiot" and threatened to take his movie somewhere else, a hollow threat that no one took very seriously. Had Bregman continued to be the front man dealing with Cubans here the negotiations

probably would have ended up in a brawl. Luckily, other movie executives with more sensitivity and brains made key telephone calls and tried to address some of the initial concerns about *Scarface*.[63]

Despite the fact that the *Herald* published op-eds in favor of the production, including a bitingly sarcastic parody of Pérez, and executive editor John McMullan stated publicly that he disagreed with Martinez and Fabricio, their columns reignited Bregman's temper. The producer vowed to the press that, for once and all, *Scarface* would not film in Miami.

A few days later, Bregman and his fellow producers ordered the advance team that was already in the city to return to Los Angeles. Fabricio, for his part, deflected any blame for escalating things with Bregman and his colleagues. He claimed that his and Martinez's columns were not inflammatory but that the producers had been looking for a reason to leave Miami and used them as an excuse.[64] Whether or not Fabricio's theory had any basis in truth, officials all over South Florida attempted to woo back the producers. Within a few days of the pullout, the city commissioners of Miami Beach unanimously voted in favor of a resolution asking the *Scarface* production team to reconsider its decision and move all filming to that city.[65] Other municipalities also formally invited them to film in their cities and towns. Columnists for the *Herald* and even national newspapers complained that cities should not be in the business of censoring artists of any medium. At the September 9, 1982, meeting of the City Commission, the top agenda item, at Pérez's request, was a discussion of the filming of *Scarface*. Pérez actually withdrew the item prior to the meeting, but a boisterous crowd that included officials from other Dade County municipalities appeared at the meeting to denounce Pérez's efforts.[66]

Scarface did not stay entirely out of Miami after fall 1982. In spring 1983, eight months after the blowup between Bregman, Pérez, and the columnists, some of the actors and crew returned to Miami to shoot additional exterior scenes that could not be replicated in Los Angeles, but the production team kept a low profile and barred all Miami press from the set because of hard feelings from the previous fall.[67] In the end, very little of the finished film, with the exceptions of the scene with the chainsaw-wielding Colombians and one where Tony propositions Elvira beside her pool, was filmed in Miami.[68] The crew also captured a few important establishing shots when they revisited the city, but the vast majority of *Scarface* was shot on the Universal Studios lot and locations around Los Angeles, resulting in a film that attempts to use Miami as an allegory for a nation that is out of control because of drugs but that features very little of the city itself.

At one point in the tense negotiations about whether filming would take place in Miami, the producers and the film's detractors haggled over whether a disclaimer could assuage Cuban American concerns regarding stereotyping. In post-production, the filmmakers *did* include a brief disclaimer that appears at the very end of the film's five-minute credits:

> Scarface is a fictional account of the activities of a small group of ruthless criminals. The characters do not represent the Cuban/American community and it would be erroneous and unfair to suggest that they do. The vast majority of Cuban/Americans have demonstrated a dedication, vitality and enterprise that has enriched the American scene.

It is difficult to ascertain why, in the end, De Palma and company would include this language, considering that there was no love lost between the producers and some representatives of the local Cuban American community, and, in the end, they owed nothing to Miami city officials. It was, however, not unprecedented as a response to criticism from an interest group. In 1980, for example, director William Friedkin begrudgingly included a brief disclaimer at the start of *Cruising*, another controversial Al Pacino film, to appease criticism from gay rights groups who had been protesting the film from its early phases of production.[69]

In any case, the Cuban American community of South Florida was not riled when *Scarface* was released in December 1983. The *Herald* once again ran a series of articles on the film and found much to criticize, but also reported that the predominant Cuban American reaction to the film was curiosity rather than outrage. Early in 1984, Spanish-language *Réplica*, the same magazine that had decried Pérez's melee with the producers in 1982, published a long, positive review, illustrated with production stills from the film provided by the studio. Shortly after the movie's premiere, a reporter asked Demetrio Pérez's assistant whether the commissioner had been among the Miami-area audiences who were packing the theaters; she replied that he had not yet seen the controversial film. "He tried over the weekend," she said, "but the lines were too long."[70]

With the benefit of hindsight, it is tempting to read Pérez's anti-*Scarface* campaign as a fool's errand. His actions seem to have made him no friends in the city he passionately served, whereas the film did respectably well at the box office and went on to become an icon of American filmmaking, as I describe below. His constituents and colleagues publicly derided him for months after the *Scarface* crew left Miami. SALAD and other organizations distanced themselves from him in English- and Spanish-language media, so that, in the end, he appeared solely responsible for the tax revenue—and, more difficult to measure, prestige—that the city lost in the process.

But is there another way of looking at it? Chon Noriega, among others, has described a deep history of media activism in which Latinx individuals, organizations, and communities have fought for fairer representation. One classic example from Noriega's *Shot in America*, a foundation study of Latinx media activism in the mid- to late twentieth century, involved Mexican American media activism against the Frito Bandito, a corporate mascot that appears tame in comparison to Tony Montana.[71] Subsequent work on Latinx media activism, including excellent work by Arcelia Gutiérrez, among others, has shown the power of Latinx audiences to organize—or at least speak out en masse—against underrepresentation and misrepresentation.[72] Unfortunately for Pérez, public opinion was not on his side and he could not attract even a vocal minority to his cause.

Even so, Pérez *was* engaging in media activism. Like Italian-Americans who mobilized against *The Godfather* (1972) and the various queer media activists who, a few years before *Scarface*, protested against the making of *Cruising* (1980) in New York City, Pérez forced serious conversations about a marginalized community's right to have a say in how it is represented.[73] On one hand, Pérez was actually more successful than earlier attempts by minority groups to have their say, considering that he took on and then scared off Hollywood producers. His campaign also helped to inspire a new committee, Facts About Cuban Exiles (FACE), that sought to improve the Cuban American image among the broader public. Decades later, FACE is still doing this work, with a mission "to promote, foster and improve the reputation and image of persons of Cuban origin and their descendants in the United States, and worldwide."[74] On the other hand, like *The Godfather* and *Cruising*, *Scarface* did get made. It was as much of a brutally negative depiction of an imagined Marielito as Pérez must have feared. And Cuban Americans barely complained when it was released.

Pérez's media activism has become part of the lore around the making of the film. Several of the key players in making *Scarface* have exaggerated the Cuban American response to the film's production, suggesting that Cubans protested en masse. In Noah Baumbach and Jake Paltrow's documentary on the director, De Palma reminisces that "first we started and got run out by the Cubans. They just ran us out of town. They didn't like what the script was about—they thought we were making all Cubans gangsters." Oliver Stone gives a bit more detail in his memoir, *Chasing the Light*. He is correct in remembering Pérez's demands for script changes making Tony a communist agitator but, like De Palma, he also misreports wide-scale protest of the movie among the Cuban community. "As I remember it,"

Stone writes, "we were there less than two weeks before Cuban exile community leaders managed to get us thrown out of the city."[75] This differs dramatically from the City Commission records and the Cuban American press, but it reflects how the filmmakers saw themselves as making a movie designed to push buttons.

REWRITING *SCARFACE*

Cuban Americans might not have protested as much as expected at the time that *Scarface* was released, but latinidad is nonetheless a defining characteristic of *Scarface*. Screenwriter Oliver Stone was already known for his left-of-center political outlook when he wrote *Scarface* and yet the film reflects the conservative vision that circulated in the news media that painted the Marielitos as less deserving of sympathy than previous waves of migrants from Cuba. As scholars in Latinx studies, Cuban studies, and related fields have argued, the Marielitos came to represent the worst possible results of the fallout of strained relations between the United States and Cuba. The Marielitos were—and have remained—a lightning rod in debates around refugees, the criminalization of immigrants, and tensions between the waves of Cuban migrant communities.

Colombians fare especially poorly in the *Scarface* screenplay. As with other narcomedia texts from the 1980s, the movie's characters use "Colombian" as a shorthand for drug trafficking and criminality. Early in the film, Tony is visibly dismayed when, for one of their first jobs together, he and Manny are hired to buy cocaine from some Colombians. Manny asks him why he looked the way that he did when they were told about the job. "I don't fucking like Colombians, ok?" Tony retorts. (In Stone's script the line is, "I just don't like fuckin' Columbians [sic].... They're animals!"[76]) Things get much worse from there. At the meeting with the Colombians in a flea-bitten Miami Beach hotel, Tony and his crew realize that they've been caught in a trap and that the Colombians are going to try to rob them. Then things get really violent. One of the Colombians hacks away at Tony's friend Angel (Pepe Serna) with a chainsaw, chopping him to pieces. Manny and their other accomplice Chi Chi (Ángel Salazar) get to the Colombians before they can wield the chainsaw against Tony. Tony and company slay the Colombians and leave with the coke. It becomes both their first score and Tony's ticket into the stratosphere of high-level traffickers.

Several decades later in an interview De Palma gave when receiving a lifetime achievement award, he described to Alec Baldwin some of the challenges he faced during the complicated shoot. At one point, an important set had burned and Pacino was injured, delaying the production. "Here

I had a [burned] set, no Al . . . but I had a lot of Colombians to kill," he recalled.[77] De Palma was joking, but the generic-ness with which he described Colombians reflects how the movie—and several other movies and television series, including *Miami Vice*—treats characters of that nationality. In *Scarface*, Colombians appear as they frequently did in the news media of the time: not as individuals but as a nameless mass descending on South Florida, ruthless villains for the War on Drugs. Here, as we will see later in this book, Anghard N. Valdivia's take on Latinx stereotyping in popular media is useful. "At issue is not the use of stereotypes—that is nearly inevitable—but the reduction of a particular group to a small number of stereotypes that serve to marginalize or demonize a group of the population."[78] *Scarface* does just this work of marginalizing and demonizing through a limited field of vision.

Then there is Pacino's over-the-top performance of Cuban-ness. The actor's heavy accent, explosive line delivery, and physical posturing have been alternately embraced, mocked, and reviled since the film was released. All of this is heightened by costuming, including expensive but tacky suits later in the film, that underscores Tony's transformation from street thug to kingpin. Around the time of *Scarface*'s release, many critics and interviewers posited that Pacino's Tony reflected his own "Latin" ethnicity as an Italian American. Their logic was that, as a person of Mediterranean origin, he possessed a Latin temperament and sensibility. Pacino repeated this idea, which he associated with where he grew up, telling a *Rolling Stone* interviewer that "coming from the South Bronx, being, in a sense, Latin myself, I have a certain connection to the Latin feeling."[79] Latin connections notwithstanding, the performance soon became notorious for its lack of nuance. Pauline Kael's description of the film in her 1983 *New Yorker* review also applies specifically to Pacino: "The picture is peddling primitive machismo at the same time that it is making it absurd," she wrote.[80] Then and now, many reviewers faulted Pacino's performance for veering into caricature. However, it is worth noting that it might have tapped into the dominant culture's view of Cuban refugees, since, as Jillian Marie Jacklin and other scholars have noted, so much of the media coverage construed the Marielitos in dehumanizing terms.

Pacino is not the only actor who performs latinidad in *Scarface*. Steven Bauer, a Cuban émigré himself, gives a more subdued performance as Manny (not unlike George Raft as Manny's counterpart in the original film). In an interesting counterpoint to the endlessly depraved Tony, Manny demonstrates a high level of business acumen and, especially later in the film, a level-headed calm in the face of the many storms Tony creates as he grows more and more unhinged. Bauer's performance is one of the most subtle in the film. The same cannot be said of the performance of Mary Elizabeth Mastrantonio as Gina, which somewhat resembles Pacino's in terms of exaggerated accent and mannerisms. Mastrantonio, Italian American like Pacino, plays Gina as what might be called "fiery," a film trope associated with Latinas since the beginning of the medium (and with Italians, from Hawkes's *Scarface* to the present). As in the original film, incestuous undertones color the relationship between brother and sister.

All three versions of *Scarface* can be read as morality plays—but with different morals. The first film was considered dangerous by the Hays Office and censorship boards, but not because it subverted the system of identifying the good guys and the bad guys. In fact, the film includes storylines of two groups that attempt to bring order to Chicago's violent chaos: journalists and the police. At the end of Hawks's film, it is the cops who put an end to Tony Camonte's reign of terror. This was a common motif for exploitation films of the thirties: titillating with sex, violence, and criminality but ultimately landing on the side of law and order. At one point, the movie was titled *The Shame of the Nation* and sometimes screened as *Scarface: The Shame of the Nation*. This moralistic bent deviated from its source material, the hard-boiled 1930 novel by Armitage Trail, which is full of corrupt public officials, including a chief of detectives who is on the make. Hawks, however, eliminated any hint of police corruption. The filmmakers' attempt to infuse the film with "good guys" and its law-and-order ending reflected the limits of what was possible to depict in a Hollywood film of the early thirties.

The remake, however, does return to Trail's pessimistic view of crime and justice. The only cop in the film, Bernstein (Harris Yulin), is on the take; he tries to extort Tony and winds up dead. The absence of any good guy to cheer for might explain why critics and some audiences were initially hostile toward the film. According to many sources, audiences at the film's premiere booed at De Palma's dedication of his movie to original writer and director Howard Hawks and Ben Hecht, expressing their distaste for its glorification of its corrupt protagonist, which Hawks and Hecht carefully avoided. A distrust of the system is a theme throughout the movie: Tony refers to members of the political, media, and banking establishments as "whores" and aggrandizes himself for "telling the truth, even when I'm lying." In what some critics have read as a metaphor for Stone and De Palma's attitudes toward the movie establishment, Tony and Elvira make a scene in a fancy restaurant in front of wealthy and powerful patrons. "Say goodnight to the bad guy," Tony shouts on his way out the door. He comes to embrace his "bad guy" reputation, but for all the wrong reasons: He does so under the hubristic notion that he is "bad" because he tells the truth, not because he hurts people.

The shared DNA of the three versions of the story is especially evident in their endings. Each ends with Tony's brutal death: In the novel, he is shot by his brother, a detective with the Chicago Police Department; the 1932 film eliminates the storyline of fraternal rivalry and has Tony die in a spray of gunfire from the police; in De Palma's remake, he is killed by Sosa's South American foot soldiers. The novel and two films are also linked by an overarching theme: their main characters' desperate grab for the American Dream. Most versions of the movie's poster, as well as subsequent VHS and DVD box art, include the tagline: "He loved the American Dream. With a vengeance." In all three versions, Tony's willingness to do anything to get ahead puts him at odds with his immigrant family, especially his mother, who always represents humble Old World attitudes in contrast to his fast-paced, modern ambitions. The Trail novel puts it this way:

> While he loves his parents with the fierce, clan-love of the Latin, he did not respect their ideas. There were many logical reasons for that—their inability to learn English well, their inability to keep step with the times and the country, their bewilderment—even after twenty years—at the great nation which they had chosen for their new home, the fact that even with his father working hard every day and his mother tending the little store they had only been able to make a bare living for the large family. So why should he accept their ideas or ethics? Where had those ideas gotten them? Tony didn't intend to live like this all his life; he meant to be a big shot.[81]

The 1932 film dramatizes this tension whenever Tony visits his mother, who is always cooking in her kitchen. The generational conflict is deepened through the character of Tony's sister Cesca, who also bristles at her mother's traditionalism (and Tony's overprotectiveness) by dressing provocatively, partying, and moving into an apartment with Tony's right-hand man Guino (George Raft). Similar dynamics shape De Palma's film as well.

SCARFACE AND ICONICITY

It would be difficult to overestimate the importance of *Scarface* to the body of texts that I call "narcomedia." In the course of researching this book, I came to think of the film as the starting point for many of the tropes that concern me in these pages: the immigrant narrative paired with drug trafficking, the excesses of the poor boy who gets rich, the kingpin who is ultimately undone by his own product. *Scarface* was not the first time that Hollywood or popular culture depicted cocaine. Nor did De Palma and his collaborators invent the idea of a Latinx kingpin. Yet, it has endured over four decades in ways that no one could have predicted in the early 1980s. This is all the more remarkable when one considers that the movie was initially only a minor success at the box office, earning a respectable but certainly not spectacular $65 million upon its initial release.

In the intervening years, however, the 1983 *Scarface* has grown into nothing less than a cultural phenomenon. Countless pop culture texts have paid homage to the film—from a character in Guy Ritchie's *Lock, Stock, and Two Smoking Barrels* (1998) confessing that everything he knows about the drug trade he learned from *Scarface* to a passable impression of Tony Montana by Chris Tucker in the movie *Friday* (1995). Saddam Hussein and his sons were reputedly such loyal fans of the movie that they named their money-laundering holding company "Montana Management" as an homage to their favorite fictional character.[82]

Scarface has inspired other narcomedia texts as well, including several video games. The game *Scarface: The World Is Yours* most closely resembles the film, although it rewrites the ending so that Tony survives and must regain control of Miami's drug trade, destroy rival gangs, and restore his reputation in the criminal underworld. It is in the upper echelon of games that are voiced by well-known actors, including Robert Loggia and Steven Bauer from the film. In addition, Tony Montana and his catchphrases have grown in popularity as tattoo motifs. In 2021, Universal Pictures licensed the Tony Montana image to Spanish retailer Pull&Bear, a global retail chain that draws heavily from US popular culture in its motifs. The store sold sweatshirts with larger-than-life portraits of Tony with a single tear streaming down his cheek (a still from a scene late in the movie), among other *Scarface*-branded apparel.

Recent narcomedia TV series have been especially keen to acknowledge De Palma's movie as a touchstone and source of inspiration, creating some fascinating intertextual layers. For example, the second season of *Narcos: Mexico* touches upon the introduction of crack to the United States. Quavos, a visiting drug dealer (a cameo by rapper Quavos, who, before guest starring, wrote a song about *Narcos* as part of the rap trio Migos) demonstrates the substance to some of his Tijuana contacts, but refuses to use it himself when a group of women smoke it at a party. "I know you don't understand this," he tells one of the Mexican women as she offers him the pipe, "but I'm going to tell you like a bad bitch told Tony: 'Don't get high

1.2. Decades after the film's release, Tony Montana is a popular motif for tattoos. Alamy Photo.

on your own supply.'" One of his associates adds, "That's Michelle fucking Pfeiffer, that's *Scarface*," referencing one of Elvira's lines from *Scarface*. "Tony should have listened," concludes Quavos.[83] The moment is meant as a bit of levity in a deadly serious show, but also serves as one of several references to *Scarface* in the *Narcos* universe. The previous episode included a plot point in which kingpin Félix Gallardo receives a tiger as a gift, presumably a reference to Tony's tiger in *Scarface* and, as in that movie, intended as a metaphor for Félix's excesses. At another point in the series, characters are watching the film. In a personal interview, *Narcos* co-creator Carlo Bernard told me that the writers of the series were quite intentional about referencing *Scarface* as well as *The Godfather* and *Goodfellas* (1990), describing these texts as having a "shared language."[84] At the peak of *Breaking Bad*'s popularity in the early 2010s, Vince Gilligan, the show's creator and showrunner, told several interviewers that he pitched the series as what happens when "you take Mr. Chips and turn him into Scarface," referencing both the De Palma film and a beloved schoolteacher

1.3. The iconic scene from *Scarface* set in Tony and Elvira's ostentatious bathroom has inspired countless memes and at least one rap video. Alamy Photo.

character.[85] Gilligan paid subtle tribute to *Scarface* by casting several actors from the film as recurring characters in the series, including Steven Bauer and Mark Margolis. *Breaking Bad* nods to *Scarface* even more explicitly in its fifth season, when a character is concerned to find her family laughing and cheering along with the movie's violent ending.[86]

Scarface has been an especially enduring source of inspiration in rap and hip-hop cultures. As Dimitri A. Bogazianos puts it in his book on rap music and crack, "In all of rap's gangster mythology there is perhaps no more overused imagery than Brian De Palma's 1983 movie, *Scarface*, especially its last scene."[87] In music videos, several rap and hip-hop artists have also recreated the famous bathtub scene in which a cigar-chomping Tony clashes with Elvira while sitting in a gold-plated tub. In the film, the over-the-top setting is meant to signify Tony's hubris, but for the artists who appropriate the scene, it seems to signify that they are at the top of their games. Nas refers to himself as "Scarface" and to Jay Z as "Manolo" in his 2002 track, "Last Real Nigga Alive." Rapper Brad Terrence Jordan, a member of the influential hip-hop group Geto Boys, performed under the name Scarface from the late 1980s until he ran for Houston City Council in 2019. A special DVD release in 2005 featured an eighteen-minute documentary produced by Def Jam Recordings, *Scarface: Origins of a Hip Hop Classic*, that included interviews with Jordan, as well as Sean Combs, Snoop Dogg, Eve, and other rap and hip-hop artists who describe how the film influenced them. Reflecting on his career in the 2015 documentary *De Palma*, the director acknowledges that rap and hip-hop cultures gave the film a surprising second life years after its initial release. As I will argue regarding depictions of Pablo Escobar in rap and hip-hop, Tony Montana has moved from antihero to hero in many of these depictions, reflecting the long-standing influence of gangster media on rap culture, which by the 1990s was increasingly saturated with rags-to-riches gangster narratives of young men navigating a world where few moral choices were black and white.

In a fascinating example of life imitating art, several real-life narcos have also paid homage to *Scarface* over the years. In 2012, Italian police confiscated a life-size bust of Pacino as Tony Montana as part of a raid on the home of a suspected drug boss outside Naples.[88] Two years later, suburban Toronto police officers stole a three-foot statue of Tony found among the possessions of a drug suspect. The officers were forced to resign in 2019 when they admitted to the theft.[89] De Palma's film is an interpretation of another filmmaker's interpretation of a novel, but real gangsters have carried the interpretive process even further.

The enduring popularity of *Scarface* has led several Hollywood players to begin work on a remake in recent years. Universal tapped director Antoine Fuqua for the project in 2016, with reports that Mexican actor Diego Luna would star.[90] (Fuqua had previously been in talks to direct a movie about Pablo Escobar.[91]) Fuqua's *Scarface* would once again make Tony an immigrant, this time from Mexico with Los Angeles as his base. Like its predecessors, this film would have tapped into cultural anxieties about drugs and immigrants in the United States, with a new Latino bad guy. Fuqua moved on to other projects, but the idea for a third remake continues to circulate in the trade press. In De Palma's movie, Tony tells the snobby white patrons of a fancy restaurant to "say goodnight to the bad guy." But it seems that popular culture is not quite ready to turn out the lights on this highly salable and complex media property.

CHAPTER 2

MIAMI VICES

Whiteness and Otherness in Representing the Criminalized City

Almost four years to the day after the "Paradise Lost?" cover story, Miami was once again on the front of *Time* magazine . . . sort of. This time, instead of a harrowing take on South Florida as a nexus of America's problems related to drugs and immigration, the cover subject was one of the most popular TV shows in the United States, a breakout hit then in its second season: *Miami Vice* (1984–1990). The cover illustration features the show's costars, Don Johnson and Philip Michael Thomas, smiling widely against a flamingo-pink background. The headline, "Cool Cops, Hot Show," was very much in tune with much of the media coverage about *Miami Vice* in late 1985.[1] Rather than focusing on dire crime rates, immigrant threats, or gun-toting pastors, writer Richard Zoglin focuses on the show's style and glamor. "With [main characters] Crockett and Tubbs at the wheel of their Ferrari, designer jackets whipping in the wind," Zoglin writes, "the TV world had better run for cover."[2] Zoglin even quotes Mayor Maurice Ferré as calling himself a fan—a far cry from Demetrio Pérez's feud with Martin Bregman. It might have appeared to *Time* readers that the popular image of South Florida had shifted from the bleak narrative of 1981 to something sunnier.[3]

I argue in the previous chapter that *Scarface* helped to construct many of the tropes of latinidad and drug trafficking that pop culture continues to recycle decades later. I also argue that the film helped to construct the city of Miami (and, to some extent, its environs) as a character in the War on Drugs of the early 1980s, when cocaine reigned supreme as the main enemy of that war. Another product of Universal Studios, *Miami Vice*, which aired on NBC for the entire second half of the decade, helps to paint a fuller picture of Miami and latinidad in the eighties and offers insights into how media activism changed after *Scarface*.

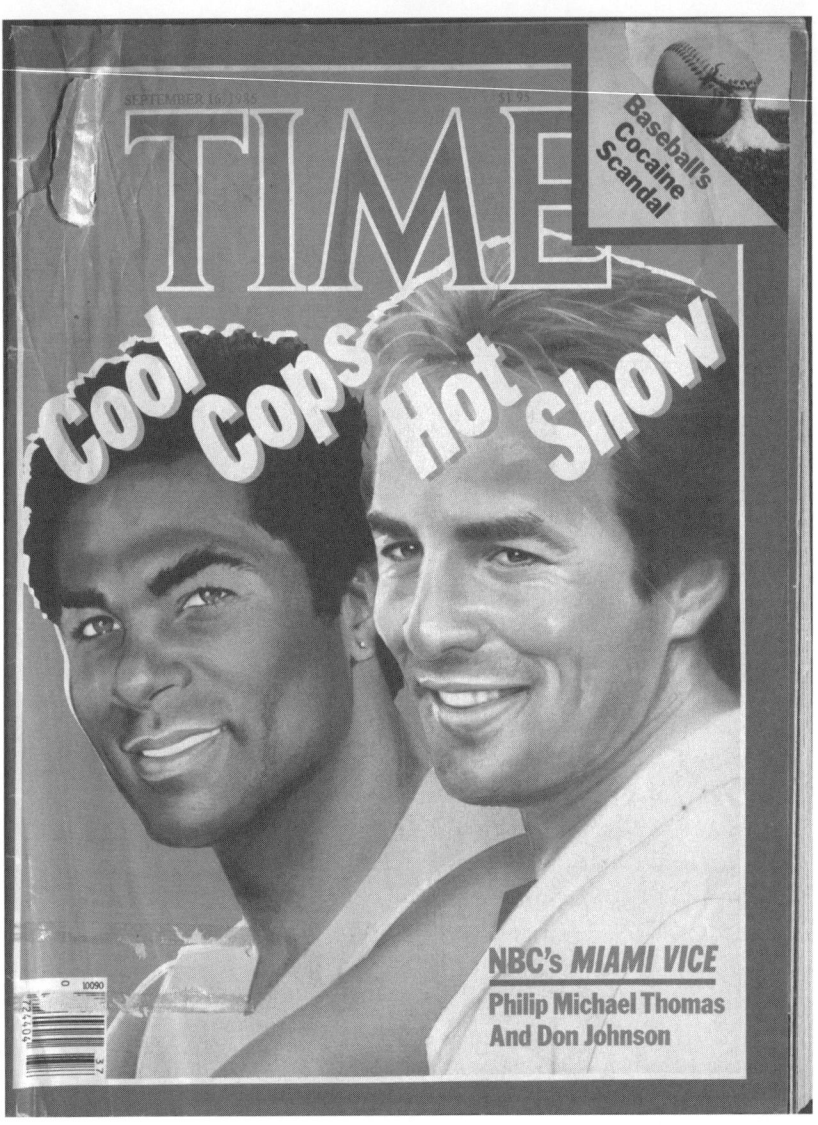

2.1. Four years after *Time* framed South Florida as "Paradise Lost," the newsmagazine touted Crocket and Tubbs as a couple of cool cops.

The later *Time* cover might imply that concerns about South Florida had subsided, but I want to stress that the show it celebrated actually told a cautionary tale about race and ethnicity that resonates with *Scarface*. Following an overview of the show and its racial and ethnic landscapes, I turn to three key representational problems that connect the series to other narcomedia texts that I examine in this book: narratives of white innocence, the centrality of the white protagonist to the series, and the politics of casting. Some of these elements are evident in *Scarface*, but *Miami Vice* provides an especially clear case study for understanding how popular media of the mid- to late 1980s reinforced dominant drug narratives even in the context of an apparently edgy mode of storytelling.

It is tempting to dismiss *Miami Vice* as a relic of the eighties—all neon lights, pastel suits, and speedboats—but the series has had a lasting influence over how many Americans see latinidad and the War on Drugs. *Miami Vice* was part of a wave of television series that depicted the social problems of the 1980s with gritty realism and ripped-from-the-headlines storylines. This spate of shows, always set in big cities, included *Hill Street Blues* (NBC, 1981—1987, on which the *Miami Vice* creator Anthony Yerkovich worked for two seasons), *St. Elsewhere* (NBC, 1982–1988), and *Cagney & Lacey* (CBS, 1981—1988). These shows and their many imitators had procedurals from previous decades in their DNA, but their focus on real-world social problems such as AIDS, urban decay, racism, and, of course, the War on Drugs gave them a 1980s sensibility. This was an iteration of ambitious, cinematic televisual fare that was often labeled "quality programming" at the time and that predates the current era of prestige television examined in later chapters.[4] These shows varied in popularity—*St. Elsewhere*, for example, owed its longevity to accolades from critics and a devoted but small core audience—but resemble one another in tone and in the somewhat liberal outlook that challenged viewers to condemn broken social and political systems rather than individuals. Like most of the series in this cycle, *Miami Vice* presents a downbeat view of American systems and institutions, depicting flawed but hard-working people whose efforts are often futile in the face of governmental corruption and neglect.

Miami Vice drew on "quality television" tropes and developed some of its own. Many of the episodes end abruptly after a climax involving violence or death, often on a freeze-frame of main character Sonny Crockett. This lack of a denouement lends a tone that is even more nihilistic and despairing than that of other cop shows of the era. Shows like *Cagney & Lacey* often featured hard-working cops going home to their families after a shift, but *Miami Vice* episodes rarely offer closure of that type. Instead, they underscore the futility of police work in a setting in which justice is rarely achieved. This sense of hopelessness culminates in the series finale, in which Crockett and Tubbs turn in their badges, quitting the force after fully realizing the depths of corruption at every level of law enforcement. Terry Kath's bluesy 1973 song, "Tell Me," accompanies a long final montage featuring some of the key moments of the previous five seasons, giving the finale an even more downbeat tone. Late in the song, background singers repeat the phrase "God bless America today," but the music and the final sequence of the series drive home the point that the good guys are losing the War on Drugs.

Miami Vice presents a compelling, if daunting, object of study partly because there is simply so much of it: The series consists of roughly 112 hour-long episodes.[5] As research for this chapter, I viewed the entire series several times over and consulted hundreds of primary and secondary sources. Still, I am not convinced that *Vice* is really a cohesive object of study. It is too sprawling and contradictory ("polysemic" in cultural studies-speak) of a text to lend itself to easy readings, even if, at the time of its release and for many years after, the show had a reputation for superficiality.[6] As Doug Kellner has put it, "Behind the high-tech glitz are multiple sites of meaning, multiple subject positions, and highly contradictory ideological problematics."[7] In my view, the show simultaneously anticipates what television scholar Jason Mittell calls the "narratively complex TV" of the 1990s and is maddeningly formulaic and repetitive.[8] Separate volumes could be written about the dominant themes of the series, from criminal justice reform to male beauty and fashion.

Miami Vice, along with its executive producer and director Michael Mann, has been the subject of dozens of academic studies, from formalist analyses to philosophical interpretations—further evidence of its surprising complexity. In the 1980s and 1990s, for example, some scholars in television studies used the series to explore questions about postmodern televisual storytelling, asking if its apparent superficiality is, in fact, one of the ways that the show makes meaning.[9]

Given the aims of this book, I am especially interested in the subject of ethnicity and race in *Miami Vice*, particularly how the show represents latinidad in relation to the War on Drugs. Its patterns of representing Latinx characters simultaneously tap into existing Latinx tropes that circulated in the popular culture of the 1980s and revise and reshape those tropes to create new patterns of representation that lasted long after the run of the series. Most academic and critical takes on the series acknowledge the political and racial context of Miami in the early 1980s. However, as we will see with later series like *Breaking Bad*, which are lauded on technical grounds and celebrated as the vision of a brilliant auteur, these studies do not provide a detailed reading of the show's racial logics. I want to ask what happens to this cultural artifact when we take an ethnic studies approach, which places race and ethnicity at the center of its critique. This chapter shows how *Miami Vice* both draws upon and creates representational practices that construct South Florida as a racially and ethnically dangerous flashpoint in the War on Drugs. It does so by examining casting practices and star power related to the show, as well as how, despite constructing a multiracial and multiethnic storyworld, *Miami Vice* consistently centers whiteness in its storytelling.

After failing to find a wide audience in its first season, during which many critics and industry observers predicted its cancellation, *Miami Vice* picked up considerable steam in summer reruns, where it capitalized on its sunny, summery setting and did not have to compete with first-run episodes of ratings juggernaut *Falcon Crest*, which aired in its time slot on CBS.[10] Creator Anthony Yerkovich and executive producer Mann took the national interest in Miami and blended ripped-from-the-headlines cop show tropes with a compelling mix of music videos, neo-noir, police procedural, melodrama, and, at times, comedy. (Below, I refer to Mann as the creative force behind the show; Yerkovich wrote the pilot but departed *Miami Vice* after the first seven episodes, and the show bears Mann's distinctive stylistic imprint, although he also departed to work on another series after season two.[11])

The series is generally considered to have declined considerably in quality after its first two seasons. Season three marked a shift in tone toward increasingly darker storylines under new executive producer Dick Wolf (best known for his mega success with *Law & Order* and its spinoffs), and season four suffered from the departure of most of its original writers. The fifth and final season featured increasingly bizarre and soap opera-like plots, including a three-episode story arc in which Crockett gets amnesia and believes that he is Sonny Burnett, his undercover alter ego. Only season two of the series ever cracked the Nielson ratings top ten—and the final two seasons failed to even make it into the top thirty. Even so, taken together, the five seasons of *Miami Vice* provide a revealing view of the city as a symbol of eighties excess, the supposed dangers of immigration and "Latinization," and the futility of the War on Drugs.

A key factor in why *Miami Vice* exists at all is the news coverage that I describe in the previous chapter.[12] There, I read *Scarface* in conversation with popular discourse about the Mariel Boatlift and South Florida's reputation as the entry point for drugs. I also address mainstream media coverage of Miami's shifting racial demographics, which are one of the discourses that *Miami Vice* informed. The series tapped into narratives of Miami in decline, but also emphasized the glamorous side of city, along with its beauty and that of its people. Michelle Pfeiffer's character performed this role in *Scarface*, but fashion, style, music, and pleasure are all over *Miami Vice*. More than that film, the series also emphasizes the tropical aesthetics of Miami (though the city is, in climatological terms, subtropical). In a short but powerful essay in the anthology *Tropicalizations*, Juan León argues that a "unique kind of tropicality has been at the heart of what modern America wants from Miami" and that development of the city depended on notions of South Florida as a distinctly American and modern tropics.[13] León's chapter focuses on literary representations of *balseros* ("raft people"), but his formulation of Miami's "questionable tropicality" is also an apt way of approaching how *Miami Vice* constructs an aesthetic of glamor that is tropical but dangerous, American but foreign.[14]

Despite this infusion of glamor, the series reflected the very serious issue of racial strife in the city. In 1980, Miami made national headlines when the acquittal of four Dade County Public Safety Department officers in the death of Arthur McDuffie, a Black insurance salesman and Marine, led to four days of rioting in the areas of Liberty City and Overtown that resulted in the deaths of at least eighteen people. The "Paradise Lost?" article in *Time*, along with other news media coverage and films like *Scarface*, grew out of perceptions of Miami as a racially volatile city in the wake of the riots. Star Don Johnson recalled the atmosphere in a 2014 *Rolling Stone* interview:

> When I got off the plane to do the pilot, you could feel the pressure cooker of violence in the air. It was one of those cases where, "Well, we ain't in Kansas no more." But it was rich and raw. The whole city was just dilapidated, and it was during that time where there was a huge transition from the old white establishment to the influx of Cubans and Hispanics. That was a gigantic factor that contributed to the riots and unrest.[15]

Although it frequently references Overtown as a particularly volatile area of the city, *Vice* explicitly mentions the riots only once in five years. Late in the fourth season, while investigating some corrupt Cuban American cops, the team learns that the dirty cops were hired for affirmative action purposes in the aftermath of the rioting.[16] Thus, the only explicit reference to the riots depicts negative consequences of anti-racist efforts that followed.

Three features distinguish *Miami Vice* from other urban crime series of the 1980s. First, Mann insisted on using original pop hits as the soundtrack of the show rather than the standard cost-saving practice of using covers or generic mood music, often giving the show the feeling of an extended music video. "The show is written for an MTV audience," director Lee H. Katzin told *Time* one year into its run, "which is more interested in images, emotions and energy than plot and character and words."[17] This MTV-style

2.2. *Miami Vice* was both emulated and ridiculed for highlighting male fashion, with star Don Johnson typically front and center. Alamy Photo.

use of music and editing contrasts sharply with other crime series of the era, which tended to cast a more somber tone through music and editing. Second, costumers dressed the show's male leads in fashion-forward pastel T-shirts and expensive Italian-made linen suits. Though somewhat unbelievable for the characters, these sartorial choices were widely influential in the mid- to late eighties, and, even decades later, the show remains synonymous with casual but extensive menswear in pastel hues. Third, *Miami Vice* features Black actor Philip Michael Thomas in the second-billed starring role. Throughout the course of the series, Thomas was paid significantly less than Don Johnson, his white costar, and, as I will explore below, his role was significantly diminished as Johnson became a major Hollywood star. Nonetheless, *Vice* did serve as a showcase for Thomas, who became a household name at the height of the show's popularity. Unlike other shows in the genre, it also capitalized on the handsome Black actor's sex appeal.

Miami Vice focuses on the professional and personal lives of undercover detectives Sonny Crockett (Johnson) and Rico Tubbs (Thomas) as they tackle drugs, prostitution, and other "vices" in the city. Crockett goes undercover as Sonny Burnett and Tubbs as Rico Cooper. The latter, while undercover, frequently affects a Jamaican or Latino accent. Some critics and scholars have interpreted Tubbs to be of Puerto Rican descent, based on his first name, the fact that he is from New York, and his Spanish-language skills, but viewers are offered almost no back story on him following the death of his brother in the pilot. I see this reading as conjecture and find that he is most frequently presented as non-Latino African American. Although several multi-episode story arcs take place over the course of *Vice*, the show typically takes a villain-of-the-week approach to its storytelling, with stand-alone episodes that wrap up by the final minute.

In the movie-length pilot, which was split into two episodes for syndication, Crockett and Tubbs, both reeling from the murder of fellow cops (Crockett's partner, Tubbs's brother), form an uneasy partnership. A Colombian cartel was behind both murders, so the detectives are united in their quest to take down the drug traffickers. Late in the pilot episode, Tubbs comes face-to-face in an armed standoff with Esteban Calderone, the Colombian kingpin who killed his brother. He flashes back to the shots that were fired in his brother's killing. (Calderone is played by playwright Miguel Piñero, one of the founders of the Nuyorican Poets Café, who also wrote one of the season's episodes.[18]) Tubbs is tempted to pull the trigger as Calderone sneers at him. "Not like this, man," cautions Crockett, and Tubbs puts down his gun, resisting his urge for extralegal justice. In the next scene, when they go to the jail in an attempt to transfer Calderone, they find that he has been released on bail. The new partners make a run to an airport, but arrive to see him board a seaplane and take off. "I'm sorry," says Crockett sincerely. "He'll be back. New name, new people, but he'll be back. Hell, this is the sunshine state, right?" He and Tubbs ride off toward the sunrise together in Crockett's now iconic Ferrari.

This ending cements the characters of Crockett and Tubbs as cynical but essentially honest cops who work within a broken system. As the culmination of the pilot, it also sets the tone for the rest of the series, as it underscores the idea that, no matter how hard the good guys work to make Miami a safer place, there will always be a new villain for next week's episode. Not surprisingly, given the popular perception of Miami that circulated in texts like *Scarface*, the villains tended to be Latinos. Crockett and Tubbs eventually do track down Calderone in the Bahamas a few episodes later, where Tubbs has an intense fling with the Colombian's artistic daughter and Crockett kills the kingpin in the climactic scene.[19] This also establishes a tone for a series where dozens of Latino bad guys threaten Crockett, Tubbs, and the general social order over the seasons.

A brief exchange between two white characters that takes place in the second season captures the treatment of Latinx characters. Jackson and Skip are preppy white young men who take to ripping off Latin American smugglers by posing as US customs agents. As "trust fund pirates," Jackson and Skip are two of several white characters who get involved in the criminal underworld but escape suspicion, at least at first, because of their race and socioeconomic status. At one point, Jackson and Skip get into a shootout with some Colombian drug runners. The melee leaves one minor character dead, leading to the following dialogue:

JACKSON: You wasted Moralez. You killed him.
SKIP: It wasn't such a big deal.
JACKSON: It was murder.
SKIP: Look, maybe we're just doing somebody a favor. These South American low-lives come up here with their dirty drug money and they breed like, like cockroaches. And they ruin the place for real Americans like you and me. Maybe, uh, we just exterminate them. Maybe we are just like Sir Francis Drake. Maybe we're good pirates.[20]

On one hand, this plot point and dialogue exchange is clearly meant as a reflection on Skip as a spoiled brat (at one point, Skip says that "trust fund babies just wanna have fun") and a racist. On the other hand, this dialogue and the scene play on the racial logic of the show over its five seasons: Latinx characters are useful as foils but ultimately expendable. The use of the word "cockroaches"—a term frequently associated with migrants from Latin America and a favorite insult of Tony Montana in *Scarface*—underscores the overarching characterization of migrants as an invasive nuisance, as does the reference to their hyperfertility, the idea that they "come here to breed" being a common xenophobic sentiment.[21] Of course, an unsympathetic character expresses this racist and xenophobic viewpoint, so one potential interpretation might be that it actually intends to expose and critique anti-Latinx violence. However, with so little to counteract or contradict it in the overarching text that is *Miami Vice*, it is difficult for me to understand it in this way.

Unlike *Scarface*, *Miami Vice* filmed almost entirely on location in its titular city and environs for its entire run. This included then-blighted Miami Beach, which served as a backdrop to many of the action scenes. City and county officials, still reeling from the debacle with the *Scarface* producers, were simultaneously nervous about the city's image and eager for the economic windfall that comes with a major studio production. They met with NBC management in August 1984 to discuss their concerns about Miami's image. (Demetrio Pérez was not invited.) Despite the fact that a Miami-Dade police lieutenant who had been consulting with the show quit in protest over its depiction of police corruption, associate producer John Nicolella assured the officials that the series depicted "good police doing good police work."[22] For the next five years of filming, the *Vice* producers did not receive complaints from city and county government officials, many of whom, for years to come, credited the show for Miami's rebirth as a glamorous destination.

Miami Vice featured a multicultural and multiethnic cast, undoubtedly intended to reflect perceptions of Miami as a racial and ethnic contact zone. This includes Thomas, one of the few Black leading actors on TV at the time (*The Cosby Show* premiered the week after the *Miami Vice* pilot aired), as well as Edward James Olmos, Saundra Santiago, Olivia Brown, and other Black and Latinx actors in supporting roles. More often than not, the show aimed to capture the tense racial relations of South Florida that dominated news media attention, so it constructed Miami's social landscape through stock racial types: Latino drug runners, Black Haitian voodoo priests, brown and Black prostitutes. Many of these stock types had appeared in the news media of the time, so audiences were already familiar with them. *Vice*'s multiracial storyworld includes episodes that take the main characters (and viewers) into different racialized settings, from Japanese crime syndicates to Seminole Indian country, providing the opportunities for these racialized Others to appear onscreen but then disappear by next week's episode.

Unsurprisingly, *Vice* plays these racialized encounters in different ways and to different ends. One sight gag from the two-hour series premiere takes place in a scene at a courthouse when a brief power outage leaves all present in the dark. When the lights go back on, the bailiff, judge, clerk, even the stenographer all have guns pointed at the defendant, who is Black. The image of multiple white people pointing guns at a Black man is jarring from a contemporary perspective, but the gag seems to directly reference the description from *Time*'s "Paradise Lost?" cover story of unlikely people arming themselves to cope with high crime rates in South Florida. The

Miami Herald news coverage of the time also frequently referenced citizens, even unlikely ones, learning how to handle guns for self-protection. The bigger idea supported by the courtroom "joke" is that white people in Miami better be ready to defend themselves against the Black and brown people in their midst, an ideology that persists decades later in "stand your ground" laws and ongoing violence against unarmed Black people.[23]

Miami Vice is, among other things, a text that places white characters and people of color in contact and conflict with one another, a hallmark of the narcomedia narrative that will be apparent in later chapters. This is an aspect of 1980s Miami that frightened some real-world observers, as I showed in the previous chapter concerning the remake of *Scarface*, and served as a source of tension in the series, as it did in other crime series of the eighties. Crockett and Tubbs frequently share a glance, a chuckle, or a joke at the expense of Black characters, such as a jive-talking informant named Noogie who appears in six episodes, or Latinx characters like series regular Izzy, a Cuban American informant and ne'er-do-well who is one of very few sources of comic relief in the entire series. At other times, they make racialized presumptions about the criminality of Black and brown characters. Crockett and Tubbs are partners, of course, but moments like these, along with the many times that Crockett gives Tubbs orders, suggest that they are not equals. In this way, *Miami Vice*, although attempting to paint a multiracial portrait of its titular city, actually reinforces color lines and social boundaries.

Color lines are reinforced, for example, through the romantic and sexual storylines involving the show's main characters. Crockett's romantic entanglements drive many of the episodes' plots and multi-episode story arcs, including early in the series when he is involved with Cuban American character Gina Calabrese. Following his tryst with Gina, with whom he has sex but does not romance, Crockett's paramours consist exclusively of white women. (Gina seems to accept Crockett's rejection.) *Miami Vice* frequently celebrates the beauty and style of brown and Black women—and Crockett constantly interacts with non-white characters in his everyday life—so the exclusivity of his romantic pairing speaks to a deeper resistance by the showrunners to really challenge the racial order. Many of Crockett's girlfriends are not whom they appear to be at first (Helena Bonham Carter as a heroin-addicted doctor, Melanie Griffith as a madam posing as a legitimate businesswoman), but they are always cool, sophisticated, and as beautiful as Crockett. Over the course of the series, he divorces one (Belinda Montgomery) and, several seasons later, marries another, a pop star named Caitlin (Sheena Easton). The only time that Crockett does go on a date with a Black woman, he is already married to Caitlin and does so undercover as Sonny Burnett in order to catch a serial killer (played by Iman) preying on men who use a video dating service.[24]

Critics have observed that the Black partners in the mixed-race buddy cop genre frequently do not have sex lives of their own, but Tubbs also romances many women over the course of five seasons.[25] Like Crockett, the show pairs him with some high-profile female guest stars, such as Pam Grier, whose appearances span several seasons, and a number of up-and-coming Black actresses. In general, Thomas appears shirtless almost as much as Johnson, so it would be inaccurate to imply that the series does not position Tubbs as a sex symbol on par with Crockett. However, Tubbs's romantic and sexual partners never include white women. He sometimes protects or helps white women, but he never romances or seduces them. As with Crockett, he does not cross the Black-white sexual color line. In fact, the only time over the course of the entire series that sex occurs between Black and white characters is during an episode focused on a Black woman who takes revenge on her white rapist.[26] Tubbs does, however, romance some non-Black women, including a Seminole woman while undercover and, earlier in the series, the daughter of kingpin Calderone. Other characters similarly adhere to these norms, though the ex-wife of Lieutenant Martin Castillo (Edward James Olmos), with whom he rekindles a sexual relationship, is Asian, and Gina has a brief but passionate affair with an IRA activist. These forms of intimacy seem to suggest that Latinx characters inhabit a liminal space in the show's sexual binary.

Vice's sexual segregation is surprising, given that that show's creators obviously positioned the series as one that would push boundaries and conventions. It is also somewhat conservative even in the context of 1980s television, considering that many shows in its overlapping genres were exploring the theme of interracial sex and romance over the course of the eighties. *Hill Street Blues*, for example, featured several such storylines in just its first season in 1981. As with other TV series that I address in later chapters, *Miami Vice* appears more conventional than its creators wanted it to be.

WHITE-CENTRISM AND WHITE INNOCENCE

Miami Vice provides the first case study for a representational practice that will be important throughout the remainder of this book, namely the practice of what I call "narrative white-centrism" that characterizes many narcomedia texts. The terms "eurocentrism" and "anglocentrism" do not quite capture what I see operating in narcomedia texts. Instead of using either of those terms, I want to posit white-centrism as a framework for understanding their deep investments in whiteness as the core of their storytelling. White-centrism in narcomedia, as we shall see, humanizes some characters while pathologizing others. White-centrism is a key narrative modality for narco storytelling across a variety of media, from film and television to video games and pulp fiction, and takes a variety of forms, including screen time, voice-over narrative, and editing, all of which tell the viewer who is central to the narrative and who supports the main story. *Miami Vice* helped to cement some of the key narcomedia tropes associated with white-centric storytelling.

As we will see later in my analysis of so-called prestige television, a recurring theme of narcomedia is the idea that drugs create encounters between white people, often suburbanites, and people of color. An underlying racial logic of this trope is that these white people are intrinsically innocent about drugs and crime, in contrast to people of color, who function as natural producers, traffickers, dealers, and consumers of narcotics. Because *Miami Vice* takes place in the world of law enforcement, which frequently operates on the presumption of white innocence and non-white guilt, it is unsurprising that this narrative is an element of the show.

An episode that aired in November 1984 typifies white innocence in the show. Titled "Glades," it focuses on Crockett and Tubbs's encounter with a white extended family, the Bramlettes, who live deep in the Everglades and work as drug smugglers.[27] Joey Bramlette, an important witness against a Colombian drug kingpin named Ruiz, has fled his police protection in Miami, so Crockett and Tubbs go undercover looking for him in the "glades," which are beautiful but full of danger—from pythons hanging from trees to backwoods locals who fear and hate outsiders. In one scene, which seems to reference the 1972 film *Deliverance*, some rednecks beat up Crockett and Tubbs and leave them lost and helpless in the swamp. When the detectives finally encounter Joey and meet the other Bramlettes in the family safe house, they learn that Ruiz "has the whole town under his thumb." The kingpin has kidnapped Joey's nine-year-old daughter, Tammy, and is threatening to kill her if Joey testifies. It turns out that Joey fled in order to lure Crockett and Tubbs to the Everglades in the hope that they would help rescue Tammy. Crockett and Tubbs, charmed by the folksy and tightly knit Bramlettes, agree to help.

The episode contrasts the Bramlettes' criminality with that of the Ruiz cartel—and of Miami in general, considering that the episode opens with a musical montage of images shot on the streets of the city that depict hookers, pimps, hustlers, and thieves all hard at work. In contrast, the Bramlettes occupy a familial compound far removed from the gritty city. Over a plate of freshly baked biscuits, members of the family explain to Crockett and Tubbs how they got ensnared in the drug trade:

CASSIE: People around here depend on each other. Least they used to.
PAUL: Hell, I can remember when my granddaddy used to deliver liquor in here during Prohibition. And I can't hardly make a living just fishing and guiding.
TUBBS: So you started running weed.
PAUL: Yeah, a man's gotta feed his family.
JOEY: It began all of six or seven years ago, just a bunch of old long-hairs running a few bails on their sailboat.
CASSIE: Nice guys, really. No guns or nothing.
. . .
PAUL: And then Ruiz shows up with his money, fast talk, and big loads.
JOEY: We got sucked in real gradual.
PAUL: Next he brings in his own little army, making threats.
CASSIE: Killing people.

The episode and this scene in particular focus on the family's mom-and-pop-style drug running as a decent business for "nice guys" that only gets morally murky when ruthless Colombians terrorize their community. When Cassie says that Ruiz has actors in the drug trade killing people, she looks genuinely surprised and horrified by what has happened to her community since he edged his way into the business. Ruiz is present in each of the courtroom scenes, dressed outrageously flashy and laughing smugly with certainty that he will get off. But he does not utter any discernible dialogue, so the audience never hears his side of the story. This juxtaposition of essentially good white people with intrinsically criminal Latinxs is a theme we will see in chapter 5, when white innocence is juxtaposed with Latinx criminality in more recent media, including TV series like *Weeds* and *Breaking Bad* and films like *Savages*.

In the episode's climax, the cops must rescue the little girl from a house guarded by several Colombians and local accomplices with semiautomatic weapons. Crockett violates his own ethical code, established in the pilot, when he shoots one of the kidnappers, a white man, at close range in front of the terrified child. Soon after, Crockett's life is saved by Clem, an elderly member of the Bramlette clan who had been teased over the course of the episode for being an ignorant, naïve old coot. The point seems to be that, despite appearances, the toothless and heavily accented Clem possesses the down-home good sense to save the day. By the episode's end, several Colombians and their local accomplices are dead, but Tammy and her parents are reunited in what is presented as a happy ending. In the denouement, Joey takes the witness stand and the episode ends abruptly, intimating (but not showing) that Joey will give the testimony that will convict Ruiz.

"Glades" is one of many episodes where the dynamics of white goodness and vulnerability are at play in *Vice*. This is not to say, however, that the show represents the good guys and bad guys in the War on Drugs in clear-cut terms across racial lines. Over the series run, many white characters wind up on the wrong side of the law, from crooked politicians to biker gangs to shady televangelists. This includes some of Crockett's love interests, which leads him to muse in one episode: "First a junkie, now a hooker. I think I've been in the business too long. I'm starting to fall for the players."[28] This means that the show's racial logics do not take a cowboys-and-Indians approach to the crime narrative by drawing clear racial lines between heroes and villains. Its logics are subtler than that.

Most obviously, Black and brown characters populate the criminal underworld of *Miami Vice* at much greater density than white characters. And, more to my point, the show, like a lot of TV and movies that would follow, is much more likely to present white actors in the drug economy as complex, three-dimensional characters. This includes the dozens of "serious" and "informational" pop culture texts that attempted to deal with drug usage throughout the eighties, a body of texts that includes, for example, the made-for-TV movie *Cocaine: One Man's Seduction*, which aired on NBC just one year before *Vice* premiered on that network. It also includes other pop culture texts, including glitzier movies like *Less Than Zero* (1987) and *Bright Lights, Big City* (1988), both based on best-selling novels and set in seemingly all-white worlds. Such texts did not aim to educate but nonetheless place white characters at their centers and frame them as victims of the afflictions of cocaine abuse rather than as the progenitors of a social problem. *Miami Vice* predates so-called prestige television by more than a decade and a half, but it already set up (and tapped into) tropes of white innocence and complexity versus brown and Black stereotypes that still make up TV drug and crime narratives.

An episode that aired two seasons later echoes the "Glades" theme of a tightly knit community being held hostage by a Colombian cartel, but within a different racialized setting. In "The Afternoon Plane," Tubbs and his girlfriend du jour Alicia (Maria McDonald) think that they have won an all-expenses-paid vacation to the gorgeous but remote (and fictional) Caribbean island of St. Gerard, but the trip turns out to be a ploy by Orlando Calderone (John Leguizamo, costumed in a white suit like so many other narcomedia kingpins) to trap Tubbs and exact revenge for the death of his father in the show's first season.[29]

The episode is notable in part because it is one of the few in the series or the genre featuring an almost entirely Black cast. In a rare shift in focus, Johnson appears for just under two minutes at the start of the episode in a framing device that sends Tubbs and Alicia to the island. Once there, Tubbs realizes that one of his old flames from New York, Sally (Margaret Avery), now lives on St. Gerard and blames Tubbs for her current predicament: It turns out that Sally was romantically involved with Esteban Calderone and was left broke and stranded on St. Gerard when he was killed by Crockett early in the series. She is also clearly still attracted to Tubbs, which seems to be reciprocated.

"The Afternoon Plane" is what the *Miami Vice* fan community calls a "Tubbs episode," meaning that it is one of the minority of episodes that focuses almost solely on Rico, with Sonny in the background. Tubbs episodes have the potential to decenter whiteness in the overall *Vice* narrative, but this particular episode also plays on tropes of Black and brown criminality. Just like many of the locals in "Glades," who live under Ruiz's thumb, the people of St. Gerard are controlled by the Calderones, who use the island as a staging ground for drug running.[30]

A key theme of the episode is the townspeople's collusion with Calderone. "We ain't never gonna have it no better," says one character. Even the local constable is on the take. In one scene, Tubbs interrupts a town hall meeting at the island church, where the locals—almost all Black—are discussing the crisis of Orlando Calderone's impending arrival. They are completely unsympathetic to Tubbs's plight and refuse him the help he needs. Afterward, he desperately walks through the town but no one will come to his aid, with the exception of a fisherman named Jacques (John Archie), who tosses Tubbs a shotgun. The unwillingness of the townspeople to take a stand against Calderone (unlike the white community in "Glades"), compounded by the dramatic tension that builds as Tubbs waits for Calderone's plane to arrive, is a clear reference to *High Noon*. Several sources report that the working title for the episode was "The Noon Plane," an even more direct reference to the classic film (though I personally like how "afternoon" connotes a rethinking and retelling of the original).

"The Afternoon Plane" represents a clever take on interesting source material, but it also reflects the subtler racial logics of the series that I mention above, especially those relating to the threats posed by Latinx and Latin American characters. On one hand, the episode recasts a beloved classic film with a Black leading man at the center of the story. On the other, the theme of white innocence is compounded by a general sense of

Latinx, well, badness. Apart from Castillo and Calabrese, *Vice* takes place in a world populated by seemingly endless Latinx villains, from street thugs to crooked cops to kingpins. The show takes a pan-Latinx approach to this badness, featuring villains from Cuban revolutionaries and counter-revolutionaries to Central American street thugs to a Chilean diplomat who deals in illegal arms. The mere mention of the word "Colombian" is used time and again over the course of the series to signify criminality, danger, or cocaine; from Calderone onward, many Colombians function as boogie men and women in the War on Drugs narratives that *Vice* advances. Contemporary understandings of the series would benefit from newer work in US-Colombian studies and what one of its progenitors, María Elena Cepeda, calls the study of "global Colombianidad."[31] A special issue of the journal *Latino Studies* is testament to the fact that further research on Colombianness in the United States is needed.[32]

Generically framing Colombians as the bad guys—and as particularly deadly ones—was very much in the zeitgeist of the early to mid-1980s. It was his daring brutality against the Colombians that set Tony Montana on course to take over the Miami cocaine trade in *Scarface*. Even lighter fare at this time, such as the 1984 sleeper hit *Romancing the Stone*, equated Colombianness with ignorance, savagery, and danger. In a late-season four clip show of *Miami Vice*, a Colombian drug dealer's girlfriend shoots and critically wounds Crockett. (It is a clip episode because Crockett's hospital bed memories consist of reused footage from previous episodes.) Generic Colombianness is compounded by generic Latinoness elsewhere in the series. Another season four episode depicts another self-contained community—a Seminole tribe of Florida—threatened by indeterminate Latin American drug runners.[33] That episode is one of a few instances in which Tubbs teams up with Black or brown people, but even in that setting, the bad guys are always Latinos.[34] White innocence can only work as a mode of representation in a diegetic world where there is so much non-white badness.

In the end, despite the apathy of the St. Gerard community, Tubbs prevails in "The Afternoon Plane" and kills both Orlando Calderone and his cousin Xavier (Antone Pagán), thus providing some closure to the plotline that began in the pilot episode. However, Alicia is also shot and the episode ends abruptly with a scene where Tubbs carries her back into their hotel. Once again, *Miami Vice* refuses to provide closure, an artistic choice that consistently sets it apart from other procedurals of the era (a less generous reading might attribute this to careless plotting, but I happen to appreciate the ambiguous endings of many of the episodes). This is the last appearance of the Calderone crime family, which has appeared since the beginning of the series and has, up to this point, seen four of its members killed on *Vice*. (A later episode beats this death toll, with five members of a Latin American crime family killed in a single episode.³⁵) "The Afternoon Plane" takes the focus off Crockett, but it does not defy the racial logics of the show: Tubbs, a Black man, has prevailed, but, as always, he stands out as exceptional among Black characters. A Black woman is probably dead. By the next episode, he is back in Miami and neither the Calderones nor the people of St. Gerard are ever heard from again in subsequent episodes. The show has once again reset itself.

WHITE-CENTRISM IN A MULTIRACIAL STORYWORLD

The theme of white innocence illuminates the show's relationship to other War on Drugs narratives examined in this book, but *Vice*'s racial politics become more complex when we consider other dimensions of the show's multiracial regular cast. Saundra Santiago as Gina Calabrese appears, in my estimation, to be the first Latina to play a leading role on prime-time network television. Gina is often in the background of the action, but she does get several story arcs over the course of the series, including episodes where she is the focus of the action (perhaps they can be called "Gina episodes"). This is the case in the season three finale, which flashes back to the murder of her mother in Havana in 1961 at the hands of a romantically possessive *castrista* and, returning to 1987, focuses on Gina's temptation to kill the man who murdered her.³⁶ Santiago plays both Gina and her mother, Elena, in the emotionally complex episode that deals with memory, healing, and revenge. The episode showcases not only Santiago's singing skills by having both Gina and Elena perform as nightclub singers, but also her acting skills in the double part. Twice over the course of the series, Gina, in order to maintain her cover, is forced into sex by kingpins and she ends up shooting her sex partner. These plot devices might appear more apt for a soap opera than a serious-minded crime drama, but the point remains that at several times over the show's run, *Miami Vice* showcased Santiago's considerable range as an actor.

Other Latinx characters round out the main cast and recurring characters. When Lieutenant Lou Rodriguez (Gregory Sierra) is killed in the fourth episode, he is replaced by the taciturn but fair Lieutenant Martin Castillo. Castillo rarely smiles, but Edward James Olmos infuses him with a sense of quiet decency in a standout performance for which he won the 1985 Emmy Award for Best Supporting Actor in a dramatic series, the second Latino actor to ever win in that category. In addition, the character of Izzy, a stereotypical Cuban American hustler who finds myriad ways to get himself into trouble—and to annoy Crockett and Tubbs—reappears every

2.3. The cast of *Miami Vice* made it one of the most multiracial and multiethnic shows of the 1980s. Alamy Photo.

few episodes to offer comic relief. Izzy is played by Martin Ferrero, who plays a cross-dressing queer villain in the series pilot, as detailed in chapter 4 of this book.

Olivia Brown was a core cast member for the entire run of *Miami Vice*, and her character, Trudy, plays a more active role in the action at the start of the series. But by the third season, Trudy spends most of her time answering telephones or doing research for Crockett and Tubbs. Gina, who had been more central to the narrative, also becomes marginal in most of season three, but has important storylines in the first and final episodes.

Trudy, in contrast to everyone else in the main cast, almost always remains in the background. She figures prominently in a fourth season episode, but only because the episode serves as a vehicle for guest star James Brown and presumably the show needed a love interest for the star (as we have seen, interracial romance was on the menu in *Miami Vice*). James Brown's character may or may not be an alien, but he has mind control powers over Trudy in an episode that frequently makes lists of the worst episodes in TV history. In general, the audience knows very little about Trudy, unlike her counterpart Gina. As if to diminish her further, the nameplate on her desk reads "Big Booty Trudy." In the opening credits, Olivia Brown received sixth billing and then fifth when another character was killed off, but writers gave her far fewer lines than anyone else in the cast.

The makers of *Miami Vice* also created limited opportunities for people of color behind the camera. Olmos directed a second season episode, his directorial debut.[37] Black Cuban-born Georg Stanford Brown, who had directed for *Hill Street Blues*, also helmed two *Vice* episodes (and would go on to win an Emmy for directing an episode of *Cagney & Lacey*). It is notable as well that the queer avant-garde multimedia artist Miguel Piñero wrote and acted for the series. Piñero had built a highly lauded career in the theater following productions of his play *Short Eyes* in the mid-seventies, a work that he had written while incarcerated in Sing Sing. By the late 1970s, he had begun to act and write for film and television and was considered by producers to be an "authentic" voice from the streets. He died at the age of forty-one before *Miami Vice* ended its run. It would be an overstatement to claim that Piñero steered *Miami Vice* toward fairer representations of its Latinx characters, but his presence in front of and behind the camera does stand out among other network television series of the early 1980s.[38]

However, it bears mentioning that, despite some opportunities the show created for its multiracial cast and crew, *Miami Vice* suffers from a problem present in so much US popular culture, even today: The non-white characters all frame the central white protagonist, Sonny Crockett. This is a centering of the white character in a multiracial underworld that we will see again in later iterations of the TV narco narrative, such as in *Weeds*, *Breaking Bad*, and, three decades later, the first two seasons of *Narcos*, when the story of the Colombian drug trade is told through the perspective of a white protagonist. Crockett's whiteness is not unimportant to how the show makes meaning. It has been noted by other critics and scholars, some of whom have found that Crockett's whiteness is underscored by other elements of the mise-en-scène. Writing in the mid-1990s, for example, Douglas Kellner found that "in terms of image construction, white is . . .

the privileged color: Crockett often wears white jackets, drives a white car, carouses on white sand beaches, and pursues white women."[39] Kellner and others have wondered if the surname Crockett is a reference to the iconic frontier whiteness of Davy Crockett, one of the "martyrs of the Alamo" in the white-centric telling of US history. The character might have a cynical outlook, and he is definitely better dressed than the Average Joe, but his name and background as a former football player for the University of Florida, along with his frequent deployment of common sense in the face of double-talk and bureaucracy, frame him as an "all-American guy," a construction that has always had whiteness at its center. He would, in fact, have been born into the sunny, prosperous, and white Florida envisioned in the 1955 "Florida: A Place in the Sun" *Time* cover story.

Despite some early success in more avant-garde stage and film work (and a certain amount of infamy for being romantically involved with Melanie Griffith when she was still a young teenager), Johnson had been struggling to establish himself as an actor since the early seventies—and was already nearing his mid-thirties—when, after the premiere season, *Vice* made him a superstar and TV icon. Many of the critics who were initially skeptical of the series in early reviews singled out Johnson as possessing a movie star appearance and charisma, predicting that he could become a bankable star even if *Vice* failed to last. When the show did take off, Johnson was its indisputable breakout star, and the subject of considerable public attention. Focus on Johnson was undoubtedly aided by his colorful personal life, as he was linked romantically with Cybill Shepherd, Uma Thurman, and Barbra Streisand. Griffith guest starred in one episode and Streisand made a cameo in another.

The series became such a showcase for Johnson that, by the middle of the third season, an episode was built around his single, "Streetwise."[40] In season four, Philip Michael Thomas's role was diminished considerably—so much so that disgruntled Thomas fans derisively began to call the series "The Don Johnson Show." In January 1989, NBC devoted an entire Friday night schedule to "Three for Crockett," consecutively airing a trio of episodes focused on the character.[41] It says a lot about the racial politics of stardom that favor white performers to note that, following *Miami Vice*, Johnson went on to star in *Nash Bridges* (CBS, 1996–2001) and then to have a career revival years later by playing smaller roles in prestigious Hollywood films, while Thomas worked only sporadically following the show's cancellation.

Over the show's run, Johnson loaned his considerable star quality to antidrug efforts. He has told reporters about his addiction to alcohol and cocaine in the seventies and early eighties many times over the decades, but has always maintained that he was sober during the entire run of *Miami Vice*.[42] In 1986, Johnson was one of several celebrities who took part in "Rock Against Drugs," a series of PSAs designed to infuse antidrug messaging with a rock-and-roll sensibility.[43] The following year, he received a hero's welcome from students at Miami Senior High School when he appeared onstage at a surprise antidrug rally with boxers Sugar Ray Leonard and Thomas Hearns, who sported hugely oversized gold boxing gloves emblazoned with the words "War on Drugs." As in most of his antidrug appearances, Johnson spoke the language of the Just Say No era. "If you want to make a success out of your life," he told the students, "stay away from drugs and alcohol."[44]

The use of Johnson in antidrug messaging correlates with the strategies employed by the National Institute on Drug Abuse (NIDA) in the mid-1980s. NIDA produced scores of pamphlets and other materials styled in a distinctly urban, multicultural fashion. Johnson was the most recognizable performer on *Miami Vice*, so it makes sense that his public image could strengthen this type of antidrug messaging, which attempted to harness popular culture, and especially television, to spread the message of Just Say No.

MIAMI VICE'S WHITE-CENTRISM IN CONTEXT

The centrality of a white character on *Miami Vice* is something that the series shares with other cop shows of the era. For example, *Hill Street Blues*, which predated *Miami Vice* by several years but overlapped with it for two, attempted to offer a new and diverse portrait of law and order in urban America, including a multiracial and multiethnic setting, but also put white characters at the center of the narrative. Aesthetically, the ambitious and groundbreaking *Hill Street Blues* is the opposite of *Miami Vice*, considering that it aimed for an air of anti-glamor, all earth tones and verité-style camerawork. But the racial and ethnic modalities of the two shows' storytelling are strikingly similar. Like Tubbs, Black and Latino cops who round out the sprawling ensemble cast of *Hill Street Blues* sometimes get complex storylines and back stories, but they are always ancillary to the white characters at the center of the series. In the first season opening credits, for example, three of the thirteen actors with a name credit are non-white, two Black performers and one non-Black Latino. *Vice* creator Anthony Yerkovich worked on *Blues* as a writer, so it is unsurprising that these otherwise different shows share a narrative style. Most episodes of *Blues* end with captain Frank Furillo (Daniel J. Travanti) and his girlfriend and later wife, public defender Joyce Davenport (Veronica Hamel), debriefing in bed or some other intimate setting about their days on their tough jobs (thus providing the denouement lacking in a typical episode of *Miami Vice*).[45] They function as the moral core of a show centering on social problems that range from rape to political corruption.

But over the course of seven seasons, hundreds more actors of color played minor supporting or guest roles as criminal characters in the usual mix of police procedural baddies: thieves, rapists, pimps, hustlers, hookers. Although *Hill Street Blues* had an obviously liberal set of values, the writers did not take the risk of centering Black, Latinx, Asian, or indigenous characters.[46] As in other series of the genre, including those with a similar political point of view, this meant that it is the show's white romantic leads, Furillo and Davenport, who grapple with the major philosophical questions involving law and order, punishment versus rehabilitation, and working for good in an inherently broken system. The couple sometimes spar over procedure but always try to do the right thing.

This leaves the guest roles, played in large part by actors of color, to represent the social problems that Furillo and Davenport debate at night in bed. The first season includes multi-episode story arcs about a Latina teenage prostitute and a Black teen mother who neglects her children (a prototypical Reagan-era "Welfare Queen") as well as several other storylines that seem to reinforce the culture-of-poverty sensibility that permeates the self-consciously progressive show. By its last two seasons, when *Miami Vice* was airing on NBC, *Hill Street Blues* began to include storylines that tapped into the War on Drugs zeitgeist of international drug trafficking, but it maintained the practice of putting white leads at its center and populating their world with Black and Latinx criminals.

An episode in the fourth season of *Miami Vice* speaks to the tension between the focus on a white protagonist and the multiracial/multiethnic world in which the show was set. In the episode's opening sequence, while responding to a domestic violence situation in a rundown apartment, Sonny inadvertently shoots a thirteen-year-old Black boy.[47] It appears that the boy, Jeffrey McAllister, was attempting to protect his mother when Sonny stormed into the apartment, gun drawn. Jeffrey points a gun at Sonny from behind a door. Sonny instinctively shoots and wounds him, but is horrified when he sees that he has shot a child. Sonny keeps a vigil by Jeffrey's hospital bed and gets pushy with the doctor about going to extreme measures to save him. As a way to deal with his guilt, Sonny makes his way to Northern Florida, where his ex-wife and their son are living with her new boyfriend. Sonny has not seen Billy in more than three years and attempts to reconnect with the boy, who tells him that his mother's boyfriend hopes to adopt him.

Sonny's shooting victim is also more complex than he first appears. As Sonny and his team investigate an influx of weapons into the Miami crime world, they learn that the gang bringing guns into the city recruits children as foot soldiers. Jeffrey, it turns out, is not an innocent kid who was simply trying to protect his mom, but a young gang member from Chicago who goes by the name of "Crossbones" and has an extensive criminal record. Black community leaders have organized to demand justice for him, but they too are being duped by the child's supposed mother and her abusive partner-in-crime. To Sonny's (and the show's) credit, when he learns the truth about "Jeffrey," he does not regret advocating for him. "It doesn't matter if he's a killer from Chicago or just a kid from Overtown," he tells his fellow cops. "He's a child. And I shot him."

Following this tender statement, Sonny and the rest of the team regroup to take down the Black Chicago street gang that has penetrated the Miami crime scene and initiated the boy into crime. The episode ends on a note that is sympathetic to Crossbones, with Crockett once again at the bedside of the still-comatose boy. It also reiterates a theme common to *Miami Vice*, other cop shows, and news reportage: the dangers of Black gangs to the city and to Black communities and the altruism of good white cops who want to eradicate them from the streets. The emotional complexity of the episode takes it beyond the typical white savior fare, but Sonny is clearly the hero and Black gang members are the villains, which speaks to the racial worldview advanced by the series.

GUEST CASTING AND BROWNFACE

None of this should suggest that Black or Latinx representations in *Miami Vice* are more progressive or liberatory than other narcomedia narratives of the 1980s. Like other series in the genres of detective shows and procedurals, *Miami Vice* relied heavily on a revolving cast of guest stars, partly because of its anthology-like narrative structure.[48] I turn now to casting in order to ask deeper questions of the show's understandings and portrayals of latinidad. Brian Herrera has shown how Latinx performers in the middle of the twentieth century navigated complex expectations from Broadway and Hollywood when it came to casting.[49] Today, casting practices have inspired social media scrutiny and increased media activism, but the *Miami Vice* casting, which would inspire outcry today, received scant attention in the 1980s. Although I do not want to hold a four decades-old text to contemporary standards, my examination of narcomedia will benefit from a consideration of how casting choices inform how we might interpret the text.

The vast majority of the Latinx guest roles over the course of *Vice*'s long run were distinctly stereotypical, consisting of kingpins, thugs, and drug dealers.[50] In one of the few seemingly non-stereotypical guest roles over the course of the entire series, Rita Moreno played an ambitious, antidrug congresswoman in a season five episode. However, her character's son gets involved in cocaine trafficking and she attempts to set up Lieutenant Castillo.[51] One of the most sympathetic portrayals of a Latino character appears in one of the "lost" episodes that did not appear in the show's original run. Repeat guest actor José Pérez (he had previously appeared as a drug dealer) portrays the "Miracle Man," a caped neighborhood crusader attempting to rid his Latinx community of drugs.[52] This appears noble at first, and it could have been an innovative storyline about community self-care, but Tubbs and fellow agent Stan Switek discover that the Miracle Man is actually mentally ill. He suffers from bipolar disorder and has adopted the Miracle Man persona as a way to deal with the grief of losing his daughter, who died of an overdose. Like most Latinx characters, the Miracle Man does not survive the episode.

The question of casting brings me to a common practice in narcomedia: brownface. Although I did not mention it per se in the previous chapter, Al Pacino's performance, despite lacking any skin-darkening makeup, has sometimes been accused of consisting of brownface because of the actor's exaggerated accent and mannerisms. I addressed the casting, including the fact that Steven Bauer is the only Latinx actor in a leading role, but brownface is something different from mere casting. It is an attempt to convey latinidad through makeup, hair, accent, costume, or mannerism, frequently in exaggerated ways. Later, in 1993, Pacino played another Latino character—a Nuyorican career criminal—in a Brian De Palma film, *Carlito's Way*. There, like in *Scarface*, the representation looks to many like brownface without makeup. Neither of these performances were atypical for narcomedia, as across the texts I examine in this book white actors frequently appear in roles that might be described as constituting brownface, including many of the film and media texts discussed in subsequent chapters of this book. Those include Cliff Curtis as Pablo Escobar in *Blow* (2001) and Catherine Zeta-Jones in *Cocaine Godmother* (2017). And, of course, beyond narcomedia, the question of brownface has been and continues to be a hot-button issue, seeming to flare up every few years when a Latinx actor is passed up for a non-Latinx white actor.

An episode that appeared late in the second season provides a good example of these practices in casting guest roles in *Miami Vice*. Titled "Free Verse," the episode focuses on a left-wing poet from an unnamed Latin American country who has a price on his head.[53] Crockett, Tubbs, and the rest of the team must protect the poet, named Hector Sandoval, from being assassinated by right-wing death squads who want to silence him. Sandoval, obviously modeled after Gabriel García Márquez, who won the Nobel Prize for literature in 1982, is played by white actor Byrne Piven.[54] Piven, also a famous acting coach at the time, plays the role with an over-the-top bravado that takes Sandoval, like other Latinx characters played by white actors (and more than a few played by Latinos), into the realm of caricature. Other than the leftist politics and outsized personality, Piven's interpretation of Sandoval does not, in the end, resemble García Márquez's public persona very much. Sandoval is a lecherous old man in a wheelchair who dazzles at a poetry reading but then goes to a nightclub where he makes a drunken scene and pulls out a gun. Later, he breaks down, revealing to Crockett and Tubbs that he is dealing with a case of writer's block.

Piven's scenery chewing and the García Márquez storyline stand out as particularly cringeworthy from my contemporary vantage point, but the episode typifies brownface among the splashier guest roles in *Miami Vice*. Although the majority of guest roles depicting Latinx characters employed Latinx actors, a good number were played by white actors with exaggerated accents or in makeup. Prior to Piven's guest appearance, Penn Jillette played a small-time Latino dealer in the second season's premiere. The following season, English actor Ian McShane portrayed a Latino drug trafficker of unknown extraction named Esteban Montoya, and in the series finale, he plays a cigar-chomping Latin American dictator. Also in the third season, Joe Urla appeared as a Cuban counterrevolutionary, acting alongside iconic salsa performer Willie Colón. In season five, Italian American character actor John Polito played a flamboyant Colombian kingpin nicknamed "El Gato" with an over-the-top approach that rivals Piven, and Jeff Meek played a stereotypical white-suited Colombian kingpin. Very few women appear in brownface over the show's run, and when they do, it is only in very small parts. The practice of casting white actors in Latino roles seems to have functioned as a way to bring higher-profile white male actors onto *Vice* that did not apply to white women.

Latinx actors almost always play supporting roles surrounding the higher-profile white guest stars in brownface. To return to "Free Verse," for example, Latinx actors play a bevy of supporting guest roles, including that of Sandoval's devoted daughter Blanca (Yamil Borges) and his ex-student, Manuel (Hector Mercado), who turns out to harbor murderous intentions for his former teacher. A then-unknown Luis Guzmán, who appeared in small roles previously, once again portrays a henchman, something he has in common with scores of Latinx actors who, over the course of the series, appear as a threatening presence with very few lines. In a rare practice for

Miami Vice, "Free Verse" ends on a positive note, as Crockett and Tubbs rescue the eccentric Sandoval and Blanca from multiple assassination attempts.

In a roundabout way, the practice of casting a white actor as the main guest character and surrounding him with Latinx actors in smaller roles echoes the Crockett-Tubbs dynamic of the show, which places the white actor at the center and the person of color at the margins. Again, this also relates to my reading of *Scarface*, which put the white star at the center but gave him a Latino wingman who was played by an actor who was himself Latino.

MIAMI AFTER *VICE*

Even though *Miami Vice* painted a dark picture of a city with a notorious reputation, the show played a key role in remaking Miami into an appealing tourist destination. Potential tourists who had been scared away in the wake of *Scarface* began to reconsider Miami as more than just a dangerous city; they came to also see it as sleek and sexy, no doubt helped by the glamorous costumes and locations used in the show. In 1986, Jack Zink observed in *Variety* that "most credit for the area's 'hot' status has gone to the high-rated Universal/NBC primetime series 'Miami Vice,' which despite initial concerns has put an appealing gloss on the region's most pronounced sore spots." Those "initial concerns" arose when city officials, journalists, and other observers once again questioned whether a crime-focused work of pop culture would further harm the region's already dubious reputation. According to Zink, "Ironically, the seed for the 'Miami Vice' turnaround may have been the political brouhaha that erupted several years ago over the 'Scarface' remake with Al Pacino.... The same issues were raised prior to 'Miami Vice's' network premiere, but the worst of the 'Scarface' agitation had spent the worst of the community's objections—actually paving the way for a tacit agreement of the tv series' presence."[55] Zink was right to note that the soft public responses to the series were connected to *Scarface* and the broader conversation about the city's image in film and television, but he did not acknowledge the fact that Pérez, Martinez, Fabricio, and others in the Cuban American community initiated this dialogue.

Miami Vice has not had the staying power of *Scarface*. Somewhere along the way, it started to be remembered as a cheesy artifact of eighties TV. But the show has never really disappeared from popular culture. The 2002 video game *Grand Theft Auto: Vice City*, part of one of the most successful game franchises in history, is clearly based on the show, immersing players in the pastel-tinted world of *Miami Vice* without actually naming the show. In the game, Philip Michael Thomas voices a character named

Lance Vance, who, like Tubbs, loses his brother in a cartel ambush early in the narrative. An official *Miami Vice* video game premiered across multiple gaming platforms two years later. In 2010, Johnson once again suited up as Sonny Crockett for a Nike commercial costarring LeBron James. Decades after the series ended, several online stores offer Crockett and Tubbs Halloween costumes, and every so often men's fashion magazines feature photo spreads inspired by the series, as *GQ Japan* did in 2013.

In 2006, Michael Mann adapted the series as a feature film starring bankable Hollywood actors Colin Farrell and Jamie Foxx as Crockett and Tubbs. The film, an early iteration of the contemporary penchant for recycling pop culture properties—or "rebooting"—hews pretty closely to the original in terms of storyline and style, though it is considerably darker and lacks the series's sense of humor about itself. It is roughly based on "Smuggler's Blues," an iconic episode of the series that originally aired in 1985.[56] Like the original *Miami Vice*, the film features a sprawling cast of Black and brown characters engaged in the drug trade. Though reviews were mixed, from a financial perspective, the movie successfully revived a seemingly dated media property. Some of the discourse around salary and billing reveals what has changed and what has remained in terms of the politics of stardom. According to the industry news sources, producers booked Farrell at a higher salary than Foxx, who had just won the Academy Award for Best Actor for *Ray* and was nominated in the Best Supporting Actor category as well. When Foxx demanded equal pay, the producers' solution was to lower Farrell's pay. However, Foxx received top billing in US advertising of the film.[57]

CONCLUSION: RENEWAL AND NOSTALGIA

In early 2019, US cable channel VH1 debuted a new reality series set in Miami. Though clearly highly produced, *Cartel Crew* purports to follow the real everyday lives of several of the descendants of some of Miami's most notorious drug traffickers. Most episodes depict a physical confrontation between female cast members or the anticipation or aftermath of their fights. The women typically fight over perceived slights or disrespect; this often involves an accusation that a cast member is not authentically connected to narco culture. *Cartel Crew* is modeled after a VH1 predecessor, *Mob Wives* (2011–2016). The earlier series created this formula by focusing on a cast of Staten Island women whose family members had been arrested and imprisoned for organized crime. *Mob Wives* also focused on themes of respect, authenticity, and honor, but from a distinctly Italian American perspective (though not all cast members personally identified as Italian American). Like the remake of *Scarface*, *Cartel Crew* takes an ethnically Italian American narrative and reshapes it as Latinx. It is one of the few reality series in TV history to have an all-Latinx cast.

The centerpiece of *Cartel Crew* is Michael Corleone Blanco, Griselda Blanco's youngest son, who is undeniably connected to an infamous narco, so his credentials are never questioned and he is treated as the star of the show. Michael Corleone Blanco—named after the character from *The Godfather* by his mother, a fan of the film, speaking again to the perceived connections between Italian American and Latinx criminality—was born in 1978 and spent most of his life in Miami. According to the *Miami New Times* and other sources, his father and all three of his older siblings were killed before he reached adulthood. Bald-headed and covered in tattoos, grownup Michael seeks to profit from his mother's bad reputation. In the years following his mother's assassination on the streets of Medellín in 2012, he launched a product line called "Pure Blanco" that features words and images associated with his mother on shirts, mugs, phone cases, and even socks. Several of the shirts depict lines or piles of cocaine and the words "blanco" or "pure" or images of Griselda Blanco. One T-shirt includes mugshots of Pablo Escobar, Griselda Blanco, and Joaquín "El Chapo" Guzmán under the words "NWA: Narcos with Attitude."[58] Around the time that *Cartel Crew* premiered, Blanco granted several interviews in which he claimed that the show and his product line in no way glorified his family's violent past but represented an opportunity to "move on" from his trauma. In *Cartel Crew* and in the product line, Michael Blanco seeks to recuperate and profit from his mother's image. He is not alone in this endeavor, as other cultural workers have begun to celebrate Griselda Blanco as the unsung "godmother" of cocaine trafficking, a pioneer who is finally getting her due, a phenomenon that I examine in chapter 4.

Although it has all of the trashy trappings that would lead many fans to describe the show as a guilty pleasure, *Cartel Crew* actually has something important to say about the legacy of cocaine trafficking in Miami. In the social world embodied by Michael Corleone Blanco and company, the 1980s represent the heyday of their loved ones' badassery (the technical term). *Cartel Crew* also taps into nostalgia for what some remember as Miami's "bad old days." *Miami Vice* reflected cultural anxieties over the city as an entry point for drugs and people by borrowing from salacious headlines in almost real time. But decades later, in retrospect, the Miami of the 1980s and 1990s has taken on a sheen of seedy glamor in the cultural imagination. Movies like *Blow* and *American Made* (2017) depict the city as having had a gritty allure, a tough but exciting setting for the cocaine cowboys. Gerald Posner's *Miami Babylon* and Roben Farzad's *Hotel Scarface*, nonfiction literary accounts of the city's debauched eighties, also seem geared toward tapping into this brand of nostalgia, as does the 2006 documentary *Cocaine Cowboys*, which spurred a sequel and then a series, and countless imitators (including, perhaps, the hit Netflix series *Narcos*). The 2006 film adaptation of *Miami Vice*, although set in the present, also plays on a seedy vision of Miami that is reminiscent of the original series. In 2014, none other than Don Johnson attempted to parlay renewed interest in *Miami Vice*'s time and place by writing and producing the pilot for a series titled *Score*, set in 1980s Miami and centered on the world of college football (a sport that Sonny Crockett had played). The series did not get picked up, but Johnson told several journalists that the time was right to remember South Florida's (and his own) heyday.[59] A few years later, actor Vin Diesel announced that his new production company's first production would be an official reboot of *Miami Vice* on NBC, its original network (which, at the time of this writing, has yet to be produced).[60]

By the late 2010s and early 2020s, crime rates hit a record low and tourism was once again booming.[61] Decades after the show went off the air, some still credit *Miami Vice* for this remarkable transformation.[62] Contemporary pop culture now presents the city as a glamorous destination, the type of place where Real Housewives go on a "girls' weekend" and where movie stars or professional athletes own the mansions originally built for drug kingpins.[63] So it can be difficult to imagine a time when locals and tourists alike perceived Miami as somewhere between charmingly derelict and downright deadly or when cartel open warfare ruled the streets and dominated the news.

For those who consume the narrative that Miami has been pacified, it might seem barely possible that, for a time in the early 1980s, many observers saw the city as teetering on the brink of total self-destruction. True, Miami retains a reputation as a flashy, sometimes decadent, city—and plenty of observers still bemoan the browning of South Florida—but it is impossible to deny that the city is experiencing a resurgence as a cultural and economic powerhouse. Its sordid past might be increasingly difficult to fathom, but some cultural workers are having a lot of fun trying.

CHAPTER 3

"THE MOST ALIVE DEAD MAN IN THE WORLD"
Plotting the Death of Pablo Escobar

On Thursday, December 2, 1993, one day after his forty-fourth birthday, Pablo Escobar and his bodyguard Alvero de Jesús, known as "Limón," were tracked to a house on a tree-lined street in the middle-class Olivos neighborhood of Medellín by a team of Colombian special agents called the "Search Bloc." Escobar had escaped from his luxurious private prison sixteen months earlier after becoming aware of a government plan to move him to a more conventional prison. He had been holed up in the safe house for some days, dictating messages for the government and the press to his family members, who were living under state protection in Bogotá. Apparently, Escobar, with no place else to go and having outlived most of his allies and burned through most of his fortune, was preparing for a partial surrender. Using new technology that could trace mobile phone calls, the Search Bloc had pinpointed Escobar's location to within, well, a block and then got lucky when a member of the team spotted him on a second-floor balcony.

The Colombian and US governments had spent hundreds of millions of dollars chasing Escobar and this was their endgame. Agents burst through the house's steel door and chased Escobar onto the neighboring rooftop, where more Colombian police had been staked out. Escobar died in a hail of bullets. Sources differ on who, exactly, fired the shots that killed him, but an autopsy report showed that he was shot three times, the fatal bullet entering his right ear and going through his brain. Escobar's son Juan Pablo insists that his father shot himself in the ear, which the drug lord had identified as his method of suicide if he were ever to be captured.[1] Others have claimed that either rival narcos or the DEA killed Escobar. The official, and widely accepted, story contends that a member of the Search Bloc fired the bullet that mortally wounded the kingpin.

A media frenzy ensued in the immediate aftermath of the shooting. Live nationwide news coverage showed the slain kingpin's body being removed from the rooftop as a crush of reporters and onlookers vied for a better viewing position. Escobar's mother appeared on the scene, insisting to the gathered media that he had been a good son and would be avenged. She screamed "murderers!" at members of the Search Bloc while, in Bogotá, her seventeen-year-old grandson Juan Pablo told reporters that he would personally murder those who had killed his father. The next day, news cameras recorded throngs of ordinary Colombians—a "raucous mob," as the *New York Times* put it—as they attempted to crowd a small chapel at Jardines Montesacro cemetery where Escobar's body was on display before burial.[2]

The house where Escobar spent his final hours, the one whose rooftop served as the scene of his death, is currently a Spanish language school owned by a Dutch expatriate who says that she did not know the history of the house when she purchased it but now wants to give it a "new meaning" that would disassociate the infamous property from Escobar.[3] On the spring-like day in January 2019 when I first visited the neighborhood with some of my own students, pupils of the language school quietly engaged in group work on the sunny balcony on which Escobar was spotted. Our party of nine was joined by dozens of others who had come to gawk at the site of Escobar's demise. The reaction of one neighbor, who paused from sweeping her porch to glare at us, was understandable. But, judging from growing fascination with Escobar and the number of guides adding it to their Pablo Escobar tour itineraries (typically paired with a visit to his hilltop grave), tourists will probably keep visiting the house. After all, Escobar's death, which was public and gory, celebrated and mourned, is a big part of why people are so fascinated with his life.

Similarly, while Escobar emerged as a focus of early narcomedia texts during his lifetime, he became a transnational fixture of the genre because of the spectacular nature of his death. The events surrounding Escobar's death have been portrayed in countless media texts, from tabloid-style TV news to well-respected nonfiction accounts.[4] The more serious-minded texts concur on the basic outline of Escobar's final day, but certain aspects of his death, especially the question of who fired the fatal shot, continue to be the subject of speculation and debate. As a result, despite the fact that the day is so well documented and that there is overall consensus about the order of events, cultural workers and media makers have chosen to highlight different aspects of how Escobar actually died. In doing so, they make different statements about what Escobar's life meant.

This chapter focuses on representations of Escobar's death as an exemplar of the deaths of kingpins and bosses across narcomedia. The great majority of the books, films, and television episodes that I discuss in this book culminate in the murders of not only the unnamed henchmen, but also of the kingpins who drove the narrative arc of the story. Researching this book has meant watching or reading about fictional characters and real historical figures who have been shot, stabbed, drawn and quartered, drowned, poisoned, strangled, blown up with homemade bombs, and mauled to death by big cats (in several texts, oddly). Photographs of many other real narcos have circulated widely in news media, including those of Pacho Herrera and Griselda Blanco, who are discussed at length in the following chapter.

Certainly, the drug business is a bloody one, and experts estimate that Escobar was directly or indirectly responsible for at least five thousand murders, but I am less interested in the gritty details of real-world murders than I am in the symbolic power of death in narcomedia.[5] This chapter shows how representations of death function in narcomedia, how they make meaning both within and beyond the genre, and how, through death, narcomedia figures are able to achieve remarkable afterlives. Death is, in fact, an essential part of narcomedia: It allows these narratives to maintain the social order by always putting the villains in their places. Of course, the failures of the War on Drugs remind us that, in reality, we can kill individual bad guys and still lose the battle against narcotics. Nonetheless, death keeps alive our collective fantasies of victory.

COLOMBIANNESS, COCAINE, AND ESCOBAR

In chapter 1, I discussed the resurgence of cocaine in the United States during the 1970s and 1980s. Tony Montana, the hubristic trafficker played by Al Pacino in *Scarface*, became the template for countless Latinx and Latin American kingpin characters who followed, including those based on real historical figures. While Montana embodied what many Americans feared about the influx of Cuban migrants, Cuba proved less central to US anxieties about cocaine as the eighties wore on. Cubans, according to popular culture of the eighties and nineties, could assimilate and even be held up as examples of the "good Latinos." Cuban Americans became a powerful Republican voting bloc in South Florida and eventually rose to prominence in national politics. As the War on Drugs accelerated, the real problem, according to both government policy and popular culture, was Colombia, and this problem was embodied in one man in particular: Pablo Escobar.

In countless pop culture tellings that have appeared since the mid-1980s, the mere mention of Colombia or Colombians serves as a shorthand for cocaine and cartels. Bruce Bagley, a political scientist writing in a 1988 *Foreign Affairs* essay, noted the attention that Colombia garnered in the US political sphere: "Colombia's emergence as a key source and trafficking country has understandably attracted a great deal of attention from US policymakers, law enforcement officials and journalists over the last decade. Indeed, in the minds of most Americans, Colombia is now essentially synonymous with drug trafficking."[6] Unlike Cuba, Colombia was already well-positioned to capitalize on the growing demand for cocaine in the United States. As an economic downturn ravaged the export-oriented economy of Medellín, already one of the nation's most industrialized metropolitan areas, drug entrepreneurs capitalized on existing industrial infrastructure and commercial routes into the United States to promote cocaine refinement and wholesale exportation.[7]

Foremost among these entrepreneurs was Pablo Escobar. Escobar was born near Medellín in 1949 and was engaging in petty crime by his teen years. By the mid-1980s, shortly after the appearances of *Scarface* and *Miami Vice*, he sat at the head of a cartel that dominated the global cocaine trade. As that industry surged, thousands of Andean farmers throughout Colombia, Peru, and Bolivia turned to coca cultivation, meaning that as Escobar's fortune grew through his export business, so too did his influence over the regional, and soon, the national economy of Colombia. Several sources describe him as the wealthiest criminal in world history, a kingpin who ran what many political scientists describe as a "narco state." As Escobar gained notoriety and both news media and pop culture fixated on his runaway success, American audiences began to generalize his public image and to perceive Colombia as a nation of drug smugglers and kingpins.

An early expression of the idea that Colombia had become synonymous with drug trafficking appeared in August 1983, a few years before Escobar's infamy reached its zenith. ABC aired an episode of its newsmagazine, *Closeup*, titled "The Cocaine Cartel." Journalist Bill Redeker narrates a series of stories exploring both the domestic market for and the international distribution of what he calls "America's $34 billion fad." Escobar appears among several Colombian crime families that the show, in a rhetorical move similar to the 1983 rewrite of *Scarface*, repeatedly suggests comprise a "new Cosa Nostra." A review of the episode was the first time Escobar's name appeared in the *New York Times*.[8] Following the initial exposure, Escobar's name, along with more generic references to Colombians, emerged as synonyms for narcotrafficking in the English-language press. By the middle of the decade, his name had appeared thousands of times in English-language media coverage of the drug trade. Infamously, *Forbes* placed Escobar on its annual list of billionaires for several years in the late 1980s, but that magazine was an outlier in framing the kingpin in somewhat glamorous terms. Most reportage focused on Escobar as an outlaw and one of the progenitors of North America's cocaine problem. In July 1992, his notoriousness reached such a level that the congressional Subcommittee on Western Hemisphere Affairs and the Task Force on International Narcotics Control held a joint hearing devoted entirely to Escobar's escape from prison and its potential effect on the international narcotics trade.[9]

A little more than a year later, the *New York Times* and other US media outlets closely followed the news coming out of Colombia as law enforcement encircled a desperate Escobar. In late October 1993, Mexican journalist Alma Guillermoprieto published a strikingly prescient article in the *New Yorker* that depicted Escobar as a man near the end. She described the combined efforts of the Search Bloc and *Los Pepes* (a vigilante group made up of some of his enemies in the narcotics trade) in hunting Escobar. Guillermoprieto painted a bleak portrait of Colombia as a nation at the brink, including a growing sentiment that the kingpin had entered his final act. "There is, nationwide," she wrote, "an impression that life will be easier for everyone if the Bloc or the Pepes finally come up with a corpse."[10] The Search Bloc killed Escobar fewer than six weeks later.

Stories and photos from December 2 depicting the raid of Escobar's Medellín safe house and the results of the gun battle that ended his life heralded the kingpin's death as the end of an era for the Colombian drug trade and for America's War on Drugs. In several widely circulated images, US DEA agents, as well Colombian special forces, gleefully posed with Escobar's bloody corpse. The spectacular nature of his death—and the fact that it symbolized American victory in the War on Drugs, however short-lived—dominated US newspapers and television for days. But the role of the United States in Colombia's internal affairs only grew after Escobar's death and the demise of his cartel, with the US government eventually directing more military aid to Colombia than to all but two other countries.[11] While Bagley doesn't mention popular culture in his work on drug policy, *Narcomedia* demonstrates the pervasiveness of US cultural productions in promoting connotations about Colombia. The tendency of US popular culture to construct white North Americans as the victims of cocaine's "seduction" and producing countries as the source of America's drug problems became a mode of externalization that largely erased the complexity of Latin American and, in particular, Colombian understandings of Escobar's legacy.

Guillermoprieto rightly predicted that Escobar's misdeeds would reverberate after he was gone. "Even when his enemies are dancing on his grave," she wrote in the *New Yorker*, "there may never be a future without Escobar, so pervasive is his influence, and not just in Medellín."[12] Although Escobar was gone by late 1993, his death would reverberate in popular culture for decades. The *New York Times* and other coverage on his death in December 1993 was, in fact, just the beginning of the countless times that the story of Escobar's bitter end would be told in American popular media, creating a large body of cultural texts like those examined below.

According to most US and Colombian sources, officials on both sides knew that Escobar's death would not curtail the international cocaine trade. By the time he was found and killed, Escobar's economic power had been severely diminished. In fact, the Cali Cartel had completely eclipsed his market share and become, by all accounts, the world's largest supplier of cocaine. A year and a half before Escobar's death, the *Time* cover story featured "The Cali Cartel: New Kings of Coke."[13] By late 1993, the government was sequestering Escobar's wife and children, who had tried and failed to flee to Germany, and the kingpin was nearly broke. Within hours of Escobar's death, US newspapers began publishing stories on the need to focus on Cali to kill the cocaine supply. Within twenty-four hours, President Bill Clinton sent Colombian President César Gaviria a congratulatory telegram, giving full credit to Colombian security forces in making the kill and pledging "cooperation in our joint efforts to combat drug trafficking."[14] But Escobar was not vanquished as neatly as his enemies hoped. The symbolic import of his demise was evident almost immediately as newspapers around the world breathlessly covered his death. Alive, Escobar was a national security threat, a global menace; in death, he became a legend.

Escobar's death has become a potent symbol in War on Drugs mythology. Colombian politicians and military operatives, as well as their US counterparts, have all gone on record since 1993 to emphasize that the assassination of Escobar was, above all, a symbolic victory in the battle against narcotrafficking. The *Washington Post*, for example, suggested as much in its reportage on Escobar's death. "Killing Escobar was a major victory for the government of Gaviria, which had been humiliated by Escobar and his ability to escape more than 1,500 men assigned to hunt him down," wrote reporter Douglas Farah.[15] In constructing the narrative as a presidential victory, Farah joined countless North American sources in acknowledging that the government had much to gain in taking out Escobar even though the Cali Cartel was, by that time, a greater threat.

Social scientists who study organized crime have a term for the strategy of killing or arresting the head of a cartel: "decapitation." In the case of Escobar, who was already broke and defeated, decapitation had *only* symbolic power. His grisly death suggested the end of an era. For North American audiences weary of the War on Drugs, it represented a much-needed victory. Mark Bowden, in *Killing Pablo*, wrote that the assassination of Escobar was not about staunching the flow of cocaine—"everyone knew that"—but about something far grander. It was a victory for "democracy, the rule of law, standing up for injustice and civilization." Pablo was simply too rich, too powerful, and too violent.[16] The United States could help to kill the Colombian boogeyman of the international drug trade, but it could not kill the competing visions of what his death represented in Colombia and abroad.

Just as the cocaine trade continued to expand after Escobar's death, so too did the cultural mythmaking around him, including a notable resurgence in popular culture since the 1990s. He also became an outsized presence in US and global media. Less than a year after his death, for example, Escobar was already the inspiration for a fictionalized character in the action thriller *Clear and Present Danger*, based on Tom Clancy's 1989 novel. As chapter 7 argues, this popularity increased even more a couple of decades later.

In 2013, Hispanic studies scholar Aldona Bialowas Pobutsky observed that a "cultural renaissance" in representations of Escobar was underway in Colombia, noting a spate of texts that appeared around the year 2000. These were mostly produced by people who knew the capo and purported to have some kind of inside knowledge or new revelations about Escobar's life and death. These include tell-all works by Escobar's brother and sister; his son; his main *sicario* (hitman), Jhon Jairo Velásquez Vásquez (aka "Popeye," who became something of an *un*contrite media gadfly following his boss's death); and Virginia Vallejo, the famous newscaster who became his lover and then a memoirist. As María Elena Cepeda puts it, "nearly thirty years after his death . . . the tensions surrounding Escobar's life testifies to the enduring power of representation."[17] In Pobutsky's view, Escobar in Colombian popular culture represents "a strong symbolic value in the process of bringing national closure to the era of the grand capos," as well as the potential to make the kingpin a "marketable commodity in Colombia and abroad" (which I, in turn, examine in chapter 7).[18] She finds that Colombian popular culture, as opposed to high culture, was quicker to reevaluate what Escobar means to the nation. As a Salvadoran newspaper put it, Escobar is now "one of the most alive dead men in the world."[19]

DEATH OF THE KINGPIN: PLOTTING PABLO'S DEATH IN *EL PATRÓN DEL MAL* AND *NARCOS*

The telenovela *El Patrón del Mal* begins with Pablo's death. The first episode, which aired on the Caracol network on May 28, 2012, opens with a title in Spanish: "Medellín, December 2, 1993. Last moments."[20] Pablo, as many Colombian viewers would know from the date, will soon meet his end. Bloated and frantic, he paces around the rooms of his safe house. A series of flashbacks shows some of Escobar's most despicable acts: his frequent and forceful threats against government officials; the assassinations of Minister of Justice Rodrigo Lara, journalist Guillermo Cano, and presidential candidate Luis Carlos Galán; and the bombings of Avianca flight 203, the offices of the newspaper *El Espectador*, the Departamento Administravo de Seguridad, and a street in Bogotá. These flashbacks are mixed with snippets of archival video footage, which include the dates that they actually took place, giving them an air of veracity. Ominous music and frenetic editing adds to the sense of impending doom. The stakes of this morality play are abundantly clear.

In the diegetic present, that day in early December 1993, Pablo has clearly taken leave of his senses even though he retains his bluster. "There's no fucking way you'll get me," he says in his very first lines, which sound like they are being broadcast over a crackly radio signal. "I'll have you all killed from the jungle. I'm going to win this." His appearance betrays this false confidence, however, as stress has taken a physical toll. Looking dyspeptic, he chugs stomach medicine and drools on himself. He punches walls and staggers around the house, pointing his pistol toward the windows. Pablo begins to dictate the terms of a possible surrender to his teenage son on the telephone, but he is interrupted by a clanging sound, signaling that the safe house has been breached. He is caught. "I've got to go," he tells his son, "because something very strange is going on." Then the screen goes black.

Beginning with the ending is a common narrative technique, especially when depicting events that loom large in the popular memory. In just under three and one-half minutes, the telenovela introduces Pablo as a villain but also reminds the viewer that he will be caught and executed in a happy ending for Colombia, as the series will suggest many hours later in its final conclusion. It takes *El Patrón del Mal* fifty-three hours to return to the scene teased in its dramatic opener. After focusing on Pablo's many misdeeds, the series dramatizes his escape from his luxuriously appointed prison, La Catedral, and his life on the run. Finally, the narrative brings the audience back to the beginning scene of the series—Pablo screaming into the phone, declaring that he will beat the government and kill his persecutors—but advances in real time to depict the last few minutes of his life.

The final episode shows little of the immediate aftermath of Pablo's death. As the Search Bloc agents who shot him realize the magnitude of what has just happened, the voices of journalists begin to relay the news to the nation. The soldiers congratulate one another and pose proudly with Pablo's corpse. A crowd gathers and the action intermixes with archival footage from the historic day depicted in the scene. Escobar's mother rushes to the scene and breaks down in tears, wailing loudly. The sequence ends abruptly when a team of medical workers carries Pablo's body off the rooftop. The editing alternates between staged and archival footage of the deceased kingpin's body, the last we see of him.

What happens next is something of a curiosity, only because it stands apart from most depictions of Escobar's death. The final four minutes of the series consist of an extended version of the theme song by Yuri Buenaventura, an upbeat urban rap number inspired by *narcocorridos*, extolling listeners to not repeat the mistakes of history.[21] "Nunca más!" ("Never again!") shouts Buenaventura, as he does in the opening credits of every episode. The song is accompanied by footage of contemporary Colombians enjoying their everyday lives: street vendors, families, workers, children. Several shots focus on their legs and feet walking forward. These shots are intermixed with archival footage of Colombia during the 1980s and 1990s, including shots of politicians and journalists who attempted to capture Escobar, and snippets from the series. In the middle of the song, Escobar's infamous smiling mugshot from his youth dissolves into an image of his middle-aged face looking more serious, which then dissolves into a post-mortem photograph of his face. *El Patrón del Mal* had always been refreshingly honest in its political perspective, and the *novela*'s ending makes a clear statement: Only through Escobar's death could Colombia be reborn. If his death was largely symbolic for the US government, *El Patrón del Mal* suggests the execution was something far more liberating for Colombians.

While the early reporting on Escobar's death in Colombia and the United States treated it as a transnational victory for the two nations, subsequent pop culture narratives across a variety of genres have fixated on US participation in the hunt for Pablo. This is a main conceit of *Narcos*, which does acknowledge the inner workings of the Colombian military police but places US DEA Agent Steve Murphy (and then Agent Javier Peña) at the center of a transnational narrative. The first two seasons of *Narcos* belong to Murphy, and it is consistent with the overall narrative that he is the one who narrates Pablo's demise. Murphy's telling of the story has been cynical throughout the first two seasons, but his narrative ultimately lands on the side of law and order, including a sense that Escobar's murder is a victory in the War on Drugs.[22] The entire second season of *Narcos* builds toward Escobar's death. Following the initial season's cliffhanger, in which Pablo escapes from his plush self-constructed prison just outside Medellín, the narrative arc of season two puts Escobar on the run, at war with the government and increasingly unhinged. His appearance has changed considerably from his somewhat sexy presentation in the first season, and he now looks similar to the Pablo depicted in *El Patrón del Mal*, plump and deranged.

But even while the last episodes of the season focus on the manhunt, they continue the process of humanizing Pablo, which I will discuss in the final chapter. The cold opening of the final episode consists of a dream sequence enacting Pablo's fantasy that he is elected president of Colombia, an ambition the real Escobar frequently professed. The episode also includes a dreamy scene in which Pablo, tired of being caged in his safe house, heads out to the streets of Medellín, where he takes pleasure in everyday things like buying an ice cream cone. He is joined by his beloved partner in crime and cousin, Gustavo Gaviria, who has been dead since the first season. They talk of old times, and Pablo tearfully admits that losing Gustavo was the beginning of the end for him, a common motif for TV finales. Despite looking terrible, Pablo feels so invincible—or delusional, depending on one's reading—that he takes off his sunglasses for the conversation, unafraid to be recognized in a crowded plaza.

Then, inevitably, comes the end for Pablo, as it must in all tellings of the Escobar saga. As in other versions, the Search Bloc finally pinpoints his exact location and agents mobilize at the safe house. They flush Pablo and his bodyguard out of the house and onto the neighboring rooftop, where law enforcement agents shoot both dead. But some subtle creative choices in *Narcos* reflect a profound difference in outlook from *El Patrón del Mal* and other Colombian versions of the story. As Pablo talks for the last time with his son Juan Pablo, they discuss Pablo's birthday wish. They had missed spending his birthday together, and Pablo begins to cry when Juan Pablo tells him that he deserves the "best birthday in the world." Following this tender moment, the Search Bloc bursts in and the chase ensues. Murphy is present on the rooftop when Pablo dies. In fact, in *Narcos*, Murphy is among the first on the scene, in contrast to the telenovela, which makes no mention of the US presence in the Search Bloc's raid.

The final minutes of the season portray the immediate aftermath of Pablo's death. President Gaviria receives the news via telephone in the same room that was part of the setting where, earlier in the season, Pablo fantasized about becoming president. Pablo's mother hears about her son's death on a crowded bus; she is crushed, but the passengers surrounding her are overjoyed and their chattering turns to cheering. She rushes to the scene and cries over her son's bloodied body. A few beats later, archival footage of the real aggrieved Hermilda Gaviria speaking to journalists is juxtaposed with archival footage of Pablo Escobar's real-world misdeeds, such as the wreckage of the Avianca flight that was bombed on his orders.

As everyday Colombians celebrate, Murphy poses for a photographer on the rooftop with members of the Search Bloc and Pablo's dead body. When the camera flashes, the real photograph takes up the frame, an image that I discuss in detail below. (*El Patrón del Mal* also depicts Search Bloc members posing triumphantly for a photograph with Pablo's dead body but without any Americans present.) Immediately after, two older men in a bar—cameos by the real Steve Murphy and Javier Peña—clink their beer glasses. Murphy and Peña spent decades writing and speaking about the manhunt leading to Escobar's murder before working as consultants on *Narcos*. This brief nod seems to say "job well done" to the US federal agents whose fictional counterparts are the protagonists of the show's first two seasons. *Narcos* used archival footage prior to these final moments of season two, but the use of the real photograph and the cameos by the real Murphy and Peña break the fourth wall in an unprecedented way, reminding in-the-know viewers that the previous two seasons told a historical story in which some of the real players still have a say in its telling. More importantly, the photo and the presence of the real agents give outsized credit to Murphy and Peña for Pablo's downfall.

Despite this congratulatory mode, *Narcos* does acknowledge that, by the time of his death, Escobar was no longer the biggest profiteer in the world. In some of the last dialogue of the season, in a scene that functions as an epilogue for season two and a teaser for the one that follows, a US official addresses Peña. "In 1992, do you know how much cocaine we estimated entered the United States from Colombia? 311 metric tons. And in 1993, during the hunt for your friend Escobar? *372 metric tons*. That piece of shit's on his last legs, every one of his labs is shut down and the cocaine supply goes *up*. Imagine what happens next year."[23] In contrast to *El Patrón del Mal*'s vision of Colombia healing in the aftermath of Escobar, this is a decidedly downbeat ending, even if it is more accurate. The ending reflects the concerns of US law enforcement and opens the door for more narcomedia narratives to follow. It has no message for Colombia or Colombians, only one for US consumers: Wait until you see what's in store for the next season.

Both shows fixate on the minute details of Pablo's final moments. *Narcos* takes many liberties with the last few weeks of Escobar's life, but its creators are more careful with the death sequence. Each series gets the small but well-documented details of Escobar's final day, such as the scrambled eggs he had eaten and the clothes that he wore, exactly right. The two shows feel remarkably similar in how they build tension through editing, sound, and plotting until the release that comes with the fatal shooting of the show's villain. Both shows also effectively use archival footage to document the aftermath of Pablo's death, as if to say, "This really happened and here is the evidence." In these ways, the shows enmesh their fictional accounts with historical artifacts to convey veracity.

But different outlooks on the meanings of Escobar's death are revealed in the small creative choices behind the scenes of each series. The most revealing differences are clear in the aftermath of the rooftop killing. For the creators of *El Patrón del Mal*, Pablo's death is presented as both a finality and a fresh start. The epilogue focuses not on the ongoing narco politics and economics that would continue to shape Colombia for decades following Escobar's death, but on national healing. Smiling Colombians from all walks of life go about their business in the closing montage, seemingly as part of a post-Escobar, post-narco-state nation. The montage is somewhat jarring because it follows a long *novela* that aimed to inspire Colombian audience members to deal, finally, with the national trauma inflicted by Escobar.

Placing so much emphasis on that central character and then suggesting through an upbeat musical montage that his death was liberatory for Colombia might be misguided in that it allows viewers to avoid thinking through the broader systems of corruption that allowed the country to remain a narco-state long after Escobar's murder. In that sense, it is not entirely different from the strategy of decapitation mentioned earlier. We might, in fact, refer to this as a form of representational decapitation, wherein killing a character kills the bigger systems that they represent—a common trope in narcomedia. This might work for a superhero movie, but for the real history of Colombia, it presents a dangerously neat narrative that does not align with the decades of violence and loss that followed the collapse of the Medellín Cartel and Escobar's death.

Narcos, on the other hand, emphasizes US involvement in the killing of Escobar and presents a generally downbeat take on the futility of decapitation as a drug control strategy, which conveniently sets up the show's third season. The US-made series, which spends a considerable amount of screen time humanizing Pablo, takes a more complex (and arguably accurate) approach to what his death means in order to maintain the interest of viewers after the exit of the original kingpin. On one hand, the villain of the series succumbs and the good guys (gringo federal agents) clink a glass to his demise. On the other, the series does acknowledge through that epilogue that Escobar's death did not curtail the transnational cocaine business and implies that Colombia's and the United States's problems were far from over in the aftermath of Pablo Escobar. In this sense, *Narcos*, despite its white-centrism and occasional flights of fancy, is actually more honest about what his death means.

THE PHOTOGRAPH AND PUBLIC SPECTACLE

Narcos and *El Patrón del Mal*, like most other depictions of Escobar's death, acknowledge the elements of public spectacle that marked the occasion, especially the making of postmortem photographs. These pictures are now a well-documented element in the order of events that immediately followed his assassination. Both series show Search Bloc, and *Narcos* shows Steve Murphy, posing triumphantly with Pablo's corpse. At one level, Escobar's postmortem images serve an evidentiary function: They verify that Escobar, frequently described as the most wanted man in the world in 1993 and legendarily successful at evading capture, really was dead. On a deeper level, they have functioned as cultural sites for celebration, mourning, and entertainment.

Although Escobar's final moments before capture have been dramatized in these texts and many others, no known photographs or video document these moments. In her study of what she calls "about-to-die" photographs, Barbie Zelizer traces the peculiar power of images of people who are moments away from death. As Zelizer notes, about-to-die pictures frequently circulate in the place of images of dead bodies. For example, Princess Diana's body had been photographed after her death in 1997, but the international news media almost universally chose to publish pictures of her alive in their coverage of the accident that ended her life.[24] But in the case of Escobar, an internationally infamous figure as hated as Diana was beloved, *only* postmortem pictures are known to exist.

Escobar loved having his picture taken, and some images, such as sepia-toned photographs of him dressed as his heroes Pancho Villa and Al Capone, became iconic in their own rights.[25] In terms of iconicity, no image of Escobar can match his infamous 1977 mugshot, in which he wears a wide-collared shirt and an unrepentant smile. In that photo, taken when he was arrested for cocaine trafficking in his late twenties, Escobar appears entirely unbothered by his arrest, an early iteration of his untouchability. Today, for reasons I describe in a later chapter, the mugshot is now a popular motif for Escobar-themed merchandise, especially T-shirts. One day, as I was writing this book in my home office in Cali, Colombia, and glancing out my window, an American tourist climbed out of a taxi wearing a black T-shirt emblazoned with the image. She smiled at me when she saw me looking at the shirt, apparently thinking I was amused by her edgy sartorial choice.

Other images, such as a snapshot from 1981 depicting Escobar and his son Juan Pablo in front of the White House while on a family vacation in Washington, DC, have circulated widely in online spaces. (In the case of the White House image, the photo is often used to support the theory that the US government turned a blind eye to Escobar for much of his career as a drug trafficker.) Photography played a role in Escobar's downfall as well. When the newspaper *El Espectador* published another of his old mugshots in 1983, it sparked public scrutiny over Escobar, who had recently been elected to the Colombian Congress under the pretense that he was a legitimate businessman. The publication of the photograph is usually credited as the impetus for Escobar's ouster from Congress.

These are all socially and politically powerful images of Escobar, but postmortem images have a power unto themselves. In *Dead Matter: The Meaning of Iconic Corpses*, Margaret Schwartz argues that "the corpse is a material thing freighted with immensely powerful cultural meaning" and a "communicative object" that can, and must, be read as a text.[26] Schwartz understands that not all corpses are created equal and that some are more meaningful than others. Some even achieve iconic status. Schwartz's examples of iconic corpses include Abraham Lincoln, Eva Perón, Emmett Till, Hamza al-Khateeb, Princess Diana, and Michael Jackson, all of which she understands as bodies that performed cultural work around grief, public mourning, and social change in their respective societies. These bodies, whether as human corpses, photographs, or other representations, remained cultural touchstones long after life had left them. Although representations of Escobar's body have functioned differently from the examples offered by Schwartz, they have been similarly potent and, for lack of a better term, long-lived.

Colombian news media provide a record of how images of the body circulated in the immediate aftermath of Escobar's death, which is especially interesting to me because of the very high stakes in showing graphic images of the corpse. Luckily for me, print media also offers a lasting record of images that reveal the photographic and editorial choices that went into how to display the body. In the hours and days after his killing, the news interrupted all of Colombian television, and camera operators for the various channels did not shy away from showing Escobar's bloody corpse on the rooftop. Reporters scrambled for the best possible views of the body, climbing onto neighboring rooftops and elbowing each other on the crowded street. The cameras continued to record as his body was carefully carried off the roof and placed in a hearse to be carried to the morgue, where even more photographs were made. Starting that evening, gruesome photographs appeared on the front pages of dozens of newspapers all over Colombia.

The cover of the Friday morning *El Tiempo*, for example, featured a large picture of Escobar's mother, Hermilda Gaviria, and other members of his grief-stricken family standing over their relative's dead body in a morgue while soldiers look on. In an exceedingly private moment made public, Hermilda blankly stares ahead while another woman, possibly one of Escobar's sisters, collapses onto the mortuary slab. Another woman and man look on soberly, the woman's hand to her throat in an expression of what appears to be shock. (Escobar's wife María Victoria and his son Juan Pablo, who had functioned as something of a hot-headed family spokesperson in the last months of his father's life, are absent because they were still under sequester in Bogotá.) The corpse, still clothed in the polo shirt and jeans, is on full display on the slab. The "Hitler mustache," shaved out of his beard by members of the Search Bloc as an added humiliation after they killed him, is also clearly visible. The headline that accompanied the image, "¡Al Fin Cayo!" ("He Finally Fell!") was used by *Narcos* decades later as the title of the episode in which Pablo is killed.[27] In the same edition, *El Tiempo* included a special insert with another image of Escobar's dead body, this one depicting the scene on the rooftop: Escobar's body at the center, surrounded by members of the Search Bloc and other men in what looks like the chaos that ensued following the killing. The cover of *El Espectador*—the newspaper that had suffered greatly at the directives of Escobar as its staff worked in the 1980s to expose his crimes, including the murder of its editor Guillermo Cano and the destruction of its offices with a bomb—featured a large image of Escobar's body being carried off the rooftop as the Search Bloc stands guard and onlookers crane their necks. In the right corner of the picture, a photograph of Escobar very much alive in 1991 is superimposed over the larger image. A smaller image of Escobar's assembled family appears just below.[28]

The next week, influential news magazine *Semana* devoted much of its issue to covering what it called "the final secrets of Escobar" and included images of his corpse, including a cover image of a man posing with the body.[29] As with similar photographs published in those first weeks of December 1993, Escobar's belly lies exposed and his face is mostly obscured in a mess of hair and blood. The man who poses with him, presumably a

3.1. Colombian newspapers and magazines, such as *Semana*, prominently displayed Escobar's corpse in the immediate aftermath of his death. Image provided by *Semana*.

member of the Search Bloc, smiles broadly but his eyes are obscured with a black bar so that he can remain somewhat anonymous. Like others who posed for similar pictures, he pulls at Escobar's sleeve in an effort to expose what can be seen of his face to the camera. In this particular image, the anonymity of the living man's face contrasts strikingly with the effort to expose Escobar. Bulleted sub-headlines entice curious readers with promises that they can find information on Escobar's diary and personal letters from the final month of his life along with unknown details of the operation that killed him.

Postmortem images of Escobar served many functions after his death, and there are myriad reasons why Colombian editors chose to place Escobar's dead body on the covers of their newspapers in the days and weeks that followed. The hunt for the kingpin lasted for months and seemed hopeless at many points, so these first images might have functioned as a means of proving to Colombians that he really was dead. Many in Colombia speculated that he could not be captured, and rumors abounded (and sometimes still circulate) that Escobar had actually paid a stand-in to take the fall for him while he escaped. Or that he had several body doubles, and it was one of them who was killed on December 2, 1993. The front page of *El Tiempo*, depicting familial grief, might have been using the family members' reactions as a form of evidence, a means to verify that the body on the slab really was the real thing. *Semana*'s emphasis on finality can be understood as doing something similar, closing the door on the Escobar era. The third bullet point in its headline gestures to the question of what would come next for Colombian narcotrafficking.

The photographs that appeared in the Colombian press tended to highlight the ignominious aspects of the death scene: smiling or cheering people milling about, roof tiles in disarray, and Escobar's body, face down, splayed. Ethnographer of visual culture Jay Ruby has argued that "Since death is the last act of a person's life, it is supposed to be meaningful and dramatic, particularly on a battlefield. To die in a war for no apparent reason and without drama is unthinkable for it implies that the deceased's life was wasted."[30] The press certainly did not minimize the drama of Escobar's capture, but photographs of the scene tell a distinctly antiheroic narrative about his death. Certainly, the final moments of Escobar's life had been dramatic, but the squalor of the scene implies that they were also pathetic and undignified.

US news media covered the events somewhat differently. The *New York Times* illustrated its cover story on Escobar's death with just a small copy of the same photograph of the living Escobar from 1991 that *El Espectador* used on its cover. The more tabloid-style *New York Daily News* also included this photograph but paired it with one of the many available images of the body being taken off the rooftop. "Good Riddance" reads that paper's headline in a large bold font, a message that resembled some Colombian headlines. Other newspapers included just a note or brief article with the news. News coverage in the United States did not include close-ups of the body.

In the United States, Steve Murphy's photograph has endured, perhaps above all others, as the iconic image of Escobar's death. Murphy, contrary to the dramatization in *Narcos*, was not actually on the scene when Escobar was killed but heard from his boss in the DEA almost immediately after the fatal shot was fired. In an interview with Mark Bowden, who spoke with Murphy extensively in his research for *Killing Pablo*, Murphy recalls his commander telling him, "You better get your ass there and take pictures back."[31] Bowden describes Murphy arriving at the house in Olivos and immediately reaching for his camera:

> Murphy shouted to the men around the body and they posed gleefully, raising their rifles like big-game hunters around their trophy buck. The DEA agent snapped their picture. He then climbed out to the roof and took more pictures of Pablo's bloated body and bloody face, and more shots of the men posing around him. Then Murphy gave the camera to one of the shooters and posed alongside Pablo's body himself.[32]

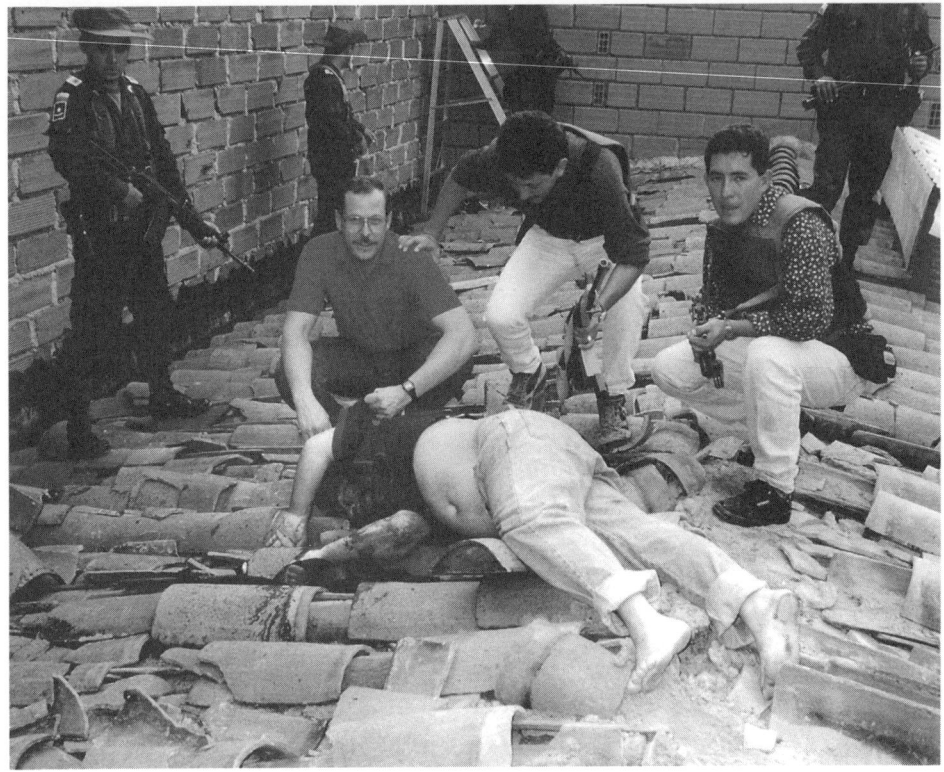

3.2. Steve Murphy posed with the corpse of Pablo Escobar on December 2, 1993. Alamy Photo.

In a subsequent interview with the *Hollywood Reporter*, Murphy claimed to be the only one on the scene with a camera until the media arrived. "The reason I was smiling," he told the reporter, "is because we knew, effective that moment, every citizen in Colombia was safer simply because one man died."[33] Bowden relates Murphy's story that the exposed film was confiscated by a Colombian officer but eventually returned to him developed, with some of the original negatives missing. According to Bowden, via Murphy, the gruesome images were initially controversial in Colombia because they implied that the DEA had killed Escobar, but copies of the pictures ended up "gracing the office walls of many in Washington and in the US military who had taken part in the successful mission."[34]

Although Murphy snapped several pictures when he arrived at the scene, I am interested here in the particular photograph that a member of the Search Bloc took when Murphy handed him his camera. In it, Murphy, wearing blue jeans and a bright red polo shirt, squats over Escobar's dead body. Murphy grasps Escobar's sleeve near his left armpit, pulling it slightly upward to expose Escobar's face to the camera. Doing so also reveals his large belly, which had grown while he was in hiding. It is clear that Murphy means to display Escobar for the camera. Although Bowden and Salazar both aptly use the word "trophy" in describing this and other pictures in Murphy's set, they do not mention the peculiarity of Murphy, a foreign agent, grasping Escobar's sleeve to show Escobar's face. It is this act, reminiscent of big game hunters posing with their quarry, that gives the image a trophy-like air.

The photograph has been reproduced elsewhere in narcomedia. It appeared on the cover of the first edition of Bowden's *Killing Pablo*, underscoring the centrality of the white agent in the text that informed *Narcos*. When Murphy and his partner Javier Peña (who, when Escobar was killed, was in Florida investigating rumors that the kingpin was in Haiti) began giving popular lectures following the success of the first season of *Narcos*, they included the photograph as one of their slides. It also illustrated several English-language newspaper and magazine articles about Murphy and Peña around the time of the *Narcos* release, sometimes with Escobar's face blurred in an attempt to make the image less graphic.

The photograph also appears in *Narcos*. As mentioned above, the series, like others, faithfully recreates the final moments of Pablo's life, leading up to his last breaths on the rooftop before a Colombian agent shoots him in the head. However, it places Murphy at the scene as Pablo dies. When he is finally dead, Steve and several members of the Search Bloc assemble around the body to pose for a photograph. A Colombian man points the camera. After it flashes, the real archival photo appears on the screen rather than the one apparently made with actors Boyd Holbrook and Wagner Moura in the fictionalized world of *Narcos*. This is another example of the series blending its fictionalized world with archival footage and images. Within the context of the death scene, it seems to echo the Colombian impulse to show that Escobar was really dead but to include (and credit) the American Murphy for the takedown. The photo appears again in the next episode, the first of the third season, when, traveling back to Colombia, Javier sits on a plane and pauses to gaze at the image—the version made in the diegetic world of *Narcos*—while thumbing through some files. So, over the course of two consecutive episodes, the series shows actors recreating the image, the archival image itself, and another actor looking at the fictionalized image. This tripling effect speaks to its iconic status and reminds viewers of the pivotal role of Murphy, a paid consultant to the show, in killing Pablo.

As noted, the Colombian press was in no way shy about publishing

3.3. As in other pop culture depictions of his life and downfall, the scene of Pablo Escobar's death is faithfully recreated in *Narcos*, including Steve Murphy posing with the body.

images of Escobar's dead body, and I have described some reasons why it was important for Colombians to circulate and consume gruesome images of the death scene. Murphy's image, however, had some particular representational politics of its own in both Colombia and the United States. First, it was not published in the immediate aftermath of Escobar's death because the negatives were confiscated and undeveloped, so they did not serve the function of proof or as an "index" of Escobar's death. It was not until years later that authors and editors would regularly use the image to illustrate their narratives of the hunt for Escobar. Second, the "stagedness" of Murphy's image challenges the documentary nature of those that appeared in the Colombian press (which are, it must be stated, also highly mediated and should not be taken for granted as "natural" or "real" depictions of the scene on the rooftop).

Jay Ruby and other scholars have noted that staging dead bodies has been a practice in war photography since the US Civil War.[35] So it makes sense that US agents invested in the War on Drugs would do the same. First, Murphy's image is fictional in the sense that it is highly staged and suggestive that Murphy was present at the killing—or even responsible for it. As Bowden's account tells it, Murphy's main role was to arrive on the scene with a camera to verify that Escobar was really dead. Second, the fact remains that it is a powerful photograph that, decades after it was taken, continues to shape what people know about Escobar. Third, Murphy's image taps into questions about the role of the United States in killing Escobar. Those two details that Bowden notes—that the picture caused speculation in Colombia that the DEA killed Escobar and that it subsequently became popular with agents as a representation of a mission accomplished—illustrate the very reasons why Colombian and international observers were dubious about whether the Search Bloc actually took down Escobar.

In his book, *La Parábola de Pablo*, a definitive history of Escobar by a Colombian source, Alonso Salazar J. maintains that Pablo's killing was only possible because of collaboration among his many enemies, led by Los Pepes but including the upper echelons of Colombian politics and society. Salazar blames Escobar's heedlessness to the vast number of people and organizations allied against him for his ultimate downfall. "Pride anesthetized his brain," he writes.

> It gave him one of the warrior's greatest ills: underestimating the enemy. He did not realize that his old and new enemies, allied against him, had enough power to kill him. Some of his men had warned him how serious it would be to kill his friends but he ignored them. The union of bandits flattered him, spurred him on, and profited from his folly.[36]

Salazar's assertion, in line with other Colombian observers, is provocative because, in a sense, it challenges the need to see or know the exact person who ended Escobar's life. Escobar's death, in other words, might be understood as a group effort, regardless of who actually pulled the trigger.

GRIEVABILITY AS WHITE-CENTRISM IN *ESCOBAR: PARADISE LOST*

The precise method of Escobar's execution might be open to debate, but it is undeniable that those who represented his death artistically or journalistically have to make some decisions regarding how they frame it in terms of affect. The 2014 film *Escobar: Paradise Lost* provides an excellent case study in the representational politics of death, victimization, and grievability. ("Grievability" refers to a hierarchy: Who, exactly, should be grieved on either an individual or societal level.) The movie's subtitle repeats the phrasing used to refer to the *Time* magazine article analyzed in chapter 1, but applies the "Paradise Lost" ideology to Colombia rather than South Florida.

Marketed as a "romantic thriller," *Paradise Lost* tells instead the story of Nick (Josh Hutcherson), a young white Canadian man who, with his brother Dylan (Brady Corbet), moves to a beachy part of Colombia to start a surfing school in the late 1980s. There he meets and falls in love with María (Spanish actor Claudia Traisac), a beautiful woman around his age. María is helping to start a community clinic that happens to be funded by her uncle, Pablo Escobar (Benicio Del Toro). A romance blossoms between Nick and María and becomes serious enough that she introduces him to her large extended family at her Uncle Pablo's birthday party. Nick had initially been impressed by Pablo's charitability, but at the elaborate gathering he questions his girlfriend about her uncle's wealth: "How'd he make all his money?" She responds matter-of-factly:

> Cocaine. People here in Colombia have been chewing coca leaves since the beginning of time. Pablo is just exporting a national product. Most of the money he makes goes to the poor. You go to any of the barrios and ask people there. They love him. Come on, dance with me.

Against Dylan's pleas, and despite the implausibility of the kingpin enlisting the help of a disinterested surfer, Nick eventually gets involved with Pablo's business.

Paradise Lost takes the artistic license frequently demonstrated in creating a fictionalized "Pablo" to another level. Incredibly, much of the plot revolves around Nick becoming indispensable to Pablo, who not only speaks English but also mentors Nick and grows to consider him part of his family. However, Nick's good fortune with the cartel undergoes a reversal when he begins to question Pablo and tries to leave Colombia with María, Dylan, and Dylan's wife, Anne. This ends badly for all involved. In the third act of the movie, Nick is on the run from Pablo's ruthless hitmen. Although Nick had heroically refused to kill anyone up to now, he fatally shoots those who are hunting him. He is also shot in the fracas. On the phone, Nick learns from Anne that Dylan has been killed just before he hears two gunshots intended for Anne and her five-month-old baby. Nick makes his way to a church in Bogotá where he and María had arranged to meet. She arrives to find him covered in blood and weak from his gunshot. She runs out screaming for help, but Pablo's henchmen have caught up with her. Underscored by dramatic violins, Nick succumbs to his wounds inside the church.

Although fictional—or, in the words of film critic Jeannette Catsoulis, "fact-studded fiction"—it touches upon some of the key events in Escobar's criminal history despite its laughable indulgences. It follows the storyline of several standard pot-boiling nonfiction accounts: A naïve gringo (albeit, in this case, one who is quick to point out that he is Canadian and not from the United States) unwittingly becomes ensnared with the Medellín Cartel and faces choices that he could not have previously imagined for himself.[37] But what interests me most about the film is Nick's death and how it contrasts with other depictions of death that this chapter has described. Nick and María embrace and weep when she realizes what is happening, and when she runs for help, the camera lingers on Nick's face as he gazes upward toward the altar, a white Canadian martyr of the Colombian drug wars. The church setting is jarring—Nick's religion or spirituality, unlike Pablo's, has not previously factored into the story—but also seems calibrated to give the story's end a grandeur and moral heft. The film does not depict Pablo's death.

Nick's death returns us to the question of grievability. (María, perhaps the only "good" Colombian in *Paradise Lost*, is also in mortal danger at the end of the film, but a quick edit leaves it unclear whether she is killed or captured and taken back to her uncle. Many reviews claim the former, but it is hard to imagine, even in a film this divorced from the history of Escobar, that Pablo would murder a beloved member of his own family.) Many Colombians die in the movie, but, unlike any of their deaths, Nick's is presented as tragedy. The same can be said for the deaths of Dylan, Anne, and their baby, even though they die offscreen. Grievability in *Paradise Lost* is another form of the white-centrism that is so common to narcomedia productions in that the film plays the death of the white protagonist as the real tragedy of the War on Drugs narrative. In other words, narcomedia narratives frequently present the deaths of white people as the real tragedies of the War on Drugs.

I am not arguing that *Escobar: Paradise Lost*—or any other text—must construct Escobar's death as a tragedy. As a cultural figure, he has not been up for that kind of reconsideration or revisionism. Instead, in analyzing the film's depictions of death, I am interrogating the larger representational politics of death in narcomedia texts. Immediately following Nick's death, a short epilogue flashes back to a moment before the film's beginning. Nick and Dylan hike through a thick forest to discover a beautiful, untouched beach. The brothers engage in an emotional embrace, stunned

3.4. Nearly all of the Pablo Escobar tours in Medellín include a stop at his grave. Photograph by Barbara Johnston.

by the beauty of the place and completely unaware of the disaster that awaits them. This repeats a common trope in narcomedia and a theme traced in dozens of literary studies of English-language depictions of the region: Latin America is an earthly paradise ruined by the presence of Latin Americans.[38] Nick and Dylan are never out to hurt anyone, just to have a good time. They are intrinsically good. By placing the kind-hearted Nick in a depraved Colombia, where even the smart and pretty María is complicit with the drug trade, the contrast between good white North Americans and bad Latinos and Latin Americans is even starker. *Paradise*

Lost does stand apart from most depictions of Escobar, which either do not present non-Colombian, white, North American "goodness" to contrast with Pablo (e.g., *Loving Pablo*) or which present the non-Colombians involved as flawed themselves (*American Made* and, to some extent, *Narcos*). But this does not mean that *Paradise Lost* is an outlier. If anything, the movie is simply more honest in how it racializes the War on Drugs as a racial and ethnic morality play.

CONCLUSION

The dozens of Pablo Escobar tours that began to operate in Medellín following the global success of the first two seasons of *Narcos* all include a stop at Escobar's gravesite in the Jardines Montesacro cemetery, high on a hill overlooking the city of Itagüí. Escobar's corpse is not on display at the cemetery, of course, but the site, like all cemeteries, provides a space for visitors to commune with his life and death and what both meant. This cemetery is a particularly open one, well-marked and fenceless. The grave of Griselda Blanco, the woman often credited with teaching Escobar the tricks of the cocaine trade, is just a short walk away. On any given day, including the several times I have visited Jardines Montesacro, small crowds gather around Escobar's flower-covered grave, so much so that musicians and food vendors also appear. The overall atmosphere is alternately somber and festive, a testament to Escobar's unlikely surge in popularity decades after his death, the subject of this book's final chapter. Other stops on the tours attempt to discourage curious travelers. (The nearby site of his former "private prison," for example, is now an old folks' home that has prominently posted banners in a futile effort to keep out tourists.) Unlike those stops, the cemetery has no interpretive framework in place telling guests what the site means or how it should or should not be used. As a result, visitors encounter a less mediated space in which to commune with the kingpin and what his death means to Colombia, its potential to move on from the cartel era, and the War on Drugs. Escobar cannot talk to those assembled at his grave, but through narcomedia representations, his death continues to speak to us.

CHAPTER 4

DANCING TOWARD REVENGE

Queer Representation and What It Means to Be Seen in Narcomedia

On the surface, there is not much queer sexuality to be seen in narcomedia. The narratives that I have examined throughout this book have tended to be explicitly masculinist and heterosexist, constructing storyworlds in which macho men rule and women are reduced to trophies, victims, or worried, long-suffering wives and mothers. Portrayals of kingpins from Tony Montana to Pablo Escobar are almost always hypersexual in nature, but the kingpin's sexuality typically reflects an insatiable appetite for power and prestige. All of this is, well, pretty straight.

However, queer characters have, in fact, long been a staple of gangster and crime movies, even if their queerness has most often been coded rather than explicit. Critics have questioned, to cite just one example, whether Edward G. Robinson's performance as hot-headed crime boss Rico Bandello in the 1931 gangster classic *Little Caesar* had a homosexual subtext. William R. Burnett, the author of the novel on which the movie was based, complained openly about Rico's lack of a female love interest and his fixation on a handsome male friend, Joe (Douglas Fairbanks Jr.). Near the end of the film, when Rico, incensed that Joe won't partner with him in the gang, goes to shoot him. Unable to bring himself to pull the trigger, Rico instead backs away tearfully. Burnett wrote a letter to the movie's producers complaining that the character he created had been made homosexual and demanding reedits.[1] His campaign did not lead to any changes, meaning that it is up to viewers to decide the true nature of Rico's motivations. However, Burnett's complaint indicates that any homoerotic subtexts were barely submerged.

Within the context of narcomedia narratives, queer characters—explicit or coded—have almost exclusively fallen into three categories: villain, victim, or clown (or some combination of the three). Consider, for example, the pilot episode of *Miami Vice*, which hinges on the actions of Calderone's queer right-hand man, Trini Desoto (Martin Ferrero, who goes on to play the hustler Izzy for the rest of the series). After meeting Trini, Crockett describes him as "a cross between Tito Puente and Carol Channing" with "a voice a little on the 'festive' side."[2] This description typifies the show's double stereotyping of queer and Latinx characters. Trini is dangerous, but he is not to be taken seriously. Later, dressed as a female prostitute, Trini is carrying a gun in his purse when Crockett and Tubbs catch up with him. It turns out that a female killer who shot a key witness in the Calderone case earlier in the episode (as the song "Girls Just Wanna Have Fun" plays) was actually a cross-dressing Trini. After Tubbs shoots him at close range, a cop pulls the wig off Trini's dead body.[3] Trini is obviously a villain, but the episode's ending makes him both a victim and, considering that the wig reveal is a classic homophobic and transphobic trope, a clown.[4]

And yet the story of queerness in narcomedia is more complicated than the tired tropes like those associated with Trini. Queer narratives have grown more complex in some narcomedia texts in recent years, and this chapter is especially interested in modes of storytelling that challenge the villain/victim/clown logics. It explores expressions of queerness across contemporary narcomedia texts to examine how violence, victimhood, anger, and revenge have functioned as queer narratives within the genre and how these narratives relate to my bigger questions of latinidad. Moreover, it asks what it means to be seen—to demand to be looked at and understood—as a queer person in narcomedia storyworlds. Queer characters, when they go beyond the established norms, have the potential to challenge what we think we know about narco cultures and the drug trade. They also have the potential to challenge dominant perceptions of Latinx cultures as intrinsically homophobic by showing how queer individuals carve out spaces for themselves. However, as this chapter will argue, the rich potential that comes with queering narcomedia narratives has rarely come to fruition.

By positing that queer characters have grown more complex in recent years, I do not mean to suggest that the old rules no longer apply. The 2016 film *The Infiltrator* is a run-of-the-mill spy thriller with typical narcomedia tropes: a white man on a mission to take down a cartel, hyperviolent jump scares, and a sprawling international storyline. The movie is an adaptation of Robert Mazur's book, also titled *The Infiltrator*, one of dozens of memoirs by US law enforcement agents that have served as the source material for narcomedia. In the film, Bryan Cranston plays Mazur, a US

Customs Service special agent who goes undercover as a flashy alter ego, international money launderer "Bob Musella," to infiltrate the economic system that enables the Colombian cartels (as well as Panamanian dictator Manuel Noriega). As Musella, Mazur establishes a sham money laundering network aimed at enticing and then exposing the cartel, all the way up to Pablo Escobar.

Cranston, star of *Breaking Bad*, has built a career out of defying expectations, but, although he is handsome, he has not typically been cast as an object of sexual desire. So it comes as something of a shock when Javier Ospina (Yul Vazquez), one of the Colombian kingpins whose business Mazur/Musella is courting, casually gropes him when they pass one another on a staircase in what's passing as Bob's New Jersey mansion. Bob is so horrified that he rushes to the bathroom to regroup. He feels shocked and dirty. Perhaps he should have seen the pass coming, considering that Ospina embodies several hallmark traits of a queer villain already familiar to audiences. He only wears spotless all-white suits, with flamboyant gold sunglasses (even during a New Jersey winter), gaudy jewelry, and flowy scarves. He smokes effete-looking cigarillos and travels everywhere with his sexually ambiguous consigliere, Lau (Xarah Xavier).

Moments after the incident on the stairs, Bob tells his collaborators (both his undercover partner and some Colombians who made the introduction to Ospina) that he is uncomfortable because Ospina touched him. "My friend, a condition of doing business with us is doing Ospina," says Gonzalo (Rubén Ochandiano), one of the Colombians. Mazur is incredulous and horrified—even calling off the deal, and thus the secret mission—until Gonzalo lets him know that he is, well, the butt of a joke. "Got you, man!" screams Gonzalo. "He came on to me too, fucking maricón, but the cartel loves him. He is the favorite son, Mr. Bob, so even if you see him fucking a goat, which you might, you must say, 'That's a fucking nice-looking goat, man.'"[5] Just then, the menacing Ospina reappears and tells Bob that he will keep his hands off him as long as he keeps his eyes on the cartel's money, with dire consequences if he doesn't. Even after Bob is let in on the joke, he continues to eye Ospina with suspicion, his queerness providing another layer of the threat that he poses to Bob and the mission.

In the long run, however, Mazur need not have worried since, like countless eccentrically queer characters before him, Ospina meets a gruesome end. In Paris, where he and Bob are meeting with international contacts, Ospina arrives drunk and unhinged. After slurring through a lunch meeting and noticing Bob's recording device, Ospina looks like he might blow Bob's cover at any moment. Later that night, he, along with a group of business associates, arrives at a nightclub. Still out of it, Ospina takes to the dance floor, making a spectacle of himself and kissing Lau and another man passionately. He is telling Bob that his cover is blown when a gunman shoots him in the back at a very close range. Our last view of Ospina is an overhead shot of his dead body in a pool of blood on the dance floor. In Mazur's memoir, based on detailed transcripts and recordings the author collected during his mission, Ospina (spelled as "Ospiña" in the book) is targeted by narcos who fear that his drug use and sexual openness are becoming too conspicuous and threatening their operations. They openly discuss murdering him in front of Mazur and other agents, but the murder takes place off the page. "We never saw Ospiña again," is all that Mazur reports.[6] The dramatic dance floor death is an invention of the filmmakers. Although Javier Ospina is only a minor character in the movie version of *The Infiltrator*, his presence among the film's cadre of Colombian bad guys speaks to the important, if submerged, presence of queer characters in narcomedia.

I have argued that the Latino kingpin trope relies, in part, on the performance of excessive latinidad and that this excessiveness appears in the forms of clothing, greed, appetite, and religiosity. What I have not yet explained are the ways that narcomedia texts use queerness to underscore the excesses of narco cultures—and the ways that queerness itself is framed as a form of excess. The fact that Ospina dies on a dance floor, a symbol of queer pleasure and freedom, is especially revealing. Dance floors, in fact, will make several appearances in the queer representations within narcomedia texts.

An important novel exploring queerness and narco culture came from Colombian author Fernando Vallejo in 1994. *La Virgen de los Sicarios*, translated into English as *Our Lady of the Assassins*, tells the story of Fernando, a man in his fifties, who returns to his hometown of Medellín after a thirty-year absence. Fernando is appalled by the state of the city, which has devolved into a state of constant violence in the cartel era. But it is in that city that he meets and begins an affair with Alexis, a sixteen-year-old *sicario*. Like so many of the street thugs whom Fernando abhors but also desires, Alexis kills indiscriminately. At first shocked by the kid's actions, Fernando eventually comes to appreciate and encourage his companion's quickness to kill. He never pulls a trigger himself, but he sees himself and the kid as outlaw partners. Inevitably, Alexis is killed by the ubiquitous *sicarios* on motorbikes. Fernando unwittingly begins a romance with one of those assassins who, true to what the narrator has told us about the *sicarios*, does not live very much longer himself. In interviews and lectures, Vallejo has described the narrator, Fernando, as based on himself.

With shades of Thomas Mann and Jean Genet, *La Virgen de los Sicarios*—

the novel and subsequent 2000 film adaption—explores gay sex and love across generational, class, and social divides. Like a lot of narcomedia texts, the film and the novel also meditate on urban violence in Medellín at the height of the cartels' power. The book, in particular, is infamous for its grim take on the state of the city in the early 1990s, with death serving as the recurring theme. Perhaps this is unsurprising since murder is a key trope across all narcomedia, but Vallejo depicts both actual death and the metaphorical death of the city and the country. "Hombre, believe you me, living in Medellín is like ricocheting through life as a corpse," he writes in a typically dark sequence. "And so we, the living dead, wander its streets speaking of robberies, hold-ups, and other dead people, drifting ghosts dragging along our precarious existences, our useless lives, submerged in the disaster."[7] Vallejo and his young lovers become the walking dead and also, quite explicitly, "angels of death," as he calls his gun-toting protégés.

What then, does it mean, that these angels of death are openly, even aggressively queer? What function might queerness play when it dares to express itself in narcomedia? As an ambitious literary text from a Colombian writer, *La Virgen de los Sicarios* is a bit afield from my focus in this book on texts aimed at big audiences. However, it is a useful starting point for thinking about what is possible when queer subjects are more than just victims or villains in crime narratives. Vito Russo, Richard Dyer, and a number of queer media scholars have noted the extent to which queerness has been associated with death on-screen, and this branch of queer scholarship has provided a key framework for understanding the construction of the sexually nonnormative with victimization.[8] Vallejo's book is obsessed with death, and his characters are haunted by the possibilities of their impending deaths. But they also have agency. In what follows, I look for the ways that queer characters find or make agency within narrative worlds that seem, much like the material realities they depict, designed to exclude them.

RIPPED FROM THE HEADLINES

The existence of the queer narco is not a figment of the filmic or literary imagination. In fact, the documented history of the drug trade shows that queer men and women played significant roles in narcotrafficking in the United States and abroad, whether as hired *sicarios* or as some of the top bosses. Francisco Hélmer Herrera Buitrago, better known as Pacho Herrera, was fourth in command of the Cali Cartel in the early 1990s. Formed by two brothers, Gilberto and Miguel Rodríguez Orejuela, in 1977, the Cali Cartel was originally allied with the Medellín Cartel, but broke off in the late 1980s over issues related to territory and competition. Its four-person "executive board" included the Rodríguez brothers, Herrera, and José "Chepe" Santacruz Lodoño. They were known as the "Gentlemen of Cali" because of their business-like approach to trafficking, including their propensity to use bribery rather than violence, and for the fact that they were perceived to come from higher social backgrounds than most traffickers. Possibly because of their discretion, the Cali Cartel is not as famous as its counterpart from Medellín, but, by most accounts, it was as successful.

Pacho Herrera, born in 1951 and raised near Cali in the Valle de Cauca, trafficked emeralds and other jewels before he completed a degree in technical maintenance. He subsequently migrated to New York, where he worked on airplanes before he started laundering money with his brother. Purportedly mentored by Chepe Santacruz, he eventually expanded his enterprise to include cocaine smuggling. In 1983, he returned to Cali to negotiate supply and distribution rights with the Cali Cartel for New York City and subsequently worked his way up the organization. Herrera's peers in the drug trade considered him to be a specialist in the business of trafficking—especially money laundering—and he was known to have the protection of some of the most competent *sicarios* in the business. Ample evidence also suggests that Herrera was a gay man.

Herrera's homosexuality seems to have been an open secret in his milieu, but many writers and media makers in both Spanish and English have been somewhat reticent about the subject. Perhaps this is related to the fact that professing one's sexuality and the personal politics of "coming out" work differently in Latin American and Latinx diasporic contexts.[9] English-language sources, including reportage from the *New York Times* during the mid-1990s, tend to describe Herrera's lavish lifestyle without making mention of his sexual practices or identity.[10] Investigative journalist William Rempel takes a matter-of-fact approach to Herrera's sexuality in *At The Devil's Table*, his pulpy 2011 profile of Jorge Salcedo, the informant who helped take down the Cali Cartel (and provided the source material for much of season three of *Narcos*, discussed below). Rempel introduces Herrera in a scene that takes place in 1990, when Salcedo meets the Gentlemen of Cali:

> Pacho Herrera, thirty-seven, was the youngest of the four. This was one of his houses—his white palette, his sterile rooms. He looked as if he had just stepped off the pages of a fashion magazine. Pacho was the only unmarried godfather. He was homosexual. Jorge thought that Pacho had the empathetic, easygoing manner of a young priest.

What he didn't know was that the gay gangster ran the most brutal wing of the enforcers in the cartel.[11]

Whereas most similar texts skirt around the issue of Herrera's sexuality, Rempel at least addresses the matter. However, he also conveys several clichés associated with the "gay gangster," including an emphasis on his style and an obsession with his looks. (Mazur also describes Ospiña as being as good looking as a fashion model in *The Informant*, and the movie adaptation dresses the character in an all-white palette.)

And although Rempel describes the sexual exploits of many of his subjects in livid detail, he politely digresses from examining Herrera's sexual proclivities and what it might have meant to be both queer and a top leader in a renowned criminal enterprise. What Rempel and just about everyone agrees upon is the fact of Herrera's brutality, remarkable even by the standards of the drug trade. According to some Colombian sources, Pablo Escobar believed that Herrera was responsible for the bombing of his Edificio Mónaco headquarters in Medellín and tried unsuccessfully to have him killed.[12] When the Cali Cartel began to collapse in 1995, Herrera was the last to surrender. After he was assassinated in prison in 1998, pictures of his bloody corpse circulated in Colombian media, just like those depicting Escobar in the same state.

Griselda Blanco, a brutal drug trafficker referred to as "the black widow," "the godmother," "the queen of cocaine," and many more *noms de guerre* in magazine and newspaper reportage, has also frequently been called bisexual. Blanco's origins have never been definitively established, but most reporting on her life repeats the narrative that Blanco's mother induced her into prostitution when she was still a child and that, after running away at age sixteen, she engaged in petty crime and sex work before getting involved with the Medellín Cartel.[13] A few years later, she made her way to the United States, where she became a major figure in the burgeoning cocaine trade in New York and Miami. The US news media first took notice of her in 1985, when she was arrested in New York. Blanco, having been deported to Colombia following her time in prison, was shot dead outside a Medellín butcher shop on September 3, 2012.

Blanco is remembered as one of the most cunning and brutal cartel leaders. Although not as internationally infamous as Escobar, she is frequently represented as a pioneer in the business of cocaine distribution. She is credited with inventing the concept of the motorcycle assassination, a form of drive-by shooting in which the passenger on the back of a motorbike shoots a motorist or pedestrian. These shootings symbolize the worst years of the narco era to many Colombians. (The terrors wrought by the motorcycle *sicarios* are dramatized in Vallejo's *Our Lady of the Assassins* and many of the other Colombian-made narcomedia texts examined in this book; in some cities it remains illegal for two men to ride together on a motorcycle.) The sequel to *Cocaine Cowboys* helps to build Blanco's mythology, as does the *Cartel Crew* series described in chapter 2.

THE MEANINGS OF QUEER REVENGE

The effete queer villain is neither a new trope in pop culture nor one that is specific to narcomedia. As Vito Russo showed in his classic study *The Celluloid Closet*, movies have portrayed queer people as villains since the beginning of the medium. Other works in the field of queer film studies have provided countless readings of this representational practice, even in movies in which a character is not explicitly or avowedly queer—from westerns to Disney to superhero franchises, from the snotty queer maître d' to the criminal mastermind. Martin Landau's effete villain in the 1959 *North by Northwest* predates and anticipates characters like Ospina and Silva.[14]

Revenge narratives have the potential to subvert the dominant culture's misgivings about queerness, but can they be subversive within the context of a mainstream media text? Despite the presence of same-sex-oriented characters, there is nothing particularly queer about *Breaking Bad* or *Narcos*. Neither of the series' showrunners is openly queer. In fact, they fit into the somewhat macho (for Hollywood) cohort described in *Difficult Men*, Brett Martin's exploration of the straight white men who helped create the prestige television movement by producing television about straight white men.[15] Both texts play with creating sympathetic drug lords, so they could possibly be interpreted as subverting the audience's expectations about what constitutes a heroic character. But they ultimately invoke their audience to sympathize with the need to bring these monsters to justice.[16] In this sense, these shows (and their many imitators) are not as subversive as they appear to be.

A queer revenge narrative also drives some of the action in the third season of *Narcos*. Like the DEA itself, *Narcos* shifts its focus to Cali in the aftermath of Escobar's death. The upstart cartel leaders are introduced at the start of the third season with a clever montage that showcases the Cali Cartel's quartet of bosses: brothers Gilberto and Miguel Rodríguez Orejuela (Damián Alcázar and Francisco Denis), New York boss Chepe Santacruz (Pêpê Rapazote), and Pacho Herrera (Alberto Ammann). The episode also shifts the voice-over narrative from Steve Murphy to his former partner Javier Peña (Pedro Pascal). As Peña explains to the audience, while US and Colombian forces had been focused on Escobar in their joint war on cocaine, the Cali Cartel had grown into a criminal enterprise even bigger than the Medellín Cartel.

In his introductory bit, Pacho soaks in the bubbles of an opulent bathtub while taking business calls. When the person with whom he was sharing the bath steps out, we see the naked rear of a young man. The setup is standard-fare narcomedia, but the sex of Pacho's bath-time companion is presumably intended to surprise the audience, who, over the course of the prior two seasons, have only been introduced to the insatiable, heteronormative sexual appetite of Pablo Escobar. As in most representations of the drug lord, it is always women and girls who are held up as the objects of Escobar's desire and, by proxy, the desires of other narcos.

Narcos initially introduces Pacho late in its first season, when the Cali Cartel emerges as a serious competitor to Escobar's Medellín-based operation. The Gentlemen of Cali become active with Los Pepes, the vigilante group that publicly—and brutally—challenges Escobar as his control over the cocaine trade begins to wane. The audience glimpses all four godfathers, including Pacho, but they appear mostly as ancillary to the efforts to take down Escobar, especially in his battle with Judy Moncada (Cristina Umaña), the widow of one of his murdered rivals (based on real-life Dolly Moncada) over the course of the second season. In one memorable scene, Escobar's men bomb the wedding of Gilberto Rodríguez Orejuela's daughter, accelerating the rivalry between the Medellín and Cali Cartels.

It is not until the start of season three that Pacho and the Gentlemen of Cali become the focus of the series, but much is revealed about them in the first episode of the season. It establishes, for example, their more business like approach to the cocaine trade, which includes their insistence on keeping their hands clean through shell companies and money laundering practices. As opposed to Escobar, whose unending appetites contributed to his downfall, Miguel runs the operation like a CEO. Whereas Escobar could only strive to be a member of Medellín's elite, the Rodríguez brothers were accepted into Cali high society. We also get better acquainted with Pacho and, near the end of the episode, witness his queerness and his brutality in equal force.

Following a meeting in which boss Miguel introduces his new plan to go legitimate after six months, Pacho is dispatched to deal with Claudio Salazar (Carlos Camacho), an associate in the cartel who, they have discovered, has secret plans to stay in the drug trade. He finds Claudio partying with some cronies at a popular open-air disco alongside a river.[17] Wearing a black leather motorcycle jacket over one of his ubiquitous silk shirts, Pacho strides up to Claudio and appears to make a peace offering by offering

Dancing toward Revenge | 109

4.1. Pacho and his dance partner defy convention in *Narcos*, season three.

him a bottle of aguardiente. "Please, Claudio," he tells him, "accept this as a token of respect. To let bygones be bygones."[18] Claudio accepts with a handshake, agreeing that the past is in the past. But before he pours a shot, Pacho excuses himself, swaggering to the dance floor as the sultry Ángel Canales cover of the classic bolero "Dos Gardenias," which he told the bartender to play, begins.

From offstage, a young man joins Pacho on the dance floor. The camera alternates between close-ups of the lovers' faces and medium shots of the crowd, which now stands almost perfectly still, watching. Reaction shots of other patrons' faces make it clear that no one knows how to respond. Claudio himself is nervous, wiping his brow and, at one point, holding his face in his hands. But Pacho and his partner are undeterred. They dance and sway to the music, their feet in sync with one another's. Near the end of the song, they kiss passionately and lingeringly—one of the most sensual scenes in a series that has tended to treat sex as another form of the kingpin's excess. Pacho and his lover can't seem to take their hands off each other and, unlike the characters present at the bar, the camera does not flinch. Director Andi Baiz, a native of Cali, captures the sense that two men dancing is more disruptive to social convention in Cali than the brutal murders that we have already witnessed.[19]

The scene might initially appear to be a touchingly bold expression of queer desire in a hostile environment, but what happens next makes it clear that Pacho's actions are not a plaintive call for acceptance. The song comes to an end. Nothing is diminished in Pacho's swagger as he returns to Claudio's table and that bottle of aguardiente. But instead of pouring the liquor, he smashes the bottle over Claudio's head. A jump cut takes the viewer to the exhaust pipe of Pacho's motorcycle, and we soon understand that Claudio is to be drawn and quartered, each limb tied to one of four idling motorcycles by a thick rope. Pacho's dance partner restrains Claudio's drinking companion, taunting and laughing as the man begs for Claudio's life. Claudio begs too, swearing he's innocent of any crimes against the cartel. It's too late. Pacho is unmoved. He and his underlings rev their engines ominously and then accelerate in four different directions. They destroy Claudio while his friend screams and sobs in disbelief. The scene ends with Pacho driving away on his motorcycle, Claudio's severed arm trailing behind.[20]

Narcos only focuses on the Gentlemen of Cali for one season, but Pacho gets a significant amount of screen time in the ten episodes. At its psychological core, Pacho's storyline is built around his need for revenge. The murder of Claudio sets the stage for this, but Pacho's drive for revenge deepens over time. After the North Valle Cartel, run by the Salazar family, maims his brother and new lover in a shootout around the middle of the season, Pacho becomes singularly focused on payback.[21] In one memorable set piece, he sets off a car bomb outside the church where members of the Salazar clan are attending mass. After the blast kills several of the cartel's men, Pacho marches into the church, takes the pulpit, and promises the terrified parishioners that no one is safe in the North Valley until Gerda Salazar, the family matriarch and Claudio's mother, is delivered to him. Later, in the cold opening of the season finale, with his sicario lover at his side, Pacho infiltrates the Salazar compound and wreaks total havoc, killing everyone in sight. After shooting Gerda point blank in the face, he sits down on the veranda and coolly lights a cigarette. Immediately afterward, looking dapper but resigned, he surrenders in a church. The edit suggests that he can turn himself in now that he has killed on behalf of the men to whom he was closest.

What else is Pacho avenging? At several points in the season, while reflecting on his role in the cartel or his use of violence, he offers a glimpse into a backstory involving rejection from his father because of his queerness. One brief bit of dialogue, delivered to Amado Carillo Fuentes (José María Yazpik), the rising kingpin of the Juarez Cartel, particularly speaks to this.[22] Amado has been urging Pacho to betray the Rodríguez brothers and go into business with him. After telling Pacho a ribald story, Amado pushes him for an answer to his repeated attempts to get him to commit to the new endeavor. Pacho's response reveals where he found family in the face of paternal rejection:

> PACHO: My turn to tell you a story, Amado. About the time when my father found me in my room with another boy.
> AMADO: Hey, I never judged you for that stuff.
> PACHO: My father told me that I wasn't a man, that I would never be one. It was the last time he spoke to me.
> AMADO: What a fucking bastard.
> PACHO: For a long time I thought he was right. Even after I started working for Gilberto and Miguel. Up until the day some motherfucker told them I was a faggot. And that it was a mistake to let me be part of the business. You know what they did? They made me a partner. Gilberto, Miguel, and Chepe, they are my family. I can't just leave them when they need me the most.[23]

Pacho's backstory, though slim, suggests something about his motivation—and his queerness. Perhaps this is clichéd since daddy issues are overused in popular culture in general and were already plumbed late in the second season of *Narcos* when Pablo attempts to reconcile with his father before his downfall. Still, this submerged narrative is significant in that it suggests that the source of Pacho's brutality is not his queerness—as other gay bad guys have suggested throughout film history—but homophobia.

By the last few minutes of the final episode of the season, the four Gentlemen of Cali are all in prison, another victory for the DEA. In our last glimpse of Pacho, a fellow prisoner who is loyal to the North Valle Cartel shoots him in the back of the head at close range. Javier Peña's voice-over reminds us that old grudges die hard in this business. Pacho falls into the arms of the same young man who danced with him to "Dos Gardenias" before Pacho killed Claudio Salazar. His lover's horrified face is now splattered with his blood and, in a brief but telling moment, the young man quickly places Pacho's body on the ground to engage in the ensuing fight in the prison yard. This signals that the cycle of violence to which Pacho contributed so ruthlessly will continue after he is gone. Like the deaths of many queer narcomedia figures before him, and perhaps like that of the real-life Hélmer Herrera, Pacho's death feels inevitable in the world of *Narcos*.

When *Narcos* aired the scene at the disco, several LGBT-themed blogs celebrated it, and the Pacho character in general, as an expression of gay power, as if it was a coming-out scene. Both Doug Miro and Carlo Bernard, co-creators of the series, mentioned their inclusion of a gay narco as a point of pride in interviews with me. Some articles and commentators even called him a "hero" and an "inspiration" because of his unabashed expression of same-sex attraction in a hypermacho, presumably homophobic industry. These responses are misguided but understandable since it is an appealing fantasy that Herrera would have behaved in this way and because Ammann offers an incredibly sexy performance as Pacho. But the idea of a real-life "openly gay" Pacho Herrera does not match up with the discretion and secrecy practiced by the historical person, whose sexuality was much more the subject of speculation from cartel insiders than documented in any real sense. The scene is much more a product of 2010s Hollywood, which champions neoliberal politics of outness, than of Cali of the 1990s. With that in mind, it is the narrative of violent revenge rather than historical accuracy that interests me here.

Pacho's need for revenge echoes a storyline that is important to the latter seasons of *Breaking Bad*. In chapter 5, I describe the fictional character of Gus as a more complex vision of latinidad than had previously appeared in the series and that influenced its spinoff, *Better Call Saul*, to include three-dimensional Latinx characters and storylines. By outward appearances, Albuquerque businessman Gus Fring (Giancarlo Esposito) is a fastidious family man and upstanding citizen. He prepares elaborate meals in his gourmet kitchen, attends charity galas, and sits on the board of a hospital. He also puts in hours at his fast-food chain, Los Pollos Hermanos. However, this being the world of *Breaking Bad*, Gus is actually a prominent meth producer and distributor in the US Southwest. The Afro-Latino kingpin runs a highly professionalized lab that employs trained chemists to produce the purest meth on the market. For several seasons, he is also a formidable nemesis to the series antihero, Walter White, who, by the fourth season, when things really heat up between him and Gus, is making so much money cooking meth that he and his wife resort to vacuum-packing the cash and hiding it in their home's crawlspace. Gus and Walter do not trust one another, but they find a common enemy in a crime family headed by the elderly Hector Salamanca (Mark Margolis, who also appears in the 1983 *Scarface*). Gus and the Salamancas are fighting for their share of the drug trade, but Gus's ruthlessness in going after them suggests motivations that go beyond business.

The deeper source of Gus's hatred of the Salamancas is revealed late in the fourth season, over two episodes that feature flashbacks to 1989. Gus and a partner, Max (James Martinez), then living in Mexico, have just started Los Pollos Hermanos as a front for their new methamphetamine business. In the present-day of episode 8, "Hermanos," Gus is face-to-face with the infirm and nonverbal Hector in the Casa Tranquila nursing home when the first sepia-toned flashback begins.[24] Meth was a new drug for most of Latin America in the late 1980s, but Gus and Max attend a poolside meeting with kingpin Don Eladio Vuente (Steven Bauer, who, like Margolis, appears in *Scarface*) in an attempt to convince him to fund a lab. The filmmakers signal the shift in time and place by coloring the flashback scenes in sepia tones. Max and Gus make a passionate pitch, arguing for making their own product rather than merely serving as traffickers for Colombian cocaine. "It's the drug of the future," Gus asserts to a seemingly receptive Don Eladio.

But, it turns out, Don Eladio is offended by their overreach. Max and Gus had been distributing "samples" of their products to his workers in an attempt to get his attention and secure a meeting with him, which Don Eladio sees as an attempt to undermine his business. Furthermore, Eladio is skeptical of meth, which he calls "the cocaine of the poor," and wants to maintain his standing as the Mexican middleman for Colombian coke. It appears that Eladio is aggravated with Gus, who has presented himself as in charge of the business side of the meth operation (Max, a trained chemist, is the "cook"). Max starts begging him not to hurt his partner, who had "rescued me from the Santiago slums and made me the man I am today." But, in a shocking move, Eladio's consigliere—none other than a younger Hector Salamanca—pulls a gun and shoots Max in the head at point-blank range. The shooting happens just offscreen, but Gus is splattered by his companion's blood. He tries to attack Hector, but another of Eladio's men wrestles him to the ground and forces him to look at Max's body. "Look at him," insists Hector. "You did this to him. . . . My advice? Stick to the chicken." Gus weeps uncontrollably as Max's blood drains into the pool.[25]

Two episodes later, and back in the present day, Gus is again in Mexico, doing business with the cartel there, when he returns to Don Eladio's villa.[26] In the shot, he stares pensively into the pool where Max met his demise about twelve years prior. Gus has brought Jesse (Aaron Paul) and Mike (Jonathan Banks), along with a gift of fine tequila for Eladio and his crew. Eladio embraces the visitors and toasts to their presence. Gus is the first to drink, and a party ensues. Bikini-clad women make the rounds, offering the partygoers cigars (and presumably more), but Gus sits alone and once again stares into the pool. Eladio approaches and tells him that there was nothing personal in their previous dealings, but Gus excuses himself to the bathroom, where he forces himself to vomit and then, with his characteristic coolness, calmly wipes his mouth. The tequila had been poisoned, and Eladio and his men fall one by one as chaos erupts in the compound. Gus watches as Eladio takes his last breath and falls into the pool. Later, Gus returns to Hector's care facility to taunt him about taking out the entire cartel, including Hector's grandson Joaquin: "It was just you and Joaquin. He was the only family you had left. Now the Salamanca name dies with you."[27] At this point, Gus's revenge, more than a decade in the making, is nearly complete.

Fans of *Breaking Bad* disagree on how to interpret the flashbacks and the relationship between Max and Gus. Some fans are adamant that Max and Gus were just good friends and that it is a misreading to interpret Gus as queer. Such is the desire of a straight fandom to erase queer desire in its favorite show. However, there are some subtle clues elsewhere in *Breaking Bad* and its prequel that suggest otherwise. Before Don Eladio joins the meeting, Hector pees in his pool and taunts Gus and Max for liking what they see while his pants are unzipped. In an episode of *Better Call Saul*, Hector says that Gus and Max, whose restaurant translates as "The Chicken Brothers," might be referred to as "The Butt Brothers."[28] This cheap shot is just an offhand remark, but it vindicates fans who had interpreted the pair as more than friends in the original series. Later, in a more powerful and explicit representation of their same-sex love, *Better Call Saul* reveals that Gus has built an entire enclave of homes in Mexico as a memorial to Max, complete with homes, a school, a clinic, and a fountain.[29]

Gus is one of the few characters to ever kill for love in the *Breaking Bad* universe. This is heightened by the slow-burn quality of his revenge narrative, which is revealed over several seasons of the prequel series, *Better Call Saul*. In some of his first lines of that series, Gus actually negotiates to keep Hector alive. He tells Mike, who intends to kill Hector, that it is not in his interest for Hector to die "at *this* time."[30] For viewers who know how it all ends, this is a juicy beginning to Gus's long-game revenge plan, showing that his calculating pursuit of Hector has taken place over several years.

The next season, when Hector lies in a coma because of a separate plot to kill him, Gus remains resolute that vengeance will be his. He visits his hospital room and makes a long speech to the unresponsive Hector. Gus tells him that, as a boy in Chile, he coaxed the fruit out of a neglected lacuma tree, fruit that he delighted in himself and sold at market in an attempt to escape the brutal poverty of his youth. One day he discovered that a coati had decimated his beloved tree. He built a snare and waited for hours before catching the thieving animal. Though wounded, it escaped his trap and hid under his shack. "Finally, it came out," Gus remembers. "It knew I was there, but it was hungry. This time I was ready. I caught it. It fought me, but I was stronger. The merciful thing would have been to kill it. I kept it. It lived for quite some time."[31] The story of the lacuma and the coati foreshadows what happens in the next episode, when Gus schemes to keep Hector infirm and vulnerable. This crueler option, echoing what he learned as a child, sets the stage for what happens years later in *Breaking Bad* (according to the timeline shared by the two series).

During his multiple visits to threaten and taunt Hector Salamanca in the Casa Tranquila nursing home, Gus makes a repeated demand: "Look at me." Hector cannot talk and seems to be able to move only a single finger, so he possesses two means of communication: his eyes and a bell that he rings with the working digit. Gus might be demanding to be looked at so that he can see that Hector's pain is registering as Gus relates how his long-held plans for revenge are finally coming to fruition. Recall that Don Eladio made Gus watch as Hector killed Max in 1989. Or, in a reading that I prefer, his demand might suggest a need to be *seen*, a desire to be acknowledged and understood on his own terms as a queer subject. I am reluctant to locate Gus's actions within the gay rights movement's politics of visibility, but there is something to be said about the fact that Gus's past enemies had seen him and Max for what they were and punished them for it, but now Gus is in charge and an active agent in making Hector pay. Being seen can be understood, in fact, as central to Gus's revenge-driven story arc. Pacho's dance at the disco in the *Narcos* third season premiere might reflect a similar desire and demand to be seen.

Pacho and Gus both meet grisly ends. Like the real-life Herrera, Pacho is gunned down in a prison yard during the final moments of the season. Gus dies even more spectacularly in the last episode of *Breaking Bad*'s fourth season. In the scene, which was originally conceived as an ending for the series before it was renewed for a fifth season, Gus pays one last visit to Hector Salamanca at Casa Tranquila.[32] As he waits in the car for one of his men to give him the all-clear, the camera spends thirty-three seconds zooming in on Gus's face, his eyes misting over with tears, and then another thirty-three seconds as he walks toward the facility. These extra-long shots, underscored by tense piano and guitar music, make it clear that a reckoning is nigh. He enters Hector's room and has his henchman prepare a syringe of deadly poison. "Last chance to look at me, Hector," he says as he begins to inject Hector with the contents of the syringe. Hector does finally look at him, his eyes growing defiantly large, but he also begins to ring his bell madly, which detonates the bomb that Walt has planted in Hector's wheelchair. The huge explosion blows the door off its hinges, and Gus walks calmly out of the room. At first, he appears unscathed, but as the camera rotates around to his other side, it reveals the gruesome fact that half of his face is ripped off. Gus straightens his tie before he falls dead, his mission for revenge finally accomplished.

SCARFACE IN RED HEELS

Looking to another narcomedia text that deals with its protagonist's queerness will deepen my analysis of the revenge narrative as a tenet of queer narcomedia. Like all the real-life narcos examined in this chapter and throughout this book, Griselda Blanco the historical person differs from "Griselda Blanco" the character who appears in popular culture. She is less well known than many of her male counterparts, but she has been a significant presence in narcomedia—and is certain to grow in prominence when Netflix releases *Griselda*, a biopic starring Sofia Vergara, sometime after this writing.[33] As Aldona Bialowas Pobutsky notes in *Pablo Escobar and Colombian Narcoculture*, the 2010s saw a spate of interest in Blanco's story that resulted in several Spanish-language biographies, some of which made their way into US-made cultural productions. I agree with Pobutsky when she asserts that this interest in the "black widow" is undoubtedly woven into the intense interest in all things Pablo Escobar around this time.[34] However, in her chapter on Blanco, Pobutsky makes little mention of how Blanco's queer framing affects her public image.

One of the oddest examples of narcomedia takes the form of a low-budget Lifetime made-for-TV movie, *Cocaine Godmother*, which traces the life of Blanco from her young childhood to her death by assassination at the age of sixty-nine. I have mentioned Blanco previously in this book, including in the biographical sketch above and in the description in chapter 1 of Miami's image as "Paradise Lost" in the early 1980s. Miami was Blanco's home base for much of her career as a US trafficker, although she also lived and worked in New York and California. In each of these places, Blanco reaped huge profits and wreaked havoc with her violent and chaotic personal life. But in a media landscape that has obsessed over every detail of male narcos' lives, Blanco's story has remained relatively unexplored. *Cocaine Godmother* seems to want to serve as a corrective and, although less successful as a production, aims to place Blanco among the cadre of male narcos that became household names in the 2010s.

In the weeks before the movie aired in January 2018, most attention from critics and social media focused on the casting of Catherine Zeta-Jones, who plays Blanco from the age of seventeen to her death in 2012. The Oscar-winning Welsh actor brought some star quality to basic cable, but her casting inspired the usual criticisms that arise when contemporary Hollywood bypasses actors of color in casting non-white roles, as happened with the casting of Emma Stone in *Aloha* (2015) and Scarlett Johansson in *Ghost in the Shell* (2017). The filmmakers wisely did not darken Zeta-Jones's fair skin, but her accent harkens back to Charlton Heston's brownface performance in *Touch of Evil* (1958). Like Johansson, Zeta-Jones made the media rounds to defend her performance and her case for color-blind casting, arguing to several reporters that, being Welsh, she was a minority herself and was used to having to play parts outside of her own experience. The Colombian press, which typically approaches US-made narcomedia with understandable suspicion, also dismissed the movie as the *"blanqueamiento de una narca colombiana en* Hollywood"—the whitening of a female narco in Hollywood.[35] All of this hubbub was misplaced, however, since, unlike bigger productions that have faced casting controversies, *Cocaine Godmother* only made a splash because of Zeta-Jones's presence as Blanco; no major newspapers, magazines, or respected online outlets bothered to review the TV movie.[36]

Most of the recent stylistic trends in narcomedia storytelling in film and television are present in the Zeta-Jones vehicle: gritty flashbacks, interstitials that use archival footage, and voice-over narrative. Hot-headed, trigger-happy *sicarios* abound. Clearly a low-budget project, it seems content to recycle many of the tropes with which audiences are already well familiar. It does, of course, focus on a woman, which is still quite rare in the world of narcomedia. It also diverges from standard narcomedia fare by placing its lead character's abuse narrative and queerness at the center of the story. For these reasons, especially the latter, *Cocaine Godmother* should be taken seriously as a narcomedia text.

The abuse narrative appears from the first scene, which finds eleven-year-old Griselda prostituted by her mother in the slums on the outskirts of Medellín. When her mother slaps her and turns her out to the streets for talking back to her, Griselda goes to the house of a john who owes her money, shoots him dead, and absconds with his money. This brief scene—only about four-and-a-half minutes of the hour-and-forty-minute movie—serves as the prologue that establishes Griselda as a victim, but also as a person with some semblance of agency, all before the opening title and credits. Immediately after, the movie fast-forwards to New York City in the early 1970s, where Griselda is a harried young mother of three with an unappreciative husband who, like her mother, slaps her when she insults him. Again, Griselda does not passively accept the abuse, but fights back. She breaks a beer bottle over his head and kicks him out of their apartment. This pattern repeats itself throughout her adult life: When men and women hurt her, she reacts with outsized violence.

Early in the movie, shortly after she leaves her husband, her eye still bruised from his slap, Griselda meets Caroline (Jenny Pellicer) at a nightclub. Caroline is seductively dancing with a man to Eddie Palmieri's "Café," a song with a slow and sensual beat. Griselda interrupts them and leads Caroline to the bar, where she buys her a drink and renames her "Carolina." They start a romance after Griselda marries her second husband, Alberto (Juan Pablo Espinosa). As Griselda and Alberto dance at their wedding, she stares longingly at Carolina until she finally walks over and takes her in her arms. Her hand tenderly caresses Carolina's back until it reaches its resting place on her ass. As with Pacho in the disco in *Narcos*, the act of dancing with one's preferred partner becomes a way to make queer desire visible—a way to be seen.

Later that night, as Alberto dozes in another room, Griselda and Carolina have passionate sex. "This is the wedding gift I really wanted," Griselda tells her, in what is by far the most romantic sequence in the movie. *Cocaine Godmother* presents their pairing as the longest-standing amorous relationship in Griselda's life. When her young son Michael is kidnapped, Griselda takes to her bed with Carolina and cocaine as her only comforts. Although the film spends a surprisingly brief forty-seven seconds focusing on Carolina's death from a drug overdose, the overall narrative makes the argument that she was the love of Griselda's life. When she is arrested and taken into custody at the end of the film, she only asks for two photographs to be retrieved from her apartment: one of her with her three older sons and one of Carolina. She lingers over the latter for a moment longer, smiling sweetly even though she has finally been defeated by the DEA. When the arresting agent leaves her alone for a moment, she tenderly caresses the picture to the strumming of a guitar.

It is tempting to view *Cocaine Godmother* as a queer and feminist response to the machista tendencies of common narcomedia tropes. Zeta-Jones, who worked for years to get the movie made (though she must have hoped for a more prestigious platform), certainly represented it that way when she spoke to the entertainment news media. She told *Entertainment Weekly* that she became interested in Blanco when she watched *Cocaine Cowboys* on Netflix. "They kept mentioning this woman," Zeta-Jones told a reporter. "Griselda, Griselda Blanco. And these men who were very dangerous and very powerful in that dark, dark world were speaking of this woman like they revered her and still, after all these years, feared her . . . . We know about Escobar, we know about El Chapo now, we know about these key figures in this world . . . but we never hear about this woman. Who is this woman?"[37]

Like the real Blanco, who was not known for possessing a glamorous mien, the filmic Griselda bucks many of the expectations for feminine gender performance within the world of narcomedia. Women appear all over the texts examined in this book, but typically only as one of two tropes: the long-suffering wife and mother or the hypersexualized objects of male attention, as I have mentioned above. These representations tend to fall clearly along the lines of the virgin/whore dichotomy that has plagued Latina imagery in US and Latin American popular cultures, as feminist works in Latinx media studies have demonstrated. Provocative recent scholarship has shown, furthermore, that narco cultures in Colombia, Mexico, and the United States have shaped expectations around feminine dress, bodies, and behavior, creating a distinct "narco aesthetic" that requires plastic surgery, makeup, and grooming practices to hyperfeminize the female subject.[38] Narcomedia texts tend to reinforce these expectations and, when not reducing them to worried wives or mothers, present women as little more than narco arm candy. This mode of representation is as old as the gangster movie genre and grants female characters little agency, despite the varied roles they have played in the real-world drug trade. Griselda does initially use her sexuality to break into the narcotics trade, but it is her gritty determination that helps her rise to the top.

Cocaine Godmother does not water down Griselda's queerness. Her relationship with Carolina is the emotional heart of the otherwise scattered film, and Griselda and Carolina frequently physically display their affection for one another in public. Unlike Max and Gus in *Breaking Bad*, the queer love and lust between Griselda and Caroline is uninhibited, uncoded, unambiguous. Other characters blanch at their physicality with one another, but the movie presents this as an expression of the homophobia of those characters rather than something pathological or particularly dangerous about Griselda, who is, in fact, often at her most tender when interacting with Carolina. After they break up, they still engage in a mode of kinship between ex-lovers that will appear familiar to queer viewers.

Cocaine Godmother frequently swerves toward camp, which only heightens its potential for a queer reading. Almost exactly midway through the film, Griselda, now addicted to her own product but at the top of the Miami drug trade, travels to Medellín to check on her wayward husband. She dons a tacky blonde wig as a disguise and heads to a bar, where she finds him having sex with a woman in a bathroom stall. Standing on a toilet and hanging over the wall of the stall, she shoots them at close range, one for each time they admit to having had sex (though her counting is off), and then goes to the mirror to check on her appearance. "Ay," she says out loud to herself, "this was my favorite blouse." This is intended to sound like a bon mot, but is so strikingly out of character for Griselda that it reads as funny for the wrong reasons. This kind of over-the-top, so-bad-it's-good writing, paired with Zeta-Jones's unnuanced performance, gaudy costumes, and Speedy Gonzales accent, adds up to a film that simply does not work. Camp, according to Susan Sontag's classic definition, must take itself seriously. *Cocaine Godmother* does take itself seriously, but many of Griselda's words and actions are so exaggerated and grandiose that they become laughable.

On a more serious note, Zeta-Jones's Griselda is considerably less violent than the actual Blanco, who was admittedly so mind-bogglingly vicious that it is difficult to represent in a realistic manner. The real Blanco is also known to have sexually assaulted both men and women. Perhaps the filmmakers toned down Griselda in order to present a character that they imagined the mostly female Lifetime audience could cheer for. But, in the end, the character Griselda barely resembles what we know about the real Blanco, whose violence has been well documented in Spanish- and English-language media, including as the focus of the sequel to *Cocaine Cowboys*.

I am tempted to read *Cocaine Godmother* as a feminist take on the narcomedia genre, but several considerations challenge this urge. First is the matter of narration. The voice-over sporadically heard in the film is provided by DEA agent Jimmy DiPiero (Warren Christie), a minor character who engages in the typical cat-and-mouse chase with Blanco. His voice-over sounds uncannily like Steve Murphy's in the first two seasons of *Narcos*, in terms of both the sound of his voice and the writing that positions him as an omnipotent observer prone to somewhat corny aphorisms. (Sample line: "He was good at being good, but even better at being bad.") Jimmy's narration also involves frequent use of the second person, exactly like Steve's, which seems to presume that the viewer identifies with the white cop rather than any of the Latinx characters. This is to say that, ultimately, a white man has the final word in both stories. What is more, these white men ultimately represent the goals and tactics of the US government and its attempts to capture and punish the Latinx characters. *Cocaine Godmother* focuses on Griselda to the point that Zeta-Jones appears in the vast majority of the scenes, but Jimmy is granted the narrative authority that comes with voice-over narration, resulting in a film in which Griselda is the object but Jimmy is the agent (pun intended).

Second, throughout the film, Griselda's brutal actions actually constitute *reactions*. She runs away and turns to smuggling after suffering abuse from her mother and first husband. She turns to smuggling partly to escape a violent and unfulfilling domestic situation. She is vicious with Carolina when she gently questions Griselda's choices as a mother. In many ways, *Cocaine Godmother* depicts Griselda Blanco as a monster, but a monster of other people's creations. Furthermore, her ideas about women are not exactly forward-thinking. "Take some motherly advice," she tells her son Uber when they are on their way to Medellín, "Trust no one in this life. Not even your wife. Men are fooled so easily. Women are like spiders.

They'll pull you into their web until you're wrapped up so tight you can no longer breathe."

Finally, the movie spends a considerable amount of time focusing on issues related to Griselda's motherhood. Pobutsky notes that Blanco's family has made a habit of speaking out on talk shows and other media about Blanco's maternal side, promoting a narrative of her as "a desperate mother obligated to feed her offspring."[39] In *Cocaine Godmother*, Griselda is endlessly disappointed that her sons follow her into the drug trade, but she also hatches multiple schemes to improve their chances at going straight, especially when it comes to her two younger sons, Uber and Michael Corleone (whose real-life counterpart, middle-aged and devoted to his mother's legacy, later starred on VH1's reality show *Cartel Crew*). When, at one point, Carolina refers to herself as the boys' mother, Griselda turns on her, grabbing her threateningly by her necklace: "Call yourself their mother again and I'll strangle you with these pearls," she warns her before descending into maniacal laughter. Motherhood is, of course, a feminist subject matter, but in the context of *Cocaine Godmother*, the theme feels like it reduces Blanco to a tired trope of Latina-ness. Blanco lived a complex, brutal, thrilling, terrible life that is far more interesting than the worried Latina mother trope.

CONCLUSION

By now it is obvious that depictions of queer characters across narcomedia are wildly disparate. From swishing, sneering villains to a pseudo-feminist queenpin, there has never been a singular way to represent queerness in narcomedia. Even so, taken together, the representations addressed here show us that queerness inhabits some important real estate in narcomedia, even if that comes with problematic or harmful systems of representation. In chapter 2, I described how Griselda Blanco's son was attempting to profit from his mother's notoriety through various product lines and his appearances on reality television. None of his efforts include any acknowledgment of his mother's queerness. Nor did Blanco herself speak about it on the record. These silences are not surprising, given that none of the other real-life narcos ever spoke up about their sexual identities. Narcomedia texts provide a cultural space where queerness is spoken despite the real-world silences.

This chapter's introduction mentioned the potential for queer characters to transform the meanings of narcomedia. Characters like Pacho, Gus, and Griselda do have their appeal. It is easy to admire how they demand to be seen in environments that try to make them invisible. Pacho's dance in the disco, Gus's fearsomeness, and Griselda's dominance call into question the macho patriarchal systems that the vast majority of narcomedia representations take for granted. Ultimately, however, despite their queerness, none of these characters challenges the bigger systems of violence and oppression in which they operate. And, like so many of their predecessors—those villains, victims, and clowns—they die grisly deaths. I am not asking for queer heroes, but these figures would look a lot more heroic if they dismantled oppressive systems rather than profiting from them.

CHAPTER 5

DARK MATTERS

Breaking Bad *and the Suburban Crime Drama*

In August 2011, the *Playboy* culture, sex, and humor blog posted a short article titled "Five Things *Breaking Bad* Has Taught Us About the Drug Trade," listing humorous tips to help the layperson understand the complexities of the drug economy as portrayed in AMC's critically acclaimed series. In number three on the satirical list, author Will Kriegshauser advises readers that successful wannabe drug kingpins "Don't Fuck with the Mexicans."[1] This snide suggestion refers to the fact that characters from south of the US-Mexico border or with Mexican roots serve as the main impediments to the misadventures of the white protagonists in the series. In making this bold statement, Kriegshauser rehearses a well-worn vision of latinidad, a way of seeing Latinas and Latinos that has prevailed in American popular media and has been the object of Latina/o film studies for two decades.[2] Kriegshauser's intention is, of course, dark humor, but the article also reveals an important but overlooked thread woven throughout *Breaking Bad*—namely, that the series frequently stages racialized encounters between its white protagonists and Latino characters who, though always only minor characters, pose formidable threats to the protagonists' livelihoods and their lives.

This chapter examines those encounters to understand *Breaking Bad* within the broader history of representational practices portraying Latinas/os and latinidad as threats to the white body politic of the United States. Though *Breaking Bad* is not the most obvious Latino studies text, I contend that the series offers critical insight into the places that latinidad inhabits in the popular imagination of the United States. To understand these constructions of latinidad, I offer a close reading of two somewhat minor but also quite important characters who help the series protagonists learn that "fucking with the Mexicans" (and Mexican Americans and

Venezuelans, *etc.*) is a risky move in one's rise to drug kingpin. These character studies, which also show how the series draws upon a constellation of Latino images that have populated film and television for the past few decades, illuminate the challenges and possibilities of constructing a complex view of latinidad on cable television.

Over the course of five seasons, *Breaking Bad* traces the descent of Walter White (Bryan Cranston), a cash-strapped high school chemistry teacher diagnosed with terminal lung cancer, into the world of methamphetamine production and distribution. Faced with mounting medical bills, a skimpy salary, a family to support, and a dire prognosis, Walt initially hopes to dip into the drug trade just enough to secure his family's financial future but eventually becomes enthralled with the sense of power and purpose granted to him by his status as a major player in that trade. Early in the series, he enlists Jesse Pinkman (Aaron Paul), a former student with marginally more street smarts, to help him "cook" and distribute the meth. As Walt's only real connection to the drug trade, Jesse, a slacker despite his privileged suburban background, becomes a partner and foil to Walt's ambitions. Largely due to Walt's underused gifts as a chemist, he and Jesse develop the purest and most coveted form of the drug that Albuquerque's addicts—and cops—have ever seen, thus ensuring that they will become major, if somewhat incompetent, players in the drug economy of the US Southwest. As he becomes more deeply entrenched in that economy, Walt enlists his resourceful wife Skyler (Anna Gunn) and evades his brother-in-law Hank, a DEA agent (Dean Norris).

After an initially lukewarm response, critics lauded *Breaking Bad* as one of the most original series in television history. This was largely due to the choice of its creator, film and television writer, director, and producer Vince Gilligan, to turn Walt's initially pragmatic foray into the drug trade into something much darker by the end of the series. As *Breaking Bad* progresses, Walt is transformed from a hapless suburban husband and father, forced to work a humiliating night job at a car wash, into a self-possessed kingpin who comes to enjoy his work as the feared and loathed "Heisenberg" (his nom de guerre in the drug world). This bold character arc transforms a down-on-his-luck but likable hero into a brutal villain who remains in the drug business for the thrill of it—and, as we shall see, to regain his lost masculinity—rather than simply to keep his family afloat. Late in the series, when it has taken a somewhat Gothic turn and Walt's wife is terrified that his foray into the drug trade will endanger him, Walt tells her, "You clearly don't know who you are talking to, so let me clue you in: I am not in danger, Skyler. I am the danger. A guy opens his door and gets shot, and you think that of me? No! I am the one who knocks!"[3]

Undeniably, Gilligan's risk-taking has changed the landscape of cable television, in part because audiences seem to simultaneously root for and against Walt and Jesse. In a short essay in *Grantland*, Chuck Klosterman argues that the appeal of *Breaking Bad* comes from the moral questions raised by Walt's dramatic transformation from gentle suburban father to ruthless antihero. This places audiences "in the curious position of continuing to root for an individual who's no longer good."[4] As the *New Yorker* claims in a follow-up review in 2012, part of the show's magic is that it is "a radical type of television, and also a very strange kind of must-watch: a show that you dread and crave at the same time."[5] A key reason why the series, which has frequently been described as either a neo-western or western-noir, has inspired these sorts of critical reactions is because it takes a classic moral question (*How far would you go to provide for your family?*) and turns it upside down (*How good would it feel to break the law to do so?*). The Emmys and Golden Globes responded favorably to the show's contradictory pleasures by awarding it multiple prizes for acting, directing, and, in the case of the Golden Globes, best drama series.

However, the series looks somewhat different if viewed from a Latinx media studies perspective. While its quality remains intact, its vision of latinidad demands a close critical reading, one that interprets the series in relation to the history and politics of representing latinidad on television. No major critic has mentioned the racial logic that pervades the show, particularly that white encounters with Latinos drive much of its action. In fact, despite its startling narrative inventiveness, *Breaking Bad* has a deficit of originality in its treatment of Latina/o characters and themes. It tends to replay old tropes and stereotypes associated with Latinos, such as their supposedly inherent criminality, their eccentric (sometimes excessive) performances of masculinity, their nearly abject lust for revenge, and their prowess as killers. These constructions of latinidad are nearly as old as the film medium, appearing everywhere from the "Greaser" character in the 1914 cowboy short *Broncho Billy and the Greaser*, who, like many of the Latino villains in *Breaking Bad*, threatens the safety of a white community with his very presence, to Salma Hayek's turn as a terrifying queenpin in Oliver Stone's *Savages* (2012). *Breaking Bad* not only perpetuates these old filmic tropes, it also masterfully plays on contemporary anxieties regarding latinidad's relationship to dominant US culture.

Indeed, part of what makes Walt's descent into the drug economy so dramatic is the extent to which he encounters the denizens of the drug underworld who, in the diegetic world of the series, are embodied as Latinos. Here, as I do throughout this book, I purposefully gender the bad guys in *Breaking Bad* as "Latinos" since all the characters in the drug trade who serve as Walt and Jesse's nemeses are men, with the possible exception of Lydia Rodarte-Quayle (Laura Fraser), who appears in the final season. While the show does portray Latinas somewhat more sympathetically than it does their male counterparts (in the forms of Carmen, Walt's principal at his high school teaching job, and Andrea, one of Jesse's girlfriends), these parts are tiny by comparison and do not contribute in any significant way to the vision of latinidad in the series, except perhaps when Walt misreads Carmen's kindness in the workplace as sexual interest.

SUBURBAN CRIME DRAMA

Breaking Bad belongs to a body of cable television series that, following the debut of *The Sopranos* on HBO in 1997, has redefined what viewers and critics expect from the medium.[6] Prior to the mid-1990s, cable television had been the domain of movie channels and pay-per-view sports. Network TV was home to "quality programming" and popular favorites like *Miami Vice*, which ended its run in early 1990. However, *The Sopranos* inspired a wide variety of character-driven dramas that had cinematic production value but could stretch out and grow over several seasons. These shows, unlike network television and basic cable, have gone largely uncensored.[7] While some cable series since 1997 have achieved commercial success on par with *The Sopranos*—such as AMC's wildly popular *Mad Men*, a show often lauded as a cultural zeitgeist with as much to say about the early twenty-first century as it does about the 1960s—others have settled for critical accolades and relatively small but extremely dedicated fan bases. Cable networks, competing to appeal to subscribers rather than advertisers, have allowed these lower-rated but ambitious series the time to grow and thrive from an artistic perspective, fostering programs that could never survive on network television but that earn praise from critics and from the entertainment industry during awards season.

Regardless of how one defines "success" when it comes to cable programming, critics have referred to the years following *The Sopranos* as the "Cable Renaissance" and the "Golden Age of Cable" or, as Dana Polan has more cynically argued, a new era of self-declared "Quality" television that aspires to elevate the medium by appealing to intellectuals, critics, and tastemakers who turn to these texts as a means to enrich their own cultural capital.[8] This chapter, along with the two that follow, is interested in how Latinos have fared on so-called prestige television.[9]

Within the cable-programming renaissance, an aesthetic trend has emerged that places previously law-abiding and unassuming characters outside the law. Examples include *Weeds* (Showtime, 2005–2012, examined at length in the next chapter), in which a widowed but resourceful suburban mother sells marijuana to keep up with the Joneses; *Hung* (HBO, 2009–2011), which follows an unhappy and financially strapped but well-endowed teacher in suburban Detroit who resorts to prostitution to make ends meet; and *Good Girls* (NBC, 2018–2021), a network show focused on a group of suburban Michigan women who stage a robbery when they find themselves struggling to make ends meet. In its first two seasons, FX's *Fargo* takes the formula to the extreme, placing characters in an even more rural setting in more extreme situations. I posit that these series constitute a mini-genre that might be called the "suburban crime drama." This subgenre moves the action of the TV crime drama away from the city, where it had been squarely located since the days of *Dragnet* and then *Hill Street Blues* and, of course, *Miami Vice*.

Instead of simply exposing the criminal underworld or cautioning viewers of its dangers, suburban crime dramas grapple with the seductive aspects of crime and explore the ways in which crime does indeed pay, even for characters who only haplessly enter that world. Unlike run-of-the-mill cop shows or standard fare sitcoms, these shows depend on a murky sense of morality and justice. The urtext of this subgenre is *The Sopranos*, which focused in equal parts on its protagonist's home life in suburban New Jersey and his other life as a mob boss. Many of the cable shows that follow this watershed series have borrowed its key elements, such as its ambiguous moral stance, its antiheroic protagonist, its focus on complex and frequently unsettling familial relations, and its suburban setting.

Another thing protagonists in these shows share is the fact that they are white.[10] Although non-white actors are underused on both network and cable television in general, suburban crime dramas appear particularly invested in placing white protagonists front and center. This, in fact, is an essential characteristic of the subgenre. At times, such as in *Weeds* when Nancy (Mary-Louise Parker) interacts with African American wholesalers or Latinx gangs, these characters become self-consciously white, so much so that non-white characters sometimes seem to function only to highlight the whiteness of the leads. In one third-season episode, written by Roberto Benabib, who is Mexican American, Nancy first encounters Guillermo and his Chicano gang, and they ridicule her whiteness.[11] When Nancy enters the bar where they hang out, *vatos* stop and stare, but she assuredly approaches Guillermo. She switches the radio from Latin music to a station playing an alt-country song ("Nosebleed" by Illinois), climbs onto a pool table, and performs a *Coyote Ugly*-style dance, showing the intimidating

Latinos that she has moves of her own. The gag, as is often the case when *Weeds* and texts like it stage these encounters, is that the white character is far outside of her natural element in the world of drug trafficking but nonetheless finds the grit and determination that she needs.

These fish-out-of-water scenarios depend on audiences' assumptions that it is funny or dramatic or charming to see suburban white people facing the tribulations usually reserved for urban people of color. This is certainly the case in *Breaking Bad*, a series in which the main characters' surname—White—and their bland suburban tastes, including a home that meticulously recreates the workaday style of a downwardly mobile suburb, reinforce Walt's supposed unfitness for the drug trade. Although they reside within the city limits of Albuquerque, the White family is marked as distinctly suburban in the styles of their homes, their clothes, and their cars. On a deeper level, as I will assert below, Walter's whiteness is a submerged but powerful theme woven throughout the series. So is Jesse's, especially in scenes related to his family of origin. The fourth episode of the series reveals that Jesse is not a street kid, as implied by his vocabulary, wardrobe, and taste in music, but the son of an affluent family that resides in a tony part of town (several rungs up the ladder of suburban comfort from the White family home).

Another defining characteristic of the suburban crime drama is its tendency to stage racialized encounters between the good-suburban-subject-gone-bad and other more "obvious" or "natural" members of the crime and drug economies. Whereas *The Sopranos* frequently references its main characters' anxieties about ethnic stereotypes associated with Italian Americans (stereotypes perpetuated in the series itself) but rarely explicitly deals with racial conflict, subsequent series have depended on racial encounters between white protagonists and people of color to build storylines and tension.[12] The stereotypes in most suburban crimes dramas are not ancillary to the plot but essential, as they help viewers understand immediately what is at stake when white characters encounter non-white ones. These encounters sometimes inspire comedy, as in *Weeds*, when a sheltered suburban mother does business with a street-smart African American family of marijuana wholesalers who play upon and expose her naïveté. Or sometimes they make for gruesome fantasy, as in *The Walking Dead* (2010–2022), a zombie thriller in which racial politics sometimes seem to intersect with necropolitics. However, most often these meetings connote a sense of terror when a previously sheltered suburban antihero must face down characters whose racial, ethnic, and class characteristics mark them as more "natural" denizens of the criminal underworld.

Ozark, for example, places an upper-middle-class suburban Chicago family in danger when the father, Marty Byrde (Jason Bateman), a financial advisor, is unwittingly implicated in a scheme that skims money from his Mexican cartel clients. The show's action begins when an enforcer for the Navarro Cartel with the unlikely name of Camino Del Rio, known as "Del" (Esai Morales), confronts Marty, his business partner, and some of his accomplices. He kills all but Marty, who proposes a plan that takes him and his family to the Ozarks, where they engage in multiple illegal schemes to get the money that he owes the cartel for his associates' misdeeds. To the Byrde family, the locals appear rough, but nothing scares them more than the Mexicans, who prove themselves to be especially lethal even in the gruesome world of the series. Del continues to threaten them, appearing throughout the season to demand repayment and terrorize Marty.

Ultimately, Del is killed by one of the Ozarks denizens, a white woman named Darlene (Lisa Emery) who blows his head off when he calls her and her family "rednecks" in the last episode of the first season.[13] But even with Del gone in subsequent seasons, the cartel and the Mexicans in general remain the central threat to the Byrde family. When Marty comes face-to-face with Navarro in the third season, the brutal kingpin has him thrown into a medieval-looking dungeon, where he is tortured but does not break. Frequently, the Byrdes and other white characters refer to simply "the Mexicans" when expressing fear or concern over real or imagined enemies. In many narcomedia texts, national groups—especially Mexicans and Colombians—become synonymous with the cartel and shorthand for lethality and danger. In *Ozark*, this lack of specificity creates a sense that Mexicanness, in general, is dangerous. (Sample line: "Them Mexicans tried to kill you, but God had another plan."[14]) The difference between the white Byrdes and non-white characters, as in virtually all series that can be called suburban crime dramas, is that Marty and Wendy Byrde are fully developed characters rather than ethnic stock types.

Given *Breaking Bad*'s setting in Albuquerque, a majority-Hispanic city, it is unsurprising that showrunner Gilligan and his expert company of writers and directors would turn to Latinxs and latinidad as the sites of intercultural and interracial encounters that mark this genre.[15] Still, we must ask what it means to rehearse these interactions yet again in televisual storytelling. Latinxs might simply be the most convenient minority group from which to cull drama in Albuquerque, but the results—a show that consistently posits a negative vision of latinidad—speaks to broader trends in the treatment of Latinos and Latin Americans in American popular culture.

BREAKING BAD AND THE LATINO THREAT NARRATIVE

Markers of latinidad pervade the entire course of *Breaking Bad*, even in moments that do not explicitly deal with Latino characters. When Walt and Jesse must destroy their RV, which plays a key role in much of the show's early action, a mournful Spanish ballad signals the end of the beginning of their journey into the drug trade. More rousingly, in season two, an elaborate and clever *narcocorrido*, written by Pepe Garza and performed by Los Cuates de Sinaloa, tells the story of Heisenberg's (Walt's alter ego in the drug business) rise and, as predicted by the song, eventual fall, from a Mexican or Mexican American perspective.[16] Even the tattoo that adorns Jesse's back is a Mexican-looking sugar skull.

Details such as these speak to the fact that Gilligan and his team intended to make the story of *Breaking Bad* a Latin-inflected one, firmly rooted in the US Southwest but also informed by the transnational drug trade that spills out of and into Mexico. These small details add up. They not only help to give the proceedings deeper roots in Albuquerque, they also make it clear that the key intercultural, interethnic, interracial encounters to take place in the series are those between white and Latino characters. However, although the series portrays Albuquerque as a multicultural city with a vibrant border culture, it also replays long-held visions of Latinos and latinidad as inherently threatening to the body politic of that city, a mode of representation that we have already seen, for example, in the Miami of the 1980s.

In recent works in Latino media studies, Leo R. Chavez and Otto Santa Anna examine the ways that mainstream American media sources, especially those from news media sources, under-represent and misrepresent Latina/os. Santa Anna notes a marked lack of journalistic interest in Latina/o stories by constructing a content analysis of more than twelve hundred stories from 2004. His title, *Juan in a Hundred*, drolly reflects his finding that less than one percent of network news sources explicitly dealt with Latino content. Chavez, in an earlier work, contends that media practices have not merely ignored Latinas/os but have actively constructed a "Latino Threat" that is now deeply embedded in the US popular imagination. According to Chavez, "the Latino Threat Narrative posits that Latinos are not like previous immigrant groups, who ultimately became part of the nation. According to the assumptions and taken-for-granted "truths" inherent in this narrative, Latinos are unwilling or incapable of integrating, of becoming part of the national community.[17]

For Chavez, the Latino Threat Narrative functions as a deeply embedded undertone in the national debate surrounding immigration and citizenship, the key arenas traced throughout the book. But the term is also useful for understanding a broader view of latinidad that pervades US popular culture, especially film and television. These cultural forms have something to say about latinidad even in the context of seemingly "apolitical" texts, ones that do not obviously deal with questions of ethnicity, race, citizenship, and belonging. "The Latino Threat Narrative is pervasive even when not explicitly named," Chavez argues. "It is the cultural dark matter filling space with taken-for-granted 'truths' in debates over immigration on radio and TV talk shows, in newspaper editorials, and on Internet blogs."[18] Though unacknowledged by Chavez, scripted television serves as an important cultural location in which the "dark matter" of the Latino Threat bubbles to the surface. *Breaking Bad*, as a series that depends again and again on encounters between white protagonists and Latino villains, is a logical place to observe the cultural work performed by the Latino Threat Narrative.

It should be obvious by now that the patterns of under-representation and misrepresentation addressed by Chavez, Santa Anna, and other Latinx media critics are present in *Breaking Bad*. Right from the beginning of the series, Latino characters function as the main impediments to Walt and Jesse's success in the meth trade. In the first hour of the series, while on a DEA ride-along with Hank, Walt encounters two meth dealers: Emilio (John Koyama), an Asian Latino, and his cousin Krazy 8 (Domingo Gallardo Molina), a Chicano. The script self-consciously treats this as a racial encounter by having Hank and his Latino partner Steve Gomez (Steven Michael Quezada) bet on whether the lead "cook" of the operation is a "beaner." Hank, already established as an unsympathetic character in some of the first scenes of episode one, bets that Latinos are behind the operation. This suggests that Gilligan, who wrote and directed the episode, intends to wage a criticism of Latino stereotypes. After all, Hank is a blowhard and a bigot and Steve, his long-suffering partner, is Mexican American.

However, subsequent scenes put Jesse and Walt in conflict with Emilio and Krazy 8, establishing a pattern of Latino bad guys that repeats several times over the course of the series. In a comedy of errors, Walt and Jesse wind up reluctantly killing both Emilio and Krazy 8 (the latter is held captive in a basement with a bike's U-lock shackling him to a support beam before Walt brutally chokes him in a fight).[19] The disposal of their bodies by dissolving them—as well as parts of Jesse's bathtub and floors—with hydrofluoric acid in episodes two and three became a source of fascination and disgust for early fans of the show (and created a sensation that undoubtedly led to new fans), but it was simply the first time in which Walt and Jesse meet terrifying Latino nemeses and then outsmart them enough to survive and face the next in a succession of brown-skinned bad guys. Granted, some white characters also come off badly in *Breaking Bad*, such as a girlfriend of Jesse's who attempts to extort some of Walt's profits and a meth-head couple whose atrocious neglect of their child frames one episode. But, those background players notwithstanding, Latino characters function as the most consistent and deadly threats over the show's run. These minor but compelling characters reveal what *Breaking Bad* has to say about latinidad, so the character studies that follow provide a more detailed analysis of how the series—and how cable television in general, along with other televisual and cinematic representations of Latinas and Latinos—advances the idea of a Latino Threat.

TUCO'S GRILL

Following the deaths of Emilio and Krazy 8, Tuco Salamanca (Raymond Cruz), an erratic and meth-addled thug, emerges as the most important distributor in Albuquerque, a kingpin with whom Walt and Jesse must do business as they reenter the drug trade. Tuco, as expertly played by Cruz, embodies a vision of ersatz machismo that has long haunted representations of Latino men on film and television. When Tuco, desperate to evade the DEA and to restart his drug operation, kidnaps Walt and Jesse, he looks the part of the dressy but thuggish psychopathic killer that audiences have come to know from the movies. A snakeskin-patterned shirt, which looks simultaneously cheap and very expensive, clings to his thick frame, a tattoo teardrop adorns his right eye, and a flashy grill covers his top teeth. He also carries an assault rifle carelessly on his arm. At one point prior to the kidnapping, Tuco kills a henchman merely for speaking out of turn, and then, like a child, he immediately commands Walt to revive him.

So Walt and Jesse are already terrified of him when he spirits them away to a shabby cinderblock cottage in the desert where his uncle—Hector Salamanca—resides.[20] While holding them there, he continues to terrify them with guns and knives, and he evades their plan to poison him with meth tainted with ricin. Perhaps most threateningly, Tuco tells them that he plans to transport them to Mexico, where they will start a meth superlab. Incredulous, Walt explains that he can't move to Mexico because he has a wife, a son, and a baby on the way. "So what?" Tuco responds, "You'll get new ones." Tuco lays out these plans for the new endeavor in Mexico while he prepares a lunch of burritos for his uncle, Walt, and Jesse.[21] The thought of going to Mexico horrifies Walt and Jesse, who see being taken to that country as a death sentence. (They have good reason to feel this way, for things get very ugly whenever the action shifts across the border.)

All in all, Tuco is a scary sight to Walt and Jesse, partly constructed through the particularities of his performance of Latino masculinity. Through his swagger, his brutal nonchalance, and that garish grill, Tuco embodies the eccentric Latino masculinities that audiences have come to know through popular culture. In several ways, Tuco echoes Tony Montana (Al Pacino) in Brian DePalma's *Scarface*. Although he does not sit at the throne of a large and lucrative cocaine empire and is more physically imposing than his predecessor, Tuco, like Tony, is similarly flamboyant in his personal style and disturbing in his eagerness to kill. Also like Tony, he is addicted to his product. Both Tuco and Tony Montana are more threatening because they are unhinged and unpredictable, qualities associated with many filmic Latino characters, from Broncho Billy's "Greaser" to the gangbanging thugs who might kill at any moment in Joel Schumacher's *Falling Down* (1993) and Clint Eastwood's *Gran Torino* (2008).[22]

Tuco's threatening nature borders on deadly through mise-en-scène and editing that accentuates his sadistic nature, especially in episode 9, which is built around the idea that to be captured by Tuco and taken into Mexico is the worst-case scenario for Walt and Jesse. As the protagonists' plot to poison Tuco with ricin they've made in the lab, many markers of his Mexicanness fill the frame, from the bright pink paint that colors the walls of the shack to the telenovelas that blare on the television to Tuco's tacky snakeskin-patterned shirt. In short, Tuco is not only Mexican or Mexican American, he is also *hyper*-Mexican or excessively Mexican, a trope that frequently frames the Latino Threat Narrative.

The matter of Latinx (and Black) excess has been well theorized by Jillian Hernandez in *Aesthetics of Excess: The Art and Politics of Black and Latina Embodiment*. For Hernandez, aesthetics of excess emerge when social actors "engage in the remix of crafting their own bodies and representations, which trouble, seduce, and sometimes capitulate with the desirous gazes of the Euro-American West."[23] Hernandez is most interested in how Black and Latina artists, performers, and everyday people embrace excess as a mode of identification and resistance. However, those performances of excess also reflect a dominant culture that has expectations regarding proper style and restraint, as Hernandez acknowledges. Tuco could possibly be read as a masculine version of some of the feminine tropes that Hernandez examines, from young women who embrace the "chonga" style in South Florida to Nicki Minaj, all of which recast Blacks' and Latinas' embrace of dress and attitude that are supposedly "too much" as a site of social power.[24] Perhaps Tuco is not unlike them or the zoot-suiters of the early and mid-twentieth century, whose excessive use of fabric and outlandish styles attracted the ire of (and violence from) white people who saw them as dangerous to the status quo. I am, however, reluctant to embrace Tuco as disruptive of a representational system that sees Latinxs as anything but threatening, given the problems with *Breaking Bad* that I outline in this chapter. In the end, Tuco's excess makes him threatening, not empowering, and despite Cruz's performance, he seems to embody the dominant culture's fear that Latinx excess represents Latinx danger.

Ultimately, Tuco becomes another victim of the show's propensity to kill off its Latino characters. At the end of the episode, Hank stumbles upon Tuco, who has been shot by Jesse as he and Walt attempted to escape, and kills him in a firefight, increasing the Latino body count of *Breaking Bad*.[25] As with the deaths of Tony Montana and countless Latino thugs in film history, the killing of a Latino villain brings closure to the storyline and secures the safety of the greater community. In this case, it also makes the white killer a hero. Hank and his team of drug enforcement agents had identified Tuco as a prime target in their efforts to get meth off the streets of Albuquerque, so this is a major, if accidental, kill for the agent.

Hank's team celebrates his feat by giving him Tuco's grill, encased in Lucite, as a commemorative gift (the episode title, "Grilled," takes on new meaning at that moment). As Hank says, explaining the prize to Walt and Walt Jr., "It's sort of a fashion statement, I guess. You know, certain folks, attracted to shiny things." Such casual anti-Mexican racism is par for the course with Hank. However, in one of the brilliantly sensitive strokes of the series, he begins to feel guilty in the aftermath of the shootout. Hank suffers panic attacks, later expressing to his wife Marie, "Ever since that Salamanca thing—Tuco Salamanca, if ever a scumbag deserved a bullet between the eyes—it changed me. I can't seem to control it. I try to fight. . . . That's not how I'm supposed to be. That's not me. . . . I think the universe is trying to tell me something and I'm finally ready to listen." The grill, which he had held up so triumphantly, begins to look less like a trophy of a victory in the drug war and more like a sad reminder of his culpability in ending a life. Eventually, he flings it into the Río Grande—the most symbolic of rivers for Latinos in the United States—where it is later discovered by two men who appear to be Mexican migrants.[26]

These actions can be read in a number of ways as a statement about latinidad in the diegetic world of *Breaking Bad*. One reading might suggest that the anti-Mexican views that Hank spews for much of the time preceding Tuco's death are mere bluster. His rejection of the gift and his struggle over the guilt suggest a more complicated view of Tuco, whom Hank had so vehemently bashed. Perhaps Gilligan and company want viewers to believe that Hank has come to see Tuco as something other than just another soulless agent of the drug war. In other words, one might infer that Hank sees

Tuco as a human being rather than a target. In a media landscape that positions brown men as little more than moving targets in its coverage of the drug war, humanizing a character like Tuco (or Krazy 8, when he revealed his backstory) is mildly revolutionary. Alternately, a more cynical reading might conclude that Hank's guilty panic attacks only serve to further deepen a white character who is increasingly complex as the series unfolds.

Either way, there is the matter of the trophy grill's final fate in the hands of the border crossers. By having Mexican migrants find it, the writers might be making a statement about Latinos and the proverbial American Dream. The Río Grande symbolizes both the migrant experience in general and, more specifically, the difficult transitions faced by Mexicans who migrate to the United States. Placing this scene at the river ties Tuco's sad fate to the migrant experience. We do not know if Tuco is a first-, second-, or third-generation American, or whether he is American at all, but the brief appearance of his grill in the hands of a new migrant at the river suggests a cynical view of migration, as if the grill stands as a warning for what awaits these anonymous border crossers in the United States.

Tuco's death in *Breaking Bad* unleashes a series of actions involving Latinx characters that lasts several seasons. Though wheelchair-bound and nonverbal, Tuco's uncle, Hector Salamanca, who communicates only with a bell or by pointing to letters, wields tremendous power over his extended family of dealers and thugs who belong to his cartel. As if to double the Latino Threat Narrative that pervades the series, Tío Salamanca even summons two murderous twin brothers to exact revenge on Walt (and later Hank) for Tuco's murder. Before being killed by Hank, the twins kill a truckload full of undocumented Mexican migrants who run the risk of blowing their covers and viciously behead a DEA informant played by Danny Trejo with, of all implements, a machete. Like Tuco, Tío Salamanca and his large family embody several old stereotypes that popular culture has attached to Latinos and latinidad, including outrageous and overdetermined performances of machismo and a pathological devotion to family (a theme we have seen since *Scarface*). This is to say that, within a show that is groundbreaking in many respects, Tuco represents a shortcut: He does not require a backstory because, since *Scarface* in 1983, audiences have been familiar with the unhinged, over-the-top Latinx kingpin figure.

Tuco's story does not end with *Breaking Bad*. Another text in what we might call the *Breaking Bad* universe sheds even more light on Tuco's status as an iteration of the Latino threat narrative.[27] The pilot episode of *Better Call Saul* (AMC, 2015–2021), a *Breaking Bad* prequel exploring the professional origins of crooked lawyer Saul Goodman (Bob Odenkirk), ends with a brief cameo of Cruz as Tuco. Saul is still known as Jimmy McGill since

5.1. Raymond Cruz's Tuco spans the *Breaking Bad* universe to appear in the prequel, *Better Call Saul*. Alamy Photo.

the series largely follows his life before he adopts a more Semitic name that he thinks appears more lawyerly. He is in cahoots with white twins (Daniel Spenser Levine and Steven Levine) who stage accidents to extort money out of unsuspecting drivers. In the series premiere, the twins follow an older Spanish-speaking woman home, accusing her of a hit-and-run and demanding cash. They have no idea that the woman is Tuco's grandmother or that she shares her home with her grandson.[28] In the second episode, Tuco is deciding what to do with the twins when Saul enters the scene.[29] Tuco wants to kill them, but Saul talks him out of it, convincing him to just maim them. As he snaps the twins' legs, they scream and cry in horror and pain, to Tuco's great delight. The camera does not focus on the violence, however, moving instead toward Saul's troubled face. He winces, looking sickened by what he sees. Later, he is on a date in a restaurant when the snapping of breadsticks reminds him of the broken legs and sends him to the bathroom vomiting. It is good character development, establishing Saul as a sensitive but corruptible soul, but once again—like most narcomedia texts with white protagonists and non-white bad guys—it only develops the white character.[30]

Like *Breaking Bad*, *Better Call Saul* features dozens of Latinx characters beyond Tuco, providing back stories for Hector Salamanca and his clan, as well as introducing other Latinx criminals in their orbit. One of those Latinx characters, Nacho (Michael Mando), undergoes a series of complex moral questions when he is faced with Hector Salamanca's demand that he recruit his father Manuel (Juan Carlos Cantu), an honest upholsterer, into the drug trafficking business. Nacho is a high-level manager in the Salamanca cartel, but he is heartbroken by the prospect of implicating his father in his crimes. He cleverly finds a way to deprive Hector of his heart medicine, which causes the older man to have a stroke that incapacitates him for the rest of his life. Through this narrative arc, Nacho is granted many of the characteristics denied to previous Latinx characters in the *Breaking Bad* universe: intelligence, compassion, and heart. Of course, Nacho exists within a show that, like *Breaking Bad*, is first and foremost about its white protagonist and in which almost every Latinx character, apart from Hank's partner Steve, is criminalized as part of the drug trade.

GUS FRING

Nacho's morally complex narrative is predated by a character who stands as a point of departure from the Latino stock characters of the original series. Late in *Breaking Bad*, Walt and Jesse become ensnared with a more organized but no less vicious drug kingpin, Gus Fring, the character whose sexuality I analyzed in chapter 4. Gus, an apparently mild-mannered proprietor of the Los Pollos Hermanos fast food chain, is doubling as the head of a major transnational cartel by the time Walt and Jesse meet him. His cover as a bespectacled, buttoned-down, and civic-minded business owner grants him the illusion of upstanding citizenship, but it is soon revealed that he is the leader of a major cartel and looking to expand his meth operations.[31] After Walt's retirement from cooking meth, Gus makes him a lucrative offer of $3 million to come back and cook meth for a short period. By accepting the offer, Walt and Jesse become employees in an elaborate and highly organized lab that operates under the cover of an industrial laundry. But they quickly become caught up in struggles over revenge and dominance in the meth trade that arise in the aftermath of Tuco's death. Gus becomes Walt and Jesse's employer but then becomes their bitter enemy.

Gus provides a counterpoint to the representational patterns described thus far in this chapter. The character diverges dramatically from the unhinged, inherently criminal Latino gangster stereotype perpetuated by Tuco. Gus is a careful, calculating kingpin with a penchant for order and gourmet cooking. As his character unfolds, the series offers tiny glimpses of his exacting nature, such as when he trains a Pollos Hermanos employee on a piece of equipment or when, in preparation for a tense tête-à-tête with a rival cartel, he carefully prepares a tray of crudité for his guests. While Gus has a begrudging respect for Walt, whose skills as a chemist he admires and intends to draw profit from, he finds Jesse distasteful because of his wannabe gangster sensibilities and the fact that he is a drug user himself. Unlike many filmic representations of the Latino kingpin, Gus sees himself first and foremost as a businessperson, using the types of methods one learns in an MBA program to establish and grow his dominance in the meth trade. For example, when he finds out that Jesse is seeking revenge against some of Gus's low-ranking dealers for killing one of his friends, he calmly stages a business meeting between Jesse and the dealers, setting the protocol that he expects his employees to follow. Gus will, however, kill when he sees fit, as when he ruthlessly slits the throat of Victor, his main assistant, when he botches an assassination attempt on Walt and Jesse. Even then, he does so completely without bombast; he simply changes from his dressy work clothes into a hazmat suit, kills Victor, washes his hands, and changes back into his suit. Despite a propensity for violence that echoes Tuco and countless other murderous Latinos in mainstream media representations, Gus, for reasons that I will detail below, provides one of the richest characterizations of a Latino in television history.

Gus is played by Giancarlo Esposito, a veteran stage and screen actor of African American and Italian heritage who, prior to his role in *Breaking Bad*, was probably best known for playing the character known as "Bugging Out" in Spike Lee's *Do the Right Thing* (1998). In that classic exploration of interracial conflict in Brooklyn, Esposito's character, who is Black, confronts a white character who has bought a brownstone in his Black neighborhood (and, most famously, scuffed his Air Jordans). Esposito's Blackness—and the fact that he has written and spoken extensively on American racism and has played iconic Black characters—adds yet another layer to his portrayal of Gus, whose country of origin is Chile. Though his Blackness goes unremarked upon in *Breaking Bad* (except when he is referred to as "dark meat" by Hector Salamanca), the presence of an Afro-Latino character on television, especially one who is characterized in such a complicated and contradictory manner, is exceedingly rare and therefore worthy of attention. The decision to cast Esposito, as well as Esposito's acting choices, already suggest that Gilligan, his casting agents, and other creative professionals working for the show intended to construct a more original vision of latinidad in their second big villain of the series.

Gus's tenure as Walt and Jesse's chief tormenter lasts for two seasons and represents a shift in the show's vision of latinidad, nudging it toward a more complex portrait of its Latino characters. The layering of queer desire and love over the already-complicated characterization of Gus helps instigate this shift, as I discussed in the previous chapter. In addition, Gus eschews macho posturing, relying instead on cold-blooded calculations to establish his dominance in the transnational drug business. What audiences find in Gus is certainly a Latino threat, but one whose motivations exceed the mere fact of his latinidad. In this sense, *Breaking Bad* might be read as diverging from the standard view of Latino deviance invented in the early years of cinema and continuing through the character of Tuco. Those characters' violent acts often seem to stem from the simple fact that they are Latino; in contrast, Gus, like Walter White, has complex emotional reasons to fight his enemies. Some observers might note that, despite the fact that Gus is constructed as a three-dimensional and somewhat sympathetic character, he is yet another entry in a long parade of Latino villains who drive the action in *Breaking Bad*.

But the task of Latinx media studies is not to simply categorize "positive" and "negative" representations of Latinas/os or to champion those texts that we place in the positive category. Rather, our aim should be a better understanding of how cultural texts construct and disseminate their visions of latinidad, even when those imaginings perform cultural work (as in associating latinidad with criminality) that runs counter to the political aims of Latino studies. This is to say that the problem with Tuco is not that he is a negative Latino representation but that the character, however well embodied by actor Raymond Cruz and rendered onscreen by Gilligan and his team, reveals an old and comparatively uncomplicated view of latinidad, one that does not challenge its predecessors or viewers. Gus, on the other hand, seems to reflect an effort to develop a more fully realized character of color on a show that previously reserved this privilege for its white characters. He is a bad guy, but a well-written one.

KEEPING WHITE FOCUS

Despite Gus's complexity, which I examine from another perspective in chapter 4, and his compelling story arc, *Breaking Bad* returns its gaze to its white protagonists in the show's fifth and final season and in a made-for-Netflix movie titled *El Camino*, released six years after the series ended. In particular, these texts return to the psychological and moral questions that drove the original series in the first place: crime and punishment, the nature of good and evil, and the repercussions of violence. Following the gruesome death of Gus at the end of season four, the final sixteen episodes pit Walter and Jesse, who had always had an uneasy partnership, in violent opposition to one another. Stylistically and plot-wise, the show takes on increasingly gothic elements, with double-crossings and a cat-and-mouse game between Walter and Jesse. At its core, however, are Walter and Jesse's dialectically opposing responses to the extremities of the drug trade. Walter descends ever further into his depraved quest for revenge. At the same time, Jesse struggles with feelings of guilt and remorse over their misdeeds—feelings Walter experienced early into their foray with cooking meth, but has now abandoned (except when it comes to his own nuclear family). Jesse's guilt, in fact, becomes so overpowering that he is barely able to function. At one point, he drives around an impoverished neighborhood throwing cash out of his car windows. Latinx characters are almost completely absent from the season, except for two minor characters: DEA agent Steve Gomez (Steven Michael Quezada), whom the neo-Nazi gang kills late in the season, and Jesse's ex-girlfriend Andrea (Emily Rios), whom the same gang kills as part of their threats that keep Jesse cooking meth.

The *Breaking Bad* finale, written and directed by Gilligan, proved to be one of the most anticipated endings of the prestige television era, and—unlike similar texts with notoriously controversial endings, e.g., *The Sopranos* and *Lost*—it tied up many loose ends. Walt makes one final visit to his wife, giving her the GPS coordinates of where Hank's body is buried and explaining how she can trade the information to avoid prosecution. He also figures out a way to set up his family financially by threatening old business partners into setting up a trust fund that will be transferred to his son on his eighteenth birthday. After breaking into the business partners' luxurious house, Walt pauses to admire its fine furnishings; it seems that Elliott and Gretchen, the business partners, have all the comforts enjoyed by successful white people that Walt once foresaw for himself. This aspect of the finale—Walt setting up his children financially, even through duplicitous means and even within the context of an episode in which he kills several of his old enemies—underscores the white kingpin character as rational, forward-thinking, and, ultimately, devoted to his family in a way that is admirable rather than pathological (as that trait is framed in Latinx representations). There is also an air of self-actualization. When Walt talks with Skyler, he finally admits what he got out of the criminal enterprise. "I did it for me," he tells her. "I liked it. I was good at it. And I was really . . . I was alive."[32]

In the climactic scene, Walt has rigged a machine gun to shoot up the Nazis' hideout, and only he and Jesse survive the fight. Jesse strangles one of the survivors, the vicious, child-killing Todd (Jesse Plemons).

The Nazis killed Hank, and Todd was monstrously brutal, so this bloody climax functions as justice in the world of *Breaking Bad*. Walt had been hunting Jesse for most of the season, but when the opportunity to kill him presents itself, he saves him, even taking a bullet for him. As they flee the gang's hideout, among the carnage of dead Nazis, they exchange a tender glance before parting ways. Jesse drives away in a Chevy El Camino, laughing and crying simultaneously as he drives into the night, and Walter returns to the lab, where he succumbs to the gunshot wound. As several television critics noted in morning-after reviews, *Breaking Bad* might have ended with its beleaguered protagonist's death, but it actually brought closure and victory to Walter's seasons-long mission.[33] In the end, with Walter dying on his own terms and saving Jesse from the Nazis, the creators of *Breaking Bad* found a way to remain sympathetic to their antihero and ensure that Walter's death, anticipated from the first beats of the series pilot, maintains an air of nobility and even grandeur. No Latinx characters fare as well.

This, however, is not where the saga ends. The feature-length coda to the series, titled *El Camino: A Breaking Bad Movie*, picks up right where this finale leaves off, but also includes flashbacks to Jesse's captivity and dealings with the gang. *El Camino* runs for more than two hours and includes Aaron Paul as Jesse in almost every scene, but only features speaking roles for two non-white actors: an eighty-second cameo by Marla Gibbs, who plays a feisty older customer at a vacuum repair shop, and one indecipherable line spoken by a Black prostitute. I realize that it might appear disingenuous to complain that Latinos are misrepresented in the *Breaking Bad* universe and then to gripe that not enough Latinx or other actors of color appear in *El Camino*. However, the dearth of non-white characters in the movie underscores my bigger point that, in *Breaking Bad* in particular and the suburban crime drama more generally, white characters are always the focus. The absence of non-white characters is especially glaring in a film intended to bring closure to a series that relied on Latino bad guys, Tuco and Gus—and even included an original *narcocorrido* at one point.

In true *Breaking Bad* fashion, Jesse faces a number of seemingly insurmountable obstacles, dangerous foes, and near misses as he struggles to escape his past in *El Camino*, which also had a limited theatrical release (presumably to qualify for awards season). His struggles are far from over in the action that takes place after the *Breaking Bad* finale, but in the end he finds his way out of the depths that his life had taken since he started cooking with Walter White. In the final scene, a fixer establishes a new identity for Jesse and delivers him to Alaska, a place where he has long dreamed of starting over. The final shot finds him driving, once again, this time into a pristine wilderness of towering pine trees and snowy mountains toward a new beginning.

Jesse's ending in *El Camino* takes the redemption arc of the *Breaking Bad* finale even further. The series had long cultivated a perception that Jesse had a good heart under his tough exterior—or, as one critic put it, the show's "criminal conscience"—and many audience members must have found it comforting that, though scarred, Jesse survived, and got away with his crimes.³⁴ (*Better Call Saul* does something similar but in reverse, since Saul is an irredeemably sleazy criminal-for-hire throughout *Breaking Bad* but is shown as a big-hearted ne'er-do-well in the prequel.) Jesse's is one of the few happy endings for anyone in the *Breaking Bad* universe, and *El Camino* seems tailor-made for fans who had been cheering for Jesse throughout the original series. However, his redemption is another form of white-centrism and, ultimately, white innocence.

CONCLUSION

This chapter has asked what happens when we put Latinos, who are always at the margins of *Breaking Bad* (and nearly all of television), at the center of our critique and what scholars and students of latinidad might gain from working at those margins. From its beginnings, the field of television studies has explored two of the guiding questions articulated by Horace Newcomb: "How does television tell its stories?" and "What is the relation of television's stories and storytelling to American—and, by implication, any other—society and culture?"³⁵ Although Latinos have rarely been granted access to the means of television production, we have nonetheless been a part of how television tells its stories and what those stories say about dominant American culture.

It is therefore time for us to ask how television tells our stories and how we might better influence the medium's vision of latinidad. While some scholars have addressed the self-conscious "latinization" of television texts from *Chico and the Man* to *Dora the Explorer*, we must also turn to cable and network series and their visions of latinidad, especially those cable series that audiences and critics label as "quality" or "important" in a landscape of shrinking audiences but increased artistic aspirations. If we look closely at these texts, which treat Latina/o characters as, among other things, threats, foils, Others, and objects, we might better comprehend the places that latinidad inhabits in the popular imaginary of the United States. Although constructions of latinidad in Vince Gilligan's *Breaking Bad* have framed this chapter, other examples abound in the world of television, including but not limited to those series that belong to the suburban crime drama mini-genre. We might also turn to reality television, competition shows, talk shows, or, like Otto Santa Anna, to the news to better understand how the Latino image circulates and makes meaning in the medium. These televisual texts might not always be so blunt as to warn viewers not to fuck with the Mexicans, but they frequently have something to say about the dominant culture's views of and anxieties regarding latinidad. Our task, then, is to decode and unlearn these messages as a first step in rethinking grim visions of latinidad, even when they come in prestige packages.

In summer 2022, as I was finishing this book, I began to see a new mezcal advertised on social media. More specifically, I saw ads promoting special events where I could pay $300 for the chance to meet Bryan Cranston and Aaron Paul at a bar in Chicago, where they were launching their new "Dos Hombres" brand of the drink, which had been "discovered" by hipsters in the United States relatively recently. A quick search revealed that Cranston and Paul were, in fact, in the midst of a national tour, hitting bars across the country to drum up interest in their new collaboration. They had launched an ad campaign with aesthetics that evoked some of the stylistic choices of *Breaking Bad*: sepia tones, sunny vistas, and what I can only describe as "desert vibes"—a marketing pastiche referencing the show where the actors first collaborated. Several photographs appearing in the brand's well-curated Instagram feed show Cranston and Paul walking down a dusty, empty desert road, evoking the mood created by Gilligan and his creative team.

The campaign showed that, almost a decade after the finale of the series, the actors are still closely associated with the show—and with each other. But the mezcal's branding revealed something more—namely, that Cranston and Paul and their creative team were still drawing on the Latinx undertones that were constantly present in the series but relentlessly pushed to its margins. The product's name and its logo featuring two burros looking at an agave plant certainly seem intended to give it some Latin flair. And the fact that the product is an import from Mexico, not unlike some of the meth in *Breaking Bad*, is not without irony. Other images in the Instagram feed feature Mexican workers growing and processing agave and offering the finished product to the viewer. One, in particular, stands out to me: A Mexican man, who is shown elsewhere in the feed to be a worker in the agave fields, offers a bottle of the mezcal. The bottle, in the foreground of the shot, is in perfect focus, but the worker is blurrily out of focus. This is an apt metaphor for how, with a couple of notable exceptions, *Breaking Bad* depicts Latinos. The show might have taught some viewers "not to fuck with the Mexicans," but Dos Hombres Mezcal reiterates just how profitable they can be.

CHAPTER 6

BAD HOMBRES
Narcomedia at the US-Mexico Border

While a candidate for president of the United States in 2016, Donald Trump encapsulated volumes of border discourse in just two now-infamous words: "bad hombres." Trump had publicly made incendiary statements about Mexican migrants when he announced his candidacy in June 2015. In reference to those crossing the border, he told a cheering crowd, "They're bringing drugs. They're bringing crime. They're rapists. And some, I assume, are good people." Then, when answering a question about immigration reform in a televised debate with Hillary Clinton just two weeks before the election, Trump elaborated on the theme:

> We have to have strong borders. We have to keep the drugs out of the country.... One of my first acts will be to get all of the drug lords, all of the bad ones—we have some bad, bad people in this country that have to go out. We're going to get them out. We're going to secure the border. And once the border is secured, at a later date, we'll make a determination as to the rest. But we have some bad hombres here, and we're going to get them out.[1]

Although this anti-Mexican and anti-migrant sentiment was part and parcel of his campaign, the phrase "bad hombres" stuck out to many as particularly vicious, xenophobic, and racist. The TV pundits and op-ed writers had a field day, and T-shirts emblazoned with the phrase immediately went on sale. The news cycle quickly moved on, but the sentiment expressed in "bad hombres" resonated for the remainder of his campaign and in the president's attempts to build a border wall. For Trump, a key part of the message was that border control is drug control.

This chapter examines discourses of the US-Mexico border within narcomedia narratives, showing that Trump's logic actually reflects decades of representational practices that have become ingrained as "knowledge" about what the border is and what it means. As several generations of border studies have now shown, the border is one of the most potent signifiers of Otherness in American racial imaginations, marking not only social difference but also the historical inequalities that have shaped relations between Latin America and the United States.[2] A diverse array of cultural texts that appeared over the course of the War on Drugs have depicted the border as a point of entry for illegal narcotics. In some ways, even *Scarface* and *Miami Vice* are border narratives in that they focus on importing illegal substances from foreign countries and on what happens when those substances cross into the United States. In both those texts, law enforcement officials surveil and guard entry points to the country. However, I am interested here in how the actual US-Mexico border functions within narcomedia. Partly due to a shift in drug trafficking routes and drug policies in the United States, that border became an increasingly common motif in narcomedia in the late 1990s and into the 2000s.

Although this chapter focuses primarily on representations of the border and Mexicanness in narcomedia, it is crucial to also address Blackness in the texts analyzed here. Understanding Blackness in texts focusing on the border helps reveal how drug trafficking and racial formations merge in narcomedia texts, an ongoing theme of this book that crystalizes in certain of the texts examined below. In representations of the US-Mexico border, Blackness has sometimes been used as a foil against which other racial formations are measured. I do not mean to imply that Mexicanness and Blackness are mutually exclusive categories of analysis or that "Mexican" is a racial category that functions in the same way as—or even similarly to—Blackness in US representational politics. And although I am reluctant to participate in the problematic erasure of Blackness in Mexico, none of the texts that I mention in this chapter include Afro-diasporic Mexican characters in the borderlands. Therefore, it is necessary for me to analyze Blackness and latinidad in ways that they are constructed in the media texts themselves: as oppositional racial formations.

I should note also that the US-Mexico borderlands have produced vibrant *narcoculturas* with distinctive cultural forms, especially evident in *narcocorridos* and B movies that narrate the exploits of narcos as they cross the border, frequently celebrating the trafficker as a "social bandit." A number of scholars in the United States and Mexico have written on *corridos* and shown how they function as counternarratives to hegemonic constructions of narcotics.[3] When it comes to *narcocultura* on the screen, Ryan

Rashotte provides an idiosyncratic analysis of what he calls "narco cinema," referring to "low-budget direct-to-video cinema produced by Mexican and Mexican American studios, predominantly for US Latina markets."[4] However, in this chapter, as elsewhere in this book, I am most interested in how US dominant culture has framed narcotrafficking in narrative film and television. I have excluded subcultural texts, as well as documentaries, from my analysis with the caveat that those media forms often have an intertextual relationship with the more mainstream, commercial texts that I examine. (The commissioning of a *narcocorrido* about its main character by Los Cuates de Sinaloa in *Breaking Bad*'s second season is a good example of this dialogical relationship.[5])

MEXICANS COMING NORTH: A HISTORY OF REPRESENTATIONAL VIOLENCE

The US-Mexico border has been an object of fascination for moviemakers since the earliest days of the form. The border has always carried tremendous symbolic weight in US culture, so it is hardly surprising that Hollywood has a long history of exploiting the symbolic power of this place and its history. As Camilla Fojas puts it, "Since the inception of cinema, the Hollywood motion picture industry has commandeered the borderlands to tell a story about US dominance in the American hemisphere." According to Fojas, the filmic borderlands, especially in the Western genre, have always been a testing ground for US American ideals, especially those related to "integrity, moral clarity, industriousness, survivalism, confidence, and self-sufficiency."[6] She further posits that borderlands function as "zones of the uncanny" in Hollywood movies, spaces where the rules of either nation never fully apply. As she sees it, the border film is a genre unto itself, related to the western, especially, but with cinematic tropes, stock characters (including the bandit), and standard storylines of its own.

In *Broncho Billy and the Greaser* (1914), silent era superstar Gilbert M. Anderson plays the postmaster in a small border town. Anderson had played three small roles in *The Great Train Robbery* (1903), usually acknowledged as one of the first narrative films and the first western, and he co-founded Essanay Studios, which produced 148 short films featuring Anderson throughout the silent era. In his Essanay films, Anderson frequently appeared as Broncho Billy, an affable cowboy type in various settings in the Old West. *Broncho Billy and the Greaser* finds the Billy character delivering mail to a mining town populated by white settlers somewhere near the border, where he shares a flirtation with a local young woman. The tranquility of the town is interrupted when a character identified as "the halfbreed" in the opening credits but named "the greaser" in the title of the film enters the scene. White actor Lee Willard plays the greaser, who is rude, drunken, and jealous of Billy's ability to charm the white woman, who is named "the girl" in the opening credits. (I use the term "greaser" here to emphasize the pervasiveness of that slur in US popular culture; the fact that the credits use the term "halfbreed" speak to US anxieties about racial admixture in Mexico and the US-Mexico borderlands. In one scene in a saloon, a sign reads "NO DRINKS FOR INJUNS," speaking further to the racial schema of the setting.[7]) Billy chases the Mexican character out of town at gunpoint to the delight of the locals, especially his sweetheart, but later the greaser finds him in his cabin. He beats and hog-ties the hero. The girl happens to see what is going on and hurries back to town to alert the menfolk, who rush to the cabin on horseback. There they find Billy and the greaser struggling over a knife. Together, they push the greaser, a prototypical bad hombre, out of the cabin and out of the story. The audience does not see him again and the seventeen-minute film ends on a romantic note between Billy and the woman who helped rescue him.

Broncho Billy films are fascinating to watch from the perspective of film history. The tropes of the western in its infancy are visible throughout the series. We can also see the bandit, one of the oldest and most enduring Latino stereotypes, jump from newspaper pages, where he was already an established figure, to narrative film.[8] Along with narrative forms and character archetypes coming into focus, the racial logics of the western, with its wild indigenous people and its unruly Mexicans who must be banished from the Anglo frontier, are also emerging. In the broader social context of the 1910s, a decade that saw a spike in Mexican migration to the United States, the message conveyed by *Broncho Billy and the Greaser* is chilling. Its ending, though somewhat ambiguous, suggests that the greaser will be lynched by the white mob that drags him away from Billy's cabin. Importantly, the film's frontier mob justice ending implies that it is the responsibility of the entire Anglo community, and not the lone frontiersman, to rid the settlement of the Mexican threat. As Monica Muñoz Martinez's work on anti-Mexican violence in Texas has shown, this racial logic was mainstream thinking in both the time period in which the movie was released and the time it depicts.[9] Although *Broncho Billy and the Greaser* looks back on the "Old West" of a couple of generations before the film was made, Martinez's *The Injustice Never Leaves You* reminds us that anti-Mexican violence remained prevalent well into the twentieth century.

The image of the Mexican in *Broncho Billy and the Greaser* set the template for hundreds of bad hombres who would follow over the subsequent century of Hollywood filmmaking. Tony Montana in *Scarface* and Tuco

Salamanca in *Breaking Bad* and countless other swarthy border crossers who terrorize white protagonists inherited the legacy of the greaser image, which remains alive and well as a filmic trope after more than a century. As Charles Ramirez Berg and subsequent scholars have shown, other Latinx tropes would appear over the course of film history—including the Latin lover, the dark lady, the spitfire—that reinforce or contradict the image of the greaser.[10] But even as these other "types" have come and gone as dominant representations of latinidad, the greaser image has stubbornly endured as a trope Mexicanness at the border. More recent border fare does not include characters that look like Broncho Billy's nemesis, but it includes his antecedents: Mexicans who are intrinsically bad and dangerous and whose difference from white protagonists make them unassimilable to the dominant culture. In unpacking what these images mean, it is helpful to remember that the greaser is a border character.

Representations of the border as a space of danger and Otherness (and the dangers of Otherness) loaned themselves to darker Hollywood fare in the 1940s and 1950s. *Border Incident* (1949), for example, applies noirish elements to a social problem film focused on the exploitation of bracero migrant workers who are smuggled across the border. By the time of the movie's release, the Bracero Program, a labor agreement granting temporary work permissions for Mexican laborers entering the United States, was in full swing.[11] Directed by Anthony Mann, *Border Incident* is the first film of several mentioned in this chapter to feature a sympathetic Mexican cop working to expose corruption in the borderlands. Ricardo Montalban plays Pablo Rodriguez, a Mexican federal agent who crosses the border undercover as a bracero. Working with a white US counterpart (George Murphy), Pablo figures out that large US farming operations are smuggling Mexican workers into the United States and exploiting them in the fields. Murphy's character dies slowly but memorably when he is killed with a mechanized harrow, but Pablo persists and exposes the conspiracy with the help of another bracero, Juan. In the end, Pablo's Mexicanness is heroic rather than dangerous; the final scene depicts him, alongside Mexican and US officials, brokering new policies for protecting the workers.

Film scholar Dominique Brégent-Heald places *Border Incident* within a film cycle she calls "border noir," referring to a subset of film noirs that uses "the border as a narrative and visual device to signal physical and symbolic transition" and grids "the liminality of postwar North American relationships during the dynamic shifts from World War II to the Cold War."[12] Although *Border Incident* has a somewhat optimistic ending, stylistically it does resemble midcentury movies that took a more cynical approach to postwar American culture. And although it features a "positive" representation in Pablo, its setting and action still perpetuate the idea of the border as a dangerous and violent space, something that must be controlled and contained.

The most enduring of the border noir film cycle is *Touch of Evil* (1958), directed by and costarring Orson Welles. Charlton Heston plays Miguel "Mike" Vargas, another dignified Mexican federal cop, who is honeymooning with his new wife Susie (Janet Leigh) in a border town when he gets caught up in a murder investigation. Mike is especially invested in the case because he believes that the main suspect, a Mexican named Manolo Sanchez (Victor Millan), has been set up by big-talking police chief Hank Quinlan (Welles) on the US side of the border. Working with an ally on the US side, Mike eventually discovers that Quinlan has been planting evidence for years. An ironic twist at the end exposes that Sanchez really did commit the murder, but Mike's instincts about Quinlan are nonetheless proven correct, and by the movie's end, he is vindicated.

Heston plays Vargas in brownface, which makes it difficult for some contemporary viewers to take his performance seriously, but the character is wholly sympathetic and decent. His romantic pairing with Susie receives little commentary, and the characters seem to genuinely like one another and treat each other as equals. However, Mike stands out among a cadre of Mexican characters, all negatively portrayed, from the murderous Sanchez to sleazy local drug kingpin "Uncle" Joe Grandi (Armenian American actor Akim Tamiroff) and the young members of his extended family whom he pays to intimidate Susie. These roughnecks echo some of the characteristics of Broncho Billy's greaser, but are tinged with the markers of the 1950s greaser, including leather jackets, well-oiled pompadours, and dangling cigarettes. In one scene, they set up Susie to look like a junkie by drugging her and surrounding her with hypodermic needles. In another, set in a remote motel, Welles implies that this mixed gender group of greasers have raped her. The *New York Times* review claimed that the scene "should make any viewer leery of border accommodations for a long time to come."[13]

The fact that *Touch of Evil* features an honest Mexican cop and a corrupt white villain makes it somewhat unique in a time period in which Hollywood ignored, villainized, or exoticized Latinx characters, but its border setting is especially relevant to this chapter. Its residents of the borderlands are dangerous partly because it is often unclear on which side they belong. This in-betweenness is underscored by details such as the fact that several characters' names are mixes of English and Spanish and some codeswitch between the two. Welles famously opened the film with a long tracking shot that crosses the border with the doomed car driven by the soon-to-be murder victim. The mise-en-scène is packed with sounds and images meant to connote the chaos, danger, and marginality of a border town: bombs, neon signs outside cheap hotels, and trinket carts and cars sharing the street. As he checks Mike's paperwork, a border agent asks if he is on the "trail of another dope ring." This dazzling opening ends with the explosion of a bomb that sets all the subsequent action in motion—and serves as a good metaphor for some of the explosive revelations that will follow. Welles was a leftist with a special fondness for Latin America, but the casting of Heston, the use of brownface, and the presence of greaser stereotypes make it difficult to champion *Touch of Evil* as a radical departure from Hollywood. But, in some ways, it is. The film constructs crime, corruption, and violence as complex reflections of the racial, ethnic, and political landscapes of the borderlands so deftly that it remains a key object of study of Latinx film scholarship.

Representations of the border shifted considerably when Latinx filmmakers began to gain limited access to the means of film production. Gregory Nava's ambitious, sprawling *El Norte* (1983) depicted the journey of two siblings, Rosa and Enrique. Forced to flee their village in Guatemala due to political violence, the pair hope to make a better life in Los Angeles. Nava and his wife and business partner Anna Thomas produced *El Norte* independently, but the film developed a following after it aired on PBS. Of the many obstacles faced by Rosa and Enrique as they journey north, the border is particularly vexing. They get stuck in Tijuana, broke but determined to make it across the border. Like many migrant characters who precede and follow them, they must rely on the services of an exploitative *coyote* who swindles them and leaves them stranded. As they crawl through a border tunnel, they are attacked by rats. Later, Rosa dies from an infection contracted through the rat bites. The border in *El Norte* is a site of terror for migrants—who, significantly, are not Mexicans—and, unlike most earlier filmic depictions, it is clear that here the director's sympathies lie with those who cross it.

Nava went back to the border with *My Family/Mi Familia* (1995), a multigenerational family epic that he and Thomas again produced independently but that enjoyed a wider theatrical release. In an extended sequence that appears early in the film and foreshadows subsequent plotlines, family matriarch María (Jennifer Lopez) has been deported to Mexico during the Depression and, with her newborn baby Chucho, makes a long journey back to her family in Los Angeles. The border is represented in the sequence by a raging river that María and Chucho must cross as a final obstacle on their way home to Los Angeles, where María's husband José and their two other children await.[14] María and the baby are tossed from a rickety raft and become separated in the strong current. She is able to recover him and they make it across, but seeing an owl in the daylight suggests to María that baby Chucho is doomed nonetheless. From a Latinx media point of view, this is pretty standard fare: For people of Mexican descent in the United States, the filmic border represents the struggles overcome by our parents, grandparents, and ancestors. The Río Grande is not a raging river and isn't the border that María crosses, but Nava uses it as a metaphor for crossing, and the scene underscores the sacrifices that María—and, as an archetype, the Mexican American women she represents—makes to keep her family intact.

Latinx Hollywood depictions of Mexican migration that followed *My Family* have tended to construct the border in similar terms, even when the style or content of a film is quite different from Nava's work. *Born in East LA* (1987) is Cheech Marin's attempt to mine the border for laughs, a rarity on film and television that misfires in many regards but ultimately calls for interracial, interethnic, international solidarity against US militarization of the border. The melodramatic *A Better Life* (2011) shows the border as a site of traumatic family separation when a hard-working single father is deported and spends time in a migrant detention facility.

The border continues to occupy the US imagination as a place of endemic violence. Dozens of Hollywood films of the past decade have set narratives of excessive violence and disorder against the moody atmosphere of the borderlands. Nava's *Bordertown* (2006), as well as *Miss Bala* (2019), *Sicario* (2015) and its sequel *Sicario: Day of the Soldado* (2018), and *Savages* (2012), all stand out for their settings at the border and for how they present the border as a space of danger, death, and violence.

In *Savages*, directed by Oliver Stone, three white twentysomethings—an Iraq War vet with PTSD (Taylor Kitsch), a Berkeley-educated do-gooder (Aaron Taylor-Johnson), and a free-spirited rich girl (Blake Lively)—grow pot in Laguna Beach, California. They are terrorized by a Mexican queenpin (Salma Hayek) who wants to take over their market. In the trailer for the film, O, the rich girl, warns the audience that this was the kind of story where "things got so out of control." The trio runs a fashionable, outward-facing business with menus and storefronts and a Berkley-educated botanist. When a gruesome video is sent to Ben in the opening moments of the film, O asks, "Is that Iraq?" "No," replies Ben the Iraq vet. "That's Mexico." The trio, the narrator announces, "grows some of the best weed in the world." We've seen this before. Made in 2012, *Savages* comes at the height of *Breaking Bad*'s cultural stature.

Lower-budget films have also used the border as a backdrop for schlocky violence, typically deploying all the worst stereotypes about Mexicans.[15] In most of these films, Mexican cartels provide ruthless, menacing villains, and the borderlands serve as their violent playground. This mini genre of border thrillers relies on a presumption that the border is an intrinsically violent space, but these films rarely explore the historical roots of border violence or the traumatic repercussions of violence. John Sayles's *Lone Star* (1996) stands apart as arthouse fare that grapples with the legacy of the border's violent history. The film memorably ends with one character telling another to "forget the Alamo."

Narrative television has been less likely than cinema to represent the border, even in the streaming era when showrunners have been drawn to darker, more cinematic subject matter. Some notable exceptions deal with border issues or are set on the border. Mary Beltrán has shown in *Latino TV: A History* that several small-screen westerns of the 1950s, mostly aimed at kids, were set in the borderlands, and some even featured Mexican American heroes or sidekicks. However, Beltrán concludes that these series and miniseries ultimately did little to disrupt midcentury consensus culture.[16] A number of later series have dealt with the serious matter of characters' undocumented statuses and deportations, including otherwise funny sitcoms like *Superstore* (2015–2021), *Jane the Virgin* (2014–2019), and *One Day at a Time* (2017–2019). Other series have shown the border as a lawless party zone, such as in familiar arcs where characters find themselves in Tijuana to buy easily accessible drugs or get cheap plastic surgery. But few have been set in the borderlands or have depicted the border in any sustained way. One exception is FX's *The Bridge* (2013–2014), which writers relocated to the US-Mexico frontier when they adapted it from a Scandinavian series and which perhaps comes closest to filmic depictions of the border.

If narrative television had largely failed to represent the border so much as use the contemporary issues surrounding it, then reality television has provided some of the few exceptions to this rule with a suite of shows that have represented the violent policing of Latinx bodies at the border through the perspective of reality television crews following border agents around. These shows have emerged since the late 1990s, which makes sense considering that the reality genre and border hypermilitarization rapidly increased around the same time. Reece Jones has argued that shows like National Geographic Channel's *Border Wars* (2010–2013) normalize the dehumanization of Latinx migrants by centering the perspectives and narratives of the federal police who hunt them. According to Jones, the show "uses images of Predator drones, Black Hawk helicopters, hidden seismic sensors, and night vision equipment to build excitement and tension in the show."[17] Other reality shows have attempted to paint a more sympathetic portrait of undocumented migrants. This includes an episode of Morgan Spurlock's *30 Days* (2005–2008) that requires a Cuban American member of the anti-immigrant organization the Minutemen to live with an undocumented family for a month and visit the conditions of the town they left in Mexico, as well as Netflix's *Living Undocumented* (2019), which takes a deeper first-person dive into the experiences of undocumented migrants.

THE BORDERLANDS AND *TRAFFIC*'S RACIAL LOGICS

The smuggling of goods and people across the border has been a cinematic trope for decades, but representations began to shift after the year 2000, as US governmental efforts to curb drugs at the border accelerated due to the rise of Mexican cartels. Whereas drug narratives had previously focused on Colombian and other international villains in the War on Drugs and on African Americans when it came to domestic drug problems, the border became a fixture in narcomedia around the turn of the twenty-first century.

Few attempts to narrate the War on Drugs, its transnational dimensions, and its failings have been as successful as Steven Soderbergh's 2000 drama *Traffic*. In contrast to much of the cinematic fare discussed so far, *Traffic* was both critically and commercially successful, earning more than $200 million at the box office and winning four Academy Awards, including for best adapted screenplay and best director. Soderbergh's film is an adaptation of a television miniseries, *Traffik*, that aired in the United Kingdom in 1989. The original series, written by Simon Moore and directed by Alistair Reid, tells the interwoven stories of Afghani, British, German, and Pakistani players in the international opium trade whose lives become unwittingly interconnected. The original *Traffik* looks and sounds dated today, but its complex narrative, moral ambiguity, and multinational settings cement its status as a precursor to the prestige television series that emerged a decade later.

Soderbergh depicts the drug trade in three North American settings—Cincinnati, San Diego, and Tijuana. In the leafy environs of Cincinnati, Robert Wakefield (Michael Douglas) is the newly appointed drug czar of the United States who discovers that his own sixteen-year-old daughter (Erika Christensen) is a user. In San Diego, Helena Ayala (Catherine Zeta-Jones), a comfortable La Jolla wife and mother, discovers the illicit sources of her family's wealth. In Tijuana, Javier Rodriguez (Benicio Del Toro) is an honest but pragmatic cop who allies himself with the DEA after he discovers the depths of corruption on his side of the border.

There is little overlap between the narrative strands. Soderbergh resists the "it was always all connected in some cosmic sense" motif of similar films of the era that explored social problems through interwoven storylines (e.g., Paul Haggis's Oscar-winning but critically maligned *Crash* from 2004). *Traffic* also features cameos by real-life politicians and border officials who explain drug policy and border enforcement to the fictional characters (and the audience). An official memorandum produced in the early 2000s by the Drug Enforcement Agency counted the agency's participation with the filming of *Traffic* as one of its achievements. "DEA offered considerable input into the movie's portrayals of the drug situation," the memo states, "and most believed it accurately depicted the challenges law enforcement faced."[18]

Several characters cross the border over the course of *Traffic*: Javier and his partner Manolo, Helena, and Frankie Flowers (Clifton Collins Jr.), the assassin she hires to kill trafficker Eduardo Ruiz (Miguel Ferrer). In one brief scene, Robert visits the DEA's El Paso Intelligence Center to get acquainted with its procedures. He does a "walk and talk" with a real-life intelligence officer, who tells him that the cartels far outpace the DEA in terms of money and technology. Outside the center, Robert peers through binoculars at a house of a kingpin across the border. In the point-of-view shot, the building appears behind broiling heat waves and is colored in the sepia tones that result when footage is shot in (or later edited to mimic) what the film industry calls a "tobacco filter." The effects underscore the idea that Mexico is very close but also unreachable to US officials, a complaint that is as old as the War on Drugs.

Soderbergh, who also served as the director of photography on the film, uses a tobacco filter in most of the Mexican scenes, a cool blue tone for Cleveland, and natural, neutral colors for San Diego and Washington, DC, where Wakefield works. The filters come and go over the course of the film's two hour and twenty-four-minute run time, but are effective in establishing that the characters live in different spheres of the War on Drugs. The result is that the sprawling, multilayered film is easier to follow because the different national and regional settings are clearly demarcated.

But, more deeply, the filters might reify the border as a boundary that separates two distinct worlds. Tijuana and San Diego are just a dozen or so miles away from one another at their extremes, but the mise-en-scène suggests that they are far apart, with San Diego in its neutral—normal—hues. For instance, when Helena crosses the border to meet with cartel head Juan Obregón (Benjamin Bratt) in Tijuana, she enters a brown-tinted world that looks very different from that of her comfortable beachfront home, which is flooded with natural colors. Furthermore, the sepia tone of the tobacco filter also might make audiences remember vintage photographs, a technique that Nava uses in *Mi Familia* when depicting the family's origins. In *Traffic*, the result is that the Mexican side of the border is more old-fashioned, more backward, than San Diego, Cincinnati, or Washington. Alex Saragoza has argued that representations of heat have frequently been deployed to connote danger, moral laxity, corruption, and licentiousness in filmic representations of the border.[19] This is true of other texts that I have examined in this book, including *Breaking Bad*, and the coloring in *Traffic* does make the Mexican settings look hotter than other locations in the film, including when Wakefield visits the rather cool Mexico City. These three possible readings of the tobacco filter—otherworldliness, old-fashionedness, and heat—all subtly place Mexico, and specifically Tijuana, in a subordinate position to the United States. This is unsurprising in the milieu of border narcomedia, but contrasts with the otherwise liberal-mindedness of the film.

At the time that Soderbergh's *Traffic* appeared on movie screens, the US government's War on Drugs was moving away from Colombia and toward Mexico. Following the extradition and imprisonment of the heads of the Cali Cartel in the mid-1990s, along with successes at shutting down trafficking routes across the Caribbean, the DEA shifted its attention to Mexico, which by 1999 had become the key transit country for cocaine en route to US markets. *Traffic* acknowledges this shift in focus when Helena's lawyer tells her that he learned how to evade the DEA in Miami in 1985, before the United States shut down drug trafficking in Miami and the action moved to the border. "It's a big game of whack-a-mole," he says. Whereas previous iterations of narcomedia had been focused on Miami and Colombia as main geographic points of tension in the War on Drugs, *Traffic* was at the forefront of positioning the border as a trouble spot.

Traffic is also a product of the NAFTA era, a historical moment in which the border's porosity represented both opportunity and anxiety in the US public sphere. When the Canadian, US, and Mexican governments were negotiating the North American Free Trade Agreement in the early 1990s, one branch of popular criticism stemmed from the perception that it would dissolve the borders between the nations, making it easy for people and contraband—especially drugs—to enter the United States and Canada from the south. *Traffic* acknowledges the fact that popular perceptions of drug trafficking were in flux when the film was made and tied, in part, to anxieties about border porosity under NAFTA. At certain moments, this undercurrent of border anxieties bubbles to the surface. While being interrogated by DEA agents, Ruiz tells them that the policy will cripple any attempts to stanch the flow of drugs and that his job as a trafficker is just getting easier:

Look boys, this has worked for years. It's gonna continue to work for years. NAFTA makes things even more difficult for you because the border's disappearing. Do you realize for the next year or two at the outside Mexican trucking companies are gonna be able to go from the States to Mexico and back again with the same freedom as UPS, DHL, and FedEx? It's gonna be a fuckin' free-for-all. . . . You guys remind me of those Japanese soldiers left behind on a deserted island who think World War II is still going on, you know that? Let me be the first to tell you: Your government surrendered this war a long fucking time ago.

Eduardo's speech might serve, in part, as a thesis statement for the film, which focuses on the futility of the War on Drugs despite the actions of some of the well-meaning soldiers in that war. As ever, the border remains a site of danger and doom and, in the world of *Traffic*, scarily porous. Two scenes after Eduardo's speech, the camera lingers on a metal border marker that is bifurcated with labels "US" and "Mexico" on opposing sides. This shot is underscored with deep, ominous musical notes, as if the physical line that separates and unites the border, as Gloria Anzaldúa put it, is intrinsically frightening.

Since its initial release, several scholars have mined *Traffic* for what it has to say about the border and the many failings of the War on Drugs.[20] While some have noted *Traffic*'s view of Mexico and Mexicans, few have addressed the dialectical relationship between whiteness and Blackness in the film, despite the fact that the racialized ideology is essential to how *Traffic* narrates drugs and the border. Blackness is a particularly fraught theme in *Traffic*, even if only two Black characters have speaking roles. As Caroline Wakefield, the drug czar's high-achieving daughter, and her boyfriend Seth (Topher Grace), who are both white, get more deeply into drugs, they begin to venture into downtown Cincinnati to buy and use crack. They frequent a fleabag hotel that stands in sharp contrast to their suburban homes. "I love this place," says Seth. Her parents figure out that Caroline has grown addicted and send her to a bucolic rehab center, but she escapes and finds her way back to the inner city and the shoddy apartment of her Black dealer (Vonte Sweet, credited only as "Drug Dealer" but named "Sketch" in the shooting script), with whom she trades sex for drugs.

In one infamous scene, *Traffic* shows the extent to which Caroline's addiction has grown—and what race has to do with it. It opens with a point-of-view shot from Caroline's perspective of the dealer on top of her, fucking her, in an image similar to older visions of drugs as a threat to white womanhood that are evident in late-nineteenth and early twentieth-century popular culture *and* newer fare like *Savages*. His face is out of focus, and the camera—presumably like a numbed Caroline—focuses instead on a bare lightbulb in a ceiling fixture. The camera jostles with the dealer's thrusting. Then the shot changes to an over-the-shoulder shot of Caroline's face, which is completely out of focus for several seconds, underscoring again the teen's mental state. When a customer knocks on the door, the dealer climbs from the bed and heads to the door to do business. In one of two brief glimpses of nudity in the film (the other shows a naked Mexican assassin being tortured), the muscular Black man is shown from the rear, walking away from Caroline. When he returns to the filthy mattress on the floor, he catches her reaching for his stash, and instead of stopping her, he teaches her how to shoot up. Her head lolls and she falls back onto the mattress, barely conscious, and then he resumes fucking the unconscious teen.

This echoes an earlier scene in which Seth taught her how to freebase crack, but this later lesson is constructed as a racialized encounter, something consistent with many of the narcomedia texts analyzed throughout this book. The dealer's Blackness is essential to the scene. In the miniseries on which *Traffic* is based, the corresponding character of Caroline's dealer, who also introduces her to intravenous drug use, is a somewhat sensitive and verbose white man who lives in a council flat and seems to genuinely care for his clients. Soderbergh makes a choice to revise the character in terms of race and attitude, perhaps to add an additional layer of commentary about social, economic, and racial divisions that blur when well-heeled white people get involved with drugs. In other words, *Traffic* might be positing that drugs dissolve important social borders.

But this does not mean that the characters want those social borders blurred. Robert spends several days looking for her on the streets and finally resorts to recruiting Seth, whom he snatches from a high school Spanish class, for the mission. They drive back to the inner city, which Robert views with disgust:

ROBERT: I can't believe you brought my daughter to this place.
SETH: Whoa, whoa. Why don't you just back the fuck up, man? "To this place?" What is that shit? Ok, right now, all over this great nation of ours, 100,000 white people from the suburbs are cruising around downtown asking every black person they see, "You got any drugs? You know where I could score some drugs?" Think about the effect that has on the psyche of a black person, on their possibilities. God, I guarantee you, you bring 100,000 into your neighborhood, into fucking Indian Hills, and they're asking every white person they see 'You got any drugs? You know where I can score some drugs?'

Within a day, everyone would be selling. Your friends, their kids, here's why: It's an unbeatable market force, man. It's a 300 percent markup value. You can go out on the street and make $500 in two hours, come back and do whatever you want to do with the rest of your day. You're telling me that white people would still be going to law school?[21]

This is by far the longest uninterrupted speech in the rather wordy film and seems calibrated to appeal to liberal-minded viewers who understand the ironies of well-meaning white people who drive forward the illicit markets that harm so many Black communities. In other words, Seth speaks to (and perhaps *for*) the type of audience member who is likely to see a Steven Soderbergh film.

The fact that Seth, a bombastic prep school student, gives the speech indicates a significant problem for African American representational politics in *Traffic*. The dealer only speaks briefly in the film to threaten Robert when he finally does track Caroline down at the apartment. He pulls a gun on him and screams in his face: "Who the fuck do you think you are? Where the fuck do you think you are? Why the fuck shouldn't I just put your ass in a dumpster?" When Robert offers him a thousand dollars for Caroline, the dealer responds by yelling, "If I want your money, man, I will take your money."[22] These threatening lines are pretty much the extent of actor Vonte Sweet's dialogue as the dealer. His presence but relative silence, along with his lack of a name and his nudity, underscores the fact that he is more of a symbol than a person in the film.

In the British original, when Jack (Robert's corollary) confronts Caroline's dealer in his shabby apartment, they have a civil conversation about her whereabouts and the dealer gives him the phone number of the man with whom she is lying low. As Jack leaves the flat, the dealer wishes him luck in finding his daughter and adds, on a melancholy note, "I wish I had someone looking for me." Later, the dealer calls Jack to tip him off about where Caroline has been hiding out. This behavior humanizes the dealer, going beyond the usual trope of the nefarious pusher that has been featured in popular culture for more than a century.

If Soderbergh had followed the source material more closely, as he does at other critical junctures of the film's plot and dialogue, *Traffic* could have reframed the racialized stereotype of the exploitative and rage-filled Black dealer that pervades the history of American anti-Blackness so thoroughly. Alas, Soderbergh instead gives the speech about white hypocrisy to Seth and sends Caroline into the "'hood" to represent her final descent into addiction and depravity. Furthermore, Seth is not the only character who thinks out loud about what drugs mean to the US body politic. Robert, his drug czar predecessor, and the real-life politicians who appear in the film all vocalize their thoughts about drugs throughout the film, and, although they cannot identify any panacea for America's drug problem, they constantly discuss drug policy and procedure. Like verbose schoolboy Seth, they have *ideas*. Black and Latinx characters, in contrast, have drugs or jobs aimed at either selling drugs or stopping them (three characters of color are non-corrupt cops).

Later in the film, Robert breaks down while giving a perfunctory speech in the White House press room. He can't go through with the platitudes expected of his position and instead speaks from his heart. He does so much more succinctly than Seth. "If there is a War on Drugs," he says, choking back tears, "then many of our family members are the enemy, and I don't know how you wage war on your own family." He cannot bring himself to go any further with the speech and leaves the White House directly for the airport and a flight home. The last viewers see of Robert, he is at a rehab center to support Caroline's ongoing treatment for addiction. This is an upbeat ending for the Wakefield storyline but it also speaks to the racial logics described in this chapter: Caroline is safe and back where she belongs, with resources and support.

Unlike its source material, *Traffic* has little to say about the redeemability of non-white drug users. In this sense, the film exemplifies a major representational problem in narcomedia: Who are the victims of the drug trade and who deserves sympathy when they find themselves addicted? I examined the idea of "grievability" in chapter 3, and we might extend that idea to what might be called "recoverability." Who can and should recover from drug addiction? From the early 1980s—when a spate of made-for-TV movies and *After School Specials* focused on the dangers of addiction—to the present, the pop culture focus on drug use has overwhelmingly centered on white users. The drama of these texts often involves a white middle-class teen or adult who experiments with the drug, grows addicted, and then spirals downward into urban ghettos and non-white landscapes. Their low point is usually represented as it is in *Traffic*: through encounters with social, economic, and racial Others and behaviors that would have been unthinkable in their lives before the drugs. After hitting rock bottom, the addict then begins to recognize that he or she has a problem and works to rebuild his or her life. The message is that addiction is a treatable disease and the user deserves compassion rather than incarceration.

One early NBC made-for-TV movie focused on addiction aired in late February 1983 and provides an example of how mainstream depictions of drug use focused on the white user as victim. *Cocaine: One Man's Seduction*

6.1. Benicio Del Toro's Javier is one of a few "good Mexican cops" who appear in narcomedia focused on the US-Mexico border. Alamy Photo.

starred Dennis Weaver as a sweet but down-on-his-luck real estate agent who, to the bafflement of his wife and teenage son, gets hooked on the drug. As the title of the movie suggests, Weaver's character does not seek out cocaine but is convinced to try it by colleagues. The moral of the film is that cocaine is pernicious enough to threaten the comfortable lives of a white middle-class family but that help comes with filial understanding.

Countless depictions across multiple genres have described abuse since the start of the War on Drugs (and many others have shown alcohol abuse over the course of US history), but rarely has popular culture focused on non-white addicts. Apart from some notable exceptions, such as David Simon's groundbreaking TV miniseries *The Corner* (2000), depictions of addiction tend to construct white characters as the "victims" of addiction and non-white characters as the progenitors of America's drug problems.

Traffic relies on stereotypes about Blackness to make its point about addiction, but the film does include a complex and deeply human (non-Black) Mexican character, Javier, who resembles others we have seen in border narcomedia. About halfway through the film, he and his partner Manolo (Jacob Vargas, who also played the younger version of the father José in *My Family*) discover that a Mexican general, Arturo Salazar, is secretly working with the Juarez Cartel, rivals to Tijuana. Javier tells Manolo that they should keep their mouths shut regarding this potentially explosive piece of intel, but Manolo attempts to sell the information to the DEA and is killed by Salazar. Javier then goes to the DEA but is not out to profit for himself.

Fojas reads Javier as a Mexican variation on the "narc" figure that appears in many War on Drugs border films, largely because he upholds rather than challenges the well-established trope of the antidrug hero. (Don Cheadle and Luis Guzmán play DEA agents who are similarly uncorrupted by the end of the film.) In my view, Javier is a compelling figure because he stands apart from the rampant Mexican corruption that, according to *Traffic*, makes any US governmental attempt to stop trafficking an impossible task. As an honest Mexican cop who thinks beyond his own self-interest, Javier is strikingly similar to characters in two films mentioned above: Miguel Vargas in *Touch of Evil* and Pablo Rodriguez in *Border Incident*. Like Miguel and Pablo, Javier is a not unfamiliar character in narcomedia: the honest Mexican. A character who sides with the Americans, who sacrifices much, if not everything, in the face of overwhelming corruption and violence, but who alone is not enough to reform a corrupt nation or a society held hostage by cartels. However, Soderbergh accomplishes what Orson Welles and *Border Incident* director Anthony Mann could not at midcentury: He constructs the Javier character as a nuanced, morally complex Mexican and not merely a hollow stereotype. This is helped by a moving, deeply felt performance by Benicio Del Toro, who became just the second Latino to win an Oscar for Best Supporting Actor in 2001.[23]

Javier's personal decency is highlighted in two key instances. First, he honors Manolo's final wish that Javier not tell his partner Ana (Marisol Padilla Sánchez) the real nature of his death. Javier visits her in her modest home, where she has a small *ofrenda* to Manolo, and honors his dead partner's wishes by telling her that it is thanks to Manolo that the corruption was exposed. She is skeptical, but Javier gently insists that Manolo died doing "something important for Tijuana." Second, although he stands to gain monetarily from the information on Salazar, Javier makes only one altruistic request of the DEA: He asks for lights for a baseball field in Tijuana, so kids can play after dark. Unfortunately, Javier stands apart from almost all other Mexicans in the film, who are depicted as violent, corrupt, and criminal. Ana seems sympathetic, but has only a few lines. So although Soderbergh and screenwriter Stephen Gaghan do an admirable job providing a more complex portrait of the drug trade, they also repeat a narrative of Mexican criminality as old as the film medium. Ultimately, Javier functions as an exception to the rule of Mexican criminality.

WHITE WOMEN AT THE BORDER

In *Traffic*, white womanhood is something that must be protected from a downfall. Jenji Kohan's *Weeds* (2005–2012), a long-running *Showtime* series, features a white woman who flirts with danger and, as part of that process, becomes a border crosser herself. *Weeds*, as I have mentioned previously, follows the misadventures of an affluent suburban widow who starts dealing pot to maintain her family's lifestyle after her husband's sudden death. Although *Weeds* is tonally very different from *Traffic*, many of its racial dynamics echo Soderbergh's film.

Weeds follows the transformation of Nancy Botwin (Mary-Louise Parker) from grieving widow to wannabe drug queenpin over the course of eight seasons. Early in the series, Nancy forms an uneasy business relationship with an African American family that serves as her main suppliers. Heylia, Vaneeta, and Conrad James contrast sharply with the all-white residents of Agrestic, the cookie-cutter suburb where Nancy lives. Much of the action in the first season of the series involves Nancy attempting to prove herself as capable to the James family, whose members are skeptical that a white woman is cut out for the marijuana trade. She eventually does find a place for herself in the business because, as an attractive, middle-class white woman and mother, she has a natural cover. Interracial encounters are played for laughs in *Weeds*, with the Black characters frequently commenting on Nancy's whiteness and the privileges that come with her racial and class affiliations.

Despite the light tone and sitcom-length episodes, the racial logic of the television show echoes a common trope of narcomedia that we've seen elsewhere: Drugs put rich white people in contact with non-white Others, who become objects of both desire and danger. In this sense, *Weeds* is a prototype for the suburban crime drama that I examine in chapter 5, even if critics have tended to dismiss it as less serious than series like *Breaking Bad* and it has received scant scholarly attention.[24] Kohan, the creator and showrunner of *Weeds*, has described interracial, interethnic, intercultural encounters as part of her artistic raison d'être. "I'm fascinated by people interacting with the Other," she told Emily Nussbaum in a 2017 *New Yorker* profile, "forced to interact with people they'd never have to deal with in their day-to-day lives. . . . Attraction or repulsion, it's great for drama."[25] In both *Weeds* and Kohan's subsequent major series, *Orange Is the New Black* (2013–2019), the racialized encounters that the showrunner thinks are "great for drama" are mediated through the experiences of rich white women who become ensnared in criminal endeavors.[26]

Weeds repeats the idea that encounters with racialized Others are "great for drama" in seasons four and five, which find the James family written out of the series and the Botwin family relocated to the fictional beach town of Ren Mar on the US-Mexico border after Agrestic burns down. Nancy, on the run from the DEA but unable to resist the marijuana industry, starts doing business with a Tijuana cartel that is headed by the mayor of that Mexican city, Esteban Reyes (Mexican actor Demián Bichir, who also starred in *The Bridge* and *A Better Life* after his turn on *Weeds*). Like so many narcomedia productions before it, *Weeds* reminds the audience that corruption and elected office are inseparable once one is south of the border. These "border seasons" of *Weeds* aired in 2008 and 2009, in the midst of a national debate over immigration reform and border enforcement, a period that included the lead-up to Arizona SB 1070 and other legislation aimed at curtailing and criminalizing undocumented migration. (The whereabouts of the James family, whose members had been pivotal to previous seasons, goes unexplained; they essentially disappear after the fire.[27]) By relocating the setting to the border, *Weeds* taps into the cultural and political zeitgeist and gives Nancy a new cast of racialized characters to go up against.

Nancy's dealings with Mexican characters echo those she had with the James family in earlier seasons, but they are distinctively framed by the borderlands setting. This is because the border looms large in seasons four and five, either as a setting for much of the action or as an ideological construct that separates Nancy and her clan from the Mexican characters. By the time she arrives in Ren Mar, she has an established but testy working relationship with Guillermo (Guillermo Díaz), a mid-level kingpin with territory in Southern California, but the relocation introduces several more Mexican characters that menace her, including Esteban and his henchmen. Nancy makes a few trips transporting weed across the border, but the main action of these seasons involves a tunnel running from Tijuana to a retail store that she manages as a front for the cartel's drug smuggling. Nancy, used to being her own boss, is now set up as an underling to the cartel head. "What's my job here?" she asks Guillermo when he introduces her to the scheme. "To be a pretty American lady," he responds.[28] Nancy is seemingly incapable of not putting herself into harm's way, so, of course, things get more complicated.

The border narrative of seasons four and five goes beyond Nancy getting ensnared with the Tijuana Cartel. At one point, Nancy's brother-in-law Andy (Justin Kirk) and their friend Doug (Kevin Nealon) start a business of their own, working as *coyotes* and smuggling migrants across the border. This plot is played, like most plots in *Weeds*, for laughs, but also taps into the zeitgeist of early-2000s border anxieties. Andy gets the idea for human smuggling after he gets stranded in Mexico and has to make his way back to the United States, an oddly common sitcom trope. This plot also involves Andy and Doug joining a Minutemen-like group as part of their cover and Doug pursuing an undocumented woman as a love interest. (Sample line when he does find her: "I smuggled her here. I think that merits some 'cock-amole' on her 'face-adilla.'"[29])

Perhaps one way to read seasons four and five of *Weeds* is as a critique of how dominant US culture sees the border and Mexicanness. The creators and performers associated with the show have frequently described *Weeds* as satire, and it is clear in early episodes that it aims to mock suburban conformity (reinforced by clever editing in the opening credits and the use of Malvina Reynolds's "Little Boxes" as the theme song). In many ways, the character of Celia Hodes, Nancy's obnoxious neighbor, with her casual but explicit racism, materialism, and unrepentant bitchiness, appears designed to critique whiteness from the inside. The demographic category known as the "soccer mom" had caused a sensation in the 1996 presidential election; at the time, a congresswoman described it to the *New York Times* as "one of the most overused terms in America."[30] Into the next decade, pop culture grappled with the meanings of what was supposedly the most powerful demographic in the nation, and Nancy, who drives a Prius and constantly carries an iced espresso drink, embodies many of the stereotypes associated with the soccer mom. Other TV shows, such as *Desperate Housewives*, which premiered the year before *Weeds*, aimed at deflating the image of the soccer mom, and *Weeds* can be read in that vein.

Nancy, although the lead character of the series, behaves in such chaotic and contradictory ways that she is often difficult to root for, suggesting that the show aims to critique the very demographic at its center (and, presumably, the one that it hopes to court as an audience). However, Nancy's self-actualization seems to be the overarching point of the show, and over the years, she finds personal empowerment—and eventually great wealth—through her participation in the drug economy. She often expresses that she is just trying to provide for her family and recoils from the harsher aspects of the drug trade, such as late in the fourth season, when she realizes that Esteban is smuggling not just marijuana through the border tunnel but guns, heroin, and women, too. In that plotline, Nancy informs on the Mexicans with whom she's working, an iteration of the only-white-people-have-a-conscience trope that I have traced in other narcomedia.

More often than not, the show reinforces rather than challenges dominant assumptions about latinidad that we have seen to be prevalent in narcomedia. Throughout its long run, *Weeds* consistently included one-dimensional characters who are difficult to describe as anything but stereotypes. From the start, the thickly accented housekeeper Lupita (Renée Victor) is a source of frustration for Nancy because she would rather be watching Telemundo than cooking or cleaning. Lupita simultaneously embodied the stereotypes of both the Latina domestic worker and the lazy Mexican. We see just a brief glimpse of Lupita outside the Botwin house early in the series when she gossips with a relative about whether Nancy could be a drug dealer. She subsequently rifles through the family's belongings, looking for evidence. But Lupita, like most Latinx characters, never gets a storyline of her own; she only seems to exist in relation to Nancy and her family.

Other characters in *Weeds* neatly align with many of the classic Latinx stereotypes that have appeared throughout the history of narcomedia. When Sucio (Ramon Franco), one of the cartel's henchmen, is assigned as a bodyguard for Nancy's son, his body odor becomes a long-running joke among the white characters, who constantly call him smelly or stinky in a redux of the "dirty Mexican" trope that is tied to the greaser image. Another who becomes a recurring character, Ignacio (Hemky Madera), is considered quirky by the other characters because he sensitively loves animals but kills people on a whim. Esteban's ruthless fixer Pilar (Kate del Castillo) belongs to a category of stock characters that Charles Ramirez Berg calls the "dark lady" in *Latino Images in Film* (Hayek's character in *Savages* is a variation on the dark lady). Pilar meets an incredibly gruesome end when pre-teen Shane Botwin (Alexander Gould) murders her with a croquet mallet. Stereotypes offer something of a shortcut to meaning: They can provide exposition without wasting precious screen time and are useful for storytelling. But, as we have seen before and will see again, they are also dehumanizing. This mode of representing Latinos carries over and is heightened in seasons four and five.

Esteban is perhaps the clearest example of Latino stereotyping present in narcomedia since at least Tony Montana in *Scarface*. He embodies what many would expect of the kingpin: He has good looks and a sexy accent but is quick to violence and will stop at nothing to maintain his position of power. Like Tony Montana, he owns big cats (in this case, a trio of endangered lions), which function as a metaphor for the character. When feeding time comes around and a goat is taken to the lion's cage, he tells a squeamish Nancy that he likes watching the carnage. This cuts immediately to a sex scene between Esteban and Nancy, a clear reference to the fact that his animalistic instincts are part of his appeal.[31] At the end of season four, Nancy informs on Esteban, making them enemies rather than lovers. The next season focuses on the tensions between the characters, as

Esteban would have had her killed except for the fact that Nancy is pregnant by him (she tantalizes him with the idea that he could finally have a son).[32] Early in the season, in a particularly explicit scene, Esteban rapes Nancy as a demonstration of his power over her. "You don't dictate the terms of this arrangement," he tells her as he zips up his trousers.[33] Later, in a rare moment of tenderness, it seems that Esteban wants to embrace Nancy, but he drops to his knees and kisses her belly instead, making it clear that he is interested in his male heir but not in her.

Weeds does not include any Mexican or Latinx characters who defy the stereotypes mentioned above or who are "incidentally" Latinx. Although the first five seasons of the series are set in Southern California, with dozens of speaking parts, it never features Latinx characters free of one ethnic stereotype or another. The same can be said for other racial and ethnic groups, as well as queer characters. The show remains relentlessly focused on its white protagonist. Critics alternately praised and panned Parker's performance, but many agreed that the role bore heavy responsibility as the very center of the show. Observers frequently construed this as a win for women on prestige television, which skewed quite heavily male when *Weeds* aired. But it also meant that Nancy's character was developed at the expense of those surrounding her, especially non-white characters. If a viewer adapted the Bechdel Test for representations of Mexicans in *Weeds*, they would find it difficult to find moments in which Mexican characters speak to each other about something other than the white protagonist.

Weeds also never explicitly critiques the racist structures it depicts, and this is true when the action shifts to a borderlands setting. Seth's big speech in *Traffic*, however misplaced it might appear because it is delivered by a privileged white college student to a powerful white official, nonetheless openly expresses the idea that American perceptions of drugs are clouded by racist assumptions and willful ignorance. *Weeds*, though it seems to wink at the audience from time to time, makes no such statement about the racialized dimensions of the drug trade. Throughout its long run, characters try to game the system rather than question the system itself. Part of the reason this happens is the white-centrism that characterizes the show. It simply refuses to take the focus off its white characters. Even when a character like Esteban receives ample screen time, it is only in relation to Nancy: first as an object of desire, then as a dangerous pursuer. As a result, the show cannot see or understand the border beyond the wants and needs of its main characters.

In her book *Stealing the Show*, TV journalist Joy Press notes that *Weeds* predates *Breaking Bad* but has not enjoyed long-standing critical success like that show.³⁴ Press attributes this partly to the fact that *Weeds* focused on a woman and has a tacitly feminist outlook, whereas *Breaking Bad* follows the transformation of its male protagonist from science geek to swaggering kingpin. I agree in principle, but also do not find *Weeds* to veer very far off the usual treatment of white womanhood in its view of the border. Previously in this chapter I mentioned that protecting white women was a key part of the racial logics of the border in early cinema. Nancy has more agency than many of the white women who found themselves in trouble at the border in texts like *Broncho Billy and the Greaser* or *Touch of Evil*. But in many ways the border has not changed since the period of silent film: It remains a space where white women encounter racial and ethnic difference and where they are imperiled by people, especially men, on or from the Mexican side of the border. Nancy's relationship with Esteban reflects this dynamic. Although the creators of *Weeds* leaned heavily into intense irreverence, the story they tell of a white woman's relationship to the border is, in the end, conventional.

CONCLUSION

This chapter has used *Traffic* and *Weeds* to critically examine the US-Mexico border as a trope within narcomedia. Jenji Kohan's next major project after *Weeds* also features a border narrative. In the last season of *Orange Is the New Black*, set in a New York state women's prison, several of the inmates are transferred to a privatized ICE detention center for various transgressions against immigration policy. There they meet Karla (Karla Córdova), a Salvadorian migrant who will be separated from her children if she is deported. Karla is desperate to remain with her kids, who have been placed in foster care. However, despite her preparedness (she had previously worked in a law office and spends her time in detention researching her legal options), she reaches a dead end in the courts. The last viewers see of Karla, she has crossed the US-Mexico border with a small group of migrants led by a *coyote*. As she makes her way through the hot desert, Karla twists her ankle on a rock and falls down a ravine. Unable to take the risk of stopping, the other migrants move on without her, leaving her to the elements.

Karla's story arc, presented in *Orange* as a tragedy, is a far cry from the alternately farcical border in *Weeds*. Karla's ordeal might be read as a reversal of Andy Botwin's supposedly comical trek through the desert in the fourth season of *Weeds*. *Orange* suffered from many of the problems associated with white centrism, but focusing on the Latina migrant and granting her both humanity and sympathy counters some of the representational patterns that this chapter has examined. Perhaps it would be too optimistic to assume that Kohan and her crew had matured in how they went about representing the border in *Orange*, but putting Karla at the center of the narrative suggests that, by the time of its seventh season in 2019, squarely in the Trump era, the border was no longer a laughing matter.

CHAPTER 7

FROM PUBLIC ENEMY TO GLOBAL MEDIA COMMODITY
Pablo Escobar Transformed

Anyone can be a criminal, but to be an outlaw demands a following.
MARK BOWDEN, *Killing Pablo*

On February 22, 2019, the city government of Medellín destroyed one of the largest and most potent symbols of Colombia's narco history. Edificio Mónaco, the home and headquarters of Pablo Escobar's cartel from 1986–1988, had housed one of the most successful criminal enterprises in world history. Its name evoked the classy aspirations—and perhaps the sovereignty—sought by its infamous owner. Escobar and his family lived in the building's sixteen thousand-square-foot penthouse until rivals bombed it while his family was in residence, sparking a bloody war between the Cali and Medellín Cartels. At one point, the apartment had been decorated with flowers flown in from Bogotá twice per week.[1] However, for twenty-five years following Escobar's assassination by joint US and Colombian forces in December 1993, the Mónaco stood mostly empty, a behemoth monument to both its creator's hubris and his tremendous impact on Colombian history. City officials long debated what to do with the building, but repurposing it as an office building or mental health center, as they had for brief periods in the 1990s, could not diminish its notoriety. Tourists discovered Medellín by the 2010s, and the Mónaco became a popular stopping point for the dozens of narco tours on offer in the city. Finally, officials settled on the idea to destroy and replace it with a peace park dedicated to the victims of narco violence. Its destruction was televised on Colombian networks and live streamed on YouTube for viewers around the world.

7.1. Before its demolition, Edificio Mónaco stood as a monument to the narco era in Medellín. Photograph by Barbara Johnston.

I visited the Mónaco about six weeks before the municipal government destroyed it. Prior to my visit, city officials had covered the building's street-facing façade with large banners, apparently aimed at tourists, that relayed messages in both Spanish and English. One made a clear but strikingly assertive statement in English: "We must remember that we are dealing with real pain, suffering, and lost lives." Given that I was with a group of students and a guide hired through a tour company, I could not help but feel abashed as I read the banner's message, which implored foreign visitors to understand the city's bloody narcotrafficking history as the source of collective grief and trauma rather than as entertainment.

The banner resonates in part because, for decades, popular culture texts from the United States have fixated on Escobar's exploits as if they took place in the realm of fantasy, as if Escobar and his ilk were works of fiction rather than the sources of "real pain, suffering, and lost lives." Banners have been placed in sites such as this one in response to the intense interest that US popular culture has taken in the transnational drug trade more broadly. This chapter turns to the head of the most successful illegal drug cartel as a case study for understanding how a single person can take on the symbolic weight of the War on Drugs and US ideas about Colombianness. It focuses on US popular culture's fascination with Escobar from the height of his economic, social, and political power in the 1980s to the 2010s and 2020s, when US and international pop cultures saw a resurgence in his image—and a refashioning of the meanings attached to him. During this time, Escobar's image has had what María Elena Cepeda calls "a stubborn legibility in the global popular imagination."[2] Cepeda and her coeditors of a special issue of *Latino Studies* that explores the growing field of US Colombian studies posit that the Escobar narrative is the single most powerful narrative within the broader narco genres that shape US perceptions of *Colombianidad*.[3] This chapter asks how this came to be and what our ongoing attraction to Escobar means.

A complex system of signifying has taken place in the years since Escobar's death, transforming him from historical outlaw to aesthetic object and American hero. On a larger scale, as Aldona Bialowis Pobutsky describes it, the various Escobar myths have turned him into "a living construct, a crossroad of ideologies navigated and fueled by conflicting interests."[4] I want to stress that it makes good sense to consider how North Americans, the progenitors of the War on Drugs, construct and disseminate Escobar's image from a distinctly American point of view to suit distinctly American purposes. But it also makes good sense to consider how that image makes meaning beyond the context of the United States, which is why I read Escobar's image in US texts in relation to Colombian and other international contexts. In the analysis that follows, as I have with other historical figures throughout this book, I use the name "Pablo" to refer to the fictionalized character based on Escobar that appears in *Narcos* and other popular culture sources, using the first name to mark that I am referring to the *character* and not the historical *person*.

ESCOBAR, COCAINE, AND COLOMBIANNESS

Chapter 1 focused on cocaine's resurgence in the United States during the 1970s and 1980s, showing that Tony Montana, the hubristic trafficker in *Scarface*, became the template for countless Latinx and Latin American kingpin characters who would follow, including those based on historical figures. The character of Montana, played by Al Pacino, embodied what many Americans feared about the influx of Cuban migrants, but Cuba was not central to US anxieties about cocaine as the eighties wore on. According to perceptions of the eighties and nineties, Cubans could assimilate and even be held up as examples of the "good Latinos." Cuban Americans became a powerful Republican voting bloc in South Florida and eventually became influential in national politics. As the War on Drugs accelerated, the real problem, according to both government policy and popular culture, was Colombia.

From the mid-1980s to the present, the mere mention of Colombia or Colombians has served as a shorthand for cocaine and cartels. Political scientist Bruce Bagley, writing in 1988, noted the attention that Colombia was then garnering in the US political sphere. "Colombia's emergence as a key source and trafficking country has understandably attracted a great deal of attention from US policymakers, law enforcement officials and journalists over the last decade," he writes. "Indeed, in the minds of most Americans, Colombia is now essentially synonymous with drug trafficking."[5] Unfortunately, the negative connotations of Colombianness have stuck. While Bagley doesn't mention popular culture in his work on drug policy, it would have behooved him to ask what roles film, television, and other media played in producing the associations he describes.

Colombia has been the main exporter of cocaine to the United States from its reintroduction in the 1970s to the present by a large margin, so I do not mean to imply that representations of Colombian drug trafficking are not based in reality. However, I do want to challenge representational practices that flatten the complexity of this country into *just* a cocaine supplier. Colombia's incredibly profitable cocaine industry came into existence through a combination of internal political instability and a global demand, especially from the United States, for the product. The tendency of US popular culture to construct white North Americans as the victims of cocaine's "seduction" and producing countries as the source of America's drug problems is a mode of externalization very much in tune with governmental policies like Plan Colombia.

An early expression of the idea that Colombia was synonymous with drug trafficking appeared in the August 1983 episode of the ABC newsmagazine *Closeup*, mentioned in chapter 1. Near the end of the episode, reporter William Sherman, on location in Medellín, describes the activities of several "cocaine dons," including Pablo Escobar. Sherman highlights Escobar in a section focused on kingpins' charitable works and includes excerpts from an interview in which Escobar makes a dubious argument for the positive effects of "hot money" on Colombia's economy and how it benefits the poor when it trickles down.[6] A review of the episode was the first time Escobar's name appeared in the *New York Times*, which subsequently mentioned him on hundreds of occasions before his death a decade later (and has mentioned him every year since).[7]

Following the initial exposure, Escobar's name, along with more generic references to Colombians, emerged as synonyms for narcotrafficking in the English-language press. By the middle of the decade, his name had appeared thousands of times in English-language media coverage of the drug trade. Infamously, *Forbes* placed Escobar on its annual list of billionaires for several years in the late 1980s, but that magazine was an outlier in framing the kingpin in somewhat glamorous terms; most reportage focused on Escobar as a criminal and one of the progenitors of North America's cocaine problem. In July 1992, his notoriety reached such a level that the Congressional Subcommittee on Western Hemisphere Affairs and Task Force on International Narcotics Control held a joint hearing devoted entirely to Escobar's escape from prison and its potential effect on the international narcotics trade.[8]

In subsequent decades, Escobar was something of a problem in representation. Who had the right to represent a real-life public enemy and how could any artist, director, writer, or performer capture a figure who carried so much political and cultural baggage? Some of the first creative endeavors to broach the subject were through the telenovela, a televisual form that has been particularly adept at engaging Latin American audiences with pressing social issues, from race relations to homophobia to, in one recent example, the reintegration of former FARC guerillas into mainstream society in the hugely popular *La Niña*.[9] Colombian telenovela *El Patrón del Mal*, which aired on the Caracol network from May to November 2012, constructs Escobar as a national villain, focusing on politicians and journalists as the martyrs and heroes in their efforts to expose his crimes. Its point of view clearly reflects its writers and producers, who are relatives of some of his prominent victims.[10] In the context of *El Patrón del Mal* and others like it, Escobar's story becomes a morality tale about greed, unchecked power, and how long civil society can endure evil run amok. And, as Pobutsky suggests in *Pablo Escobar and Colombian Narcoculture* and elsewhere, such telenovelas provide a cultural space for thinking collectively about the traumatic events of the 1980s and 1990s.

Given the provocative themes depicted in Colombian texts, it is not surprising that the Colombian interest in representing Escobar extended to US popular culture, where his reemergence as a popular motif coincided with widespread cultural anxieties over a new national drug "epidemic" in the 2010s—this one related to prescription opioids rather than cocaine. Escobar's transmediated image in US popular culture functions differently from the way it does in Colombia, where the facts of his life are known in excruciating detail by the general public and faithfully reconstructed in texts like *El Patrón del Mal*. In US-made texts, Escobar has become a more flexible signifier, meaning that the character "Pablo Escobar" does not necessarily reference the historical person on whom he is based, but is open to interpretation, reinvention, and reimagination. This blurring between the real and imaginary Escobar has sometimes led to some rather fraught representational practices. He has, for example, been played by actors who are Spanish (Javier Bardem, *Loving Pablo*), Brazilian (Wagner Moura, *Narcos*), Puerto Rican (Benicio Del Toro, *Escobar: Paradise Lost*), and Māori (Cliff Curtis, *Blow*). Certainly, Colombian popular culture has produced variations on Escobar, but perhaps because US-based media makers need not answer to a large constituency that survived the brutality of the Colombian narco state in the 1980s and 1990s, they have been especially originative both in creating a multiplicity of Pablo characters who deviate from the historical record and in constructing new fantasies and desires about Escobar. As described below, this has led to some pushback from Colombian and Colombian-diasporic audiences.

Escobar's resurgence is possible partly because Colombian representations of the drug lord began to be translated into English media, whether as direct translations of Spanish-language representations or as English-language interpretations of recent Colombian history.[11] One striking example of the former comes from a member of the Escobar family. After creating a sensation in Colombia with a tell-all memoir, *Mi Hermano Pablo* (2008), about his time in the cartel, Escobar's brother Roberto worked with US writer David Fisher to produce a version for English-language readers, released with the rather anodyne title *The Accountant's Story*. Roberto Escobar and Fisher seem well aware of their parts in the myth-making process associated with Pablo Escobar. Fisher, in his foreword, puts it this way:

> Pablo Escobar became a legend the old-fashioned way: He shot his way to the top of the charts. True legends, like that of Pablo Escobar, grow slowly and must be nurtured. The stories told about them have to grow in scope and size until reality is simply too small to contain them. They have to burst beyond the borders of time and place and become famous enough to outlive the contemporary journalism of their life. The world has to come to know them on a first-name basis.[12]

Fisher's description of the Escobar "legend" might be understood as a craven attempt to justify the publication of yet another cartel memoir, several of which had reached English-language readers by the time *The Accountant's Story* was published in 2009. But Fisher is also exactly right: Although pop culture is often eager to label undeserving players as "legends," the real legends are the ones who achieve their status through a longer course of action, and Pablo Escobar's status in US and international popular cultures seems to confirm Fisher's thesis. *The Accountant's Story* did not match the Spanish-language *Mi Hermano Pablo* in attracting the public's attention, but its foreword rather presciently captures the myth-making process that was soon to take hold in US popular culture.

NARCOS'S AMERICAN DREAM

Escobar's slow-growing legend, nurtured by his brother and many others, accelerated when Netflix debuted *Narcos*, its seventh original drama series, on August 28, 2015. No text in recent popular culture has been as powerful at shaping Escobar's international image as *Narcos*, which begins when he is already the head of an established cartel and swiftly takes viewers to his gruesomely sensational death at the end of the second season (a scene that *El Patrón del Mal* teases in its first episode but takes 112 more installments to reach). Although Escobar is the driving force for much of the action of the first two seasons, the show's protagonists are real-life DEA agents Steve Murphy and Javier Peña, both of whom consulted with the creative team and make brief cameos late in season two. In telling the complex story of Colombian narcotrafficking through the lenses of Murphy and Peña, *Narcos* follows its source material, including Mark Bowden's *Killing Pablo* (2001).

The series also follows a pattern well established in so-called prestige television of narrating crime drama through the voices of white or US American characters. This is to say that *Narcos*, like many of its predecessors and followers, actually does not focus on Escobar as its main character, choosing instead to present DEA agents as the main players in Colombia's narcotics history. Still, examining how *Narcos* constructs its most infamous Colombian character reveals US perceptions of latinidad that pervade depictions of the War on Drugs well into the twenty-first century.

I interviewed Doug Miro, one of the co-creators of *Narcos*, in Detroit in 2017. When I asked the writer and producer how he first approached developing the character, he described Pablo as a variation on the American Dream:

> He pulled himself up from his bootstraps, a poor kid on the farm, by sheer force of will and intelligence, to being the biggest drug dealer in the world. And that is an American story if there ever was one, further romanticized by the fact that he's a criminal, and so he has

that darkness and bad boy element, and he's good looking, he has certain flair . . . he's not subtle. So that combination of flair and romanticism, and no subtlety combined with that American story—I mean he ticks all the boxes for us.[13]

Miro looked wistful as he remembered how exciting it was to develop the character. "He's all the romantic things of a criminal that we like to think about," he continued. "He throws caution to the wind, he had a dream and he found it, so he did live an American Dream."[14] Miro's description is not unlike how Brian De Palma and Oliver Stone have long described *Scarface*, which used the American Dream in its initial marketing campaign and has been understood by critics as a dark take on that theme (like the 1932 film on which it is based).

A scene midway through the third episode of the first season reflects Miro's vision for the Pablo character. The kingpin's power is growing at this point in the series. Frustrated by political obstacles to his expanding empire, especially the threat of extradition to the United States, he embarks on a political career. He has vowed to take on the nation's oligarchs—known as "The Men of Always," which is also the title of the episode—whom he has come to see as the main threats to his business interests. He builds a following among the poorer barrios of Medellín by gifting them housing and soccer fields. Like the real Escobar in 1982, Pablo gets elected to Congress as an alternate. In *Narcos*, he takes the seat when the winning candidate quickly resigns.[15]

The scene, which lasts under two minutes, takes place as Pablo is preparing to assume his seat in Congress. As a shorthand, I will refer to this sequence as "Pablo Dreaming" since that label captures its tone—and because this is what YouTuber Adrian Balint, who uploaded the scene shortly after it aired, called it. "Pablo Dreaming" alternates between two sets of action. In one, Pablo wanders hazily around a field while smoking a joint and looking reflective. In the other, he approaches the capitol, wearing slacks, a crisp white shirt, and a tan blazer. On his way to the congressional chamber, he passes under statues of Tomás Cipriano de Mosquera and Rafael Nuñez, two important nineteenth-century statesmen. Each of these alternating scenes takes place under an ominous sky with sounds of rolling thunder. A second-person voice-over from agent Steve Murphy reflects on Pablo's journey so far—and what it means that it has taken place in Colombia:

> Imagine you were born in a poor family, in a poor city, in a poor country and by the time you were twenty-eight years old you have

so much money you can't even count it. What do you do? You make your dreams come true. The problem is that nobody can control the dreams they have. Especially if you're Pablo Escobar. Especially if you grew up in Colombia. There's a reason magical realism was born in Colombia. It's a country where dreams and reality are conflated, where in their heads people fly as high as Icarus. But even magical realism has its limits . . . and when you get too close to the sun your dreams may melt away.[16]

Following this dream-like sequence, an aide approaches Pablo and tells him that he should not enter the Congress without a tie. The aide offers the one he is wearing, which was a gift from his girlfriend. As Pablo accepts it, offering some cash, he tells him that his girlfriend will be in the history books.

The scene accomplishes much within the narrative arc of the first season. It illustrates Pablo's expansive way of thinking as he attempts to wield power *through*—rather than *against*—national institutions. (Later scenes in the series, as he nears his demise, include a dream sequence in which Pablo is sworn in as president.) Escobar is not an everyday thug but an ambitious, complex character aiming at the upper echelons of Colombian society. The scene also shows the impossibility of Escobar's ambitions, since his brief congressional stint—it was over before it even started—proved to be a source of irritation and humiliation for the rest of his life. The dreamy quality of the scene is a departure for *Narcos*, which typically strives for gritty realism, but it underscores *Narcos*' characterization of Pablo as a deeply human character with dreams, aspirations, and goals.

The action with the tie, which is rooted in actual events, succinctly symbolizes that, despite the illusion of legitimacy he is cultivating, Pablo is and will remain an outsider bound by the socioeconomic conditions of his birth. As soon as the Congress convenes, Justice Minister Rodrigo Lara Bonilla displays an enlarged mugshot of Pablo, accuses him of being a criminal, and demands his immediate resignation.[17] Humiliated and furious, Pablo stands up, removes his tie, and leaves.[18] On his way out, he returns it to the perplexed aide. This ending suggests that Pablo may have endless, if ill-gotten, financial resources, but he lacks the social capital to penetrate the governing class. Lack of social capital was, in reality, a significant motivating factor for Escobar and many other narco kingpins throughout the 1980s. Following the ouster in the Congress, Pablo declares all-out war on the government and the oligarchs running the country, partly because of his humiliation. Rodrigo Lara Bonilla becomes his first political victim.

The moral logic of what happens with the tie is central to the mytholo-

7.2A. Pablo smokes and dreams as he prepares to enter Congress in a pivotal scene from *Narcos*, season one.

7.2B. He takes a tie from a friendly aide in a sequence that underscores the rags-to-riches narrative.

7.3. Wagner Moura's performance as Pablo Escobar inspired countless memes and gifs. Alamy Photo.

gizing of Escobar as a Robin Hood figure, a rich man who has not forgotten his roots. Perhaps for this reason, many other descriptions of Escobar entering Congress depict the incident with the tie with several variations. In *Loving Pablo*, to cite just one example, dozens of male onlookers offer him the ties from around their necks when a guard tries to stop him from entering. In that film, as elsewhere, the message is that Pablo is a man of the people, a little guy who grew rich and made it to the capitol, with many fans among the Colombian people. *Narcos* takes a more intimate approach, showing that Pablo is more comfortable with the helpful staffer than he is with the well-heeled plutocrats who dwell in the chambers of Congress. In this sense, the series seems content to accept Escobar's self-mythologizing as a man of the people.

Along with other images of Pablo looking contemplative, often wearing a fatherly sweater or holding a bulky early cellphone, "Pablo Dreaming" has taken on a life of its own through online fandom practices. Aficionados of the show—and of Wagner Moura's breakout performance—have reproduced the image of Pablo walking through the field, with his joint and his wistful countenance, in countless memes, gifs, and works of digital fan art.

These fandom practices also reveal the complexities of creating a character who is both menacing and appealing. TV critic Emily Nussbaum has observed the rise of what she calls "bad fans" alongside the antiheroic characters who have dominated prestige television. For Nussbaum, bad fans are the viewers who are drawn to and celebrate the violent and salacious facets of the antihero, missing the points of their cautionary tales. "This is particularly true of the much-lauded stream of cable 'dark dramas,'" writes Nussbaum, "whose protagonists shimmer between the repulsive and the magnetic. As anyone who has ever read the comments on a recap can tell you, there has always been a less ambivalent way of regarding an antihero: as a hero."[19] She notes that these fans uncritically embrace characters like Tony Soprano (*The Sopranos*), Walter White (*Breaking Bad*), or Archie Bunker (*All in the Family*), whom Nussbaum sees as bad fandom's earliest object of affection, despite the fact that these shows explicitly critique their bad behavior.

Unlike other televisual antiheroes, however, Pablo Escobar was a real person and an unequivocal villain; he has been linked to at least five thousand murders, including more than one hundred passengers on a bombed commercial flight and almost one thousand police officers in Medellín.[20] This makes the fact that he has become a popular, meme-worthy character on prestige television all the more complicated. Other real-life villains have certainly been revived in the popular imagination through recent televisual storytelling, including cult leaders and serial killers, but none have attracted bad fans, copycat documentaries, or marketing power like Pablo in *Narcos*.

RAGS TO RICHES TO REALISM

Screenwriters have every right to diverge from established history, and every *Narcos* episode begins with a disclaimer that "some of the characters, names, businesses, incidents and certain locations and events have been fictionalized for dramatization purposes." The breadth of history covered by *Narcos*—from the late 1970s to 1993—over just twenty episodes in the first two seasons makes it necessary for the writers to condense historical actions and characters.[21] It makes narrative sense, for example, that *Narcos* condenses Pablo's ill-fated political stint, which lasted from August 1982 to January 1983, into just a single day in the Congress. Having Lara humiliate him and kick him out makes for better television than the months of paperwork that it took to actually prevent the kingpin from becoming a lawmaker.

But what are the implications of fictionalizing a true story within a text that relies heavily on its rootedness in historical fact? This vacillation between truth claims and artistic license is most evident in the show's voice-over narrative. When Murphy asks viewers to imagine that they "were born in a poor family, in a poor city, in a poor country" like Escobar, does it matter that this rags-to-riches narrative does not reflect Escobar's upbringing, which was actually quite comfortable by midcentury Colombian standards? His mother was, in fact, a schoolteacher, which meant that she had an education and regular income, as well as considerable social standing. His father owned a home, as well as some land and animals. By the time that Pablo Escobar was in high school, his family lived in a newly established development that would be roughly equivalent to an American suburb.

But the rags-to-riches narrative of Escobar was not strictly the product of American showrunners. Escobar himself, and his publicists, fashioned a myth of childhood poverty as a key part of representing himself as a Robin Hood figure to those who resided in the popular barrios of Medellín—a key constituency of voters when he ran for office and a pool of foot soldiers for his business dealings. Escobar's vision of himself as a poor person with money can be understood as an attempt to fashion himself as what Eric Hobsbawm called a "social bandit." For Hobsbawm, social bandits are "peasant outlaws whom the lord and state regard as criminals, but who remain within peasant society, and are considered by their people as heroes, champions, avengers, fighters for justice, perhaps even leaders of liberation, and in any case men to be admired, helped, and supported."[22] Escobar seemed to understand the power of the social bandit and, in fact, he idolized and mimicked the likes of Pancho Villa and Al Capone, both of whom have had long posthumous reputations as Robin Hood figures. For Hobsbawm, the social bandit is an intrinsically rural figure, so the very urban Escobar probably would not fulfill his specifications for the term, even though he attempted to tap into the allure of his rural counterparts through mimicry. Of course, by the time that Escobar was gifting schools and soccer fields to the poorer barrios of Medellín, nothing about him resembled a peasant freedom fighter. But, more to the point, Escobar was *never* as poor as he pretended to have been.

In *Killing Pablo*, Mark Bowden provides an important corrective to these cultural fantasies, but media makers have tended to ignore the established history and to reiterate Escobar's false narrative of an impoverished upbringing. According to Bowden, US audiences take comfort in the fact that they can cheer for Pablo because he is an underdog and that, ultimately, they prefer that comforting narrative even when the corrective is offered. In our interview, Bowden could not resist making connections to the power of false narratives in political rhetoric. "You can say a million times that Donald Trump is a corrupt fraud of a businessman who ran every company he owned into bankruptcy," he told me, "and yet the idea that he's this miracle businessman is impermeable. You can't rid people of this idea. People adopt the stories that they like and they believe in them—and if there's someone in the world that even remotely resembles the mythological tale, they get celebrated for being an example. You can't crack that, the strength of that myth."[23]

Narcos, like Escobar himself and scores of other texts, chooses to repeat the myth rather than grapple with Pablo's actual class background. It repeats the poverty myth several times within just the one episode. Early in "The Men of Always," Pablo is convincing Valeria Velez—a thinly veiled character based on Virginia Vallejo—to help him run for Congress. He holds a copy of a fictionalized version of the Colombian newsmagazine *La Semana*, which in April 1983 ran an infamous cover story calling Escobar "Un Robin Hood Paisa"—a Medellín Robin Hood—and celebrating his public service.[24] During a sex act that includes penetrating her with a gun, he tells Valeria that he is going to run for office and that she, a well-connected journalist and member of Colombia's high society, is going to help him win. According to Pablo, he is motivated by class resentment above all else. "Those shitty oligarchs," he tells Valeria. "Those people, all of their lives don't know what it's like to wonder where their next meal is coming from. I come from nothing, Valeria, and I have more money than any of those sons of bitches." Just a few beats later, Murphy's voice-over calls him "the living embodiment of the Colombian dream." Another few beats after that, Pablo describes himself as a "poor person with money." All of this is reinforced later in the episode, during the "Pablo Dreaming" sequence, when Murphy describes Pablo as the product of an impoverished family and community.

As this chapter's epigraphic quote from Mark Bowden implies, media texts of the 2010s and 2020s have constructed narratives that subtly and not-so-subtly celebrate the bandit and the outlaw, so Escobar is an obvious choice as a pop culture antihero. These characters are so prevalent on prestige television that that genre has grown explicitly self-aware regarding the nature of criminality. Perhaps a character on the basic cable series *Fargo*, a bank robber in 1950 Kansas City, says it as well as any theorist attempting to revise Hobsbawm when she explains to her young niece why she sees herself as an outlaw rather than as a criminal:

You see, criminals play the game. Banking and family, an honest dollar for an honest day's work. Politics and voting. And the criminal, he is on the other side of that but still he plays the game. And if he plays it long enough he even starts to talk about going legit.... The outlaw, on the other hand? We reject the game. Society. Ain't nothing organized about our crime because our crime is our freedom.[25]

Given the time period depicted in this season of *Fargo*, this character would never have heard of a Colombian drug trafficker named Pablo Escobar, but both she and Pablo reside in a televisual world that wants to celebrate them as social disrupters.

NARRATION AND POINT OF VIEW

Point of view also shapes how the "Pablo Dreaming" scene makes meaning in relation to the dominant narratives that shape *Narcos*. Although it focuses on Pablo and his Icarus-like overshooting, it is Murphy's voice that narrates the sequence, asking viewers to imagine themselves in Pablo's place as a child of a poor family who wants to make his dreams come true. At this point, the series has already employed second-person voice-over from the white DEA agent, who frequently explains and condenses complex political and social conditions that lead to Colombia's ascent in the international drug trade. Boyd Holbrook plays Murphy as a swaggering but sensitive drug cop who got his start making minor marijuana busts on the streets of Miami but works his way up to the DEA's most important case. In the aftermath of the hunt for Escobar, the real Steve Murphy has told and retold the story of his involvement to countless reporters and audiences. He is a key informant in Bowden's *Killing Pablo* and, following the success of *Narcos*, he became a popular public speaker. At the time of this writing, he and his DEA partner Javier Peña co-own DEA Narcos, a company that promotes their public appearances. This is the only instance in which the voice-over purports to provide insight into either Pablo's motivations or what being Colombian might have to do with his criminal ambitions.[26]

As I have argued previously in this book, narrating Latinx and Latin American stories from the perspectives of white protagonists is not a new practice. Examples abound of films focused on Latin American narcotrafficking that are told wholly from the perspectives of white North American interlocutors: schlocky and explicitly racist fare like Chuck Norris's *Delta Force 2: The Colombian Connection* (1990); Johnny Depp's critically lauded performance in Jonathan Demme's *Blow* (2001); and the Tom Cruise vehicle *American Made* (2017). *Escobar: Paradise Lost* (2014) focuses not on the titular character but on a white Canadian surfer who is drawn into his orbit when he romances Escobar's niece. In each of these films, and dozens more like them that have depicted narcotrafficking from the early 1980s to the present, white American lead characters make their way through a drug underworld, whether as cops, smugglers, or profiteers. Colombians, other Latin Americans, and US Latinx characters languish as menacing background players. In *Narcos*, like some of the other texts mentioned here, the centrality of the white protagonist is heightened by the fact that the story is narrated in his voice; it is Murphy who decides what is important for the viewer to know about Escobar, cocaine trafficking, and Colombia.

The primacy of the white male US American experience reflects Hollywood's ongoing refusal to bank on Latinx stories and performers. The rights to Mark Bowden's *Killing Pablo* had been optioned in the early 2000s, but the film was never made, partly, according to the author, because no studio was willing to produce a film carried by a Latinx actor, even one with a main character as devilishly compelling as Escobar. Bowden told me in an interview what happened when he shared his intention of adapting the book into a feature film with a famous director. "I gave him one of the original copies of *Killing Pablo*," Bowden said. "And he told me: 'This is great but they're never going to get this made because they're all Hispanic characters and Hollywood is not into that. Hollywood isn't going to make a movie with all of these Latinos; there's got to be a role for Tom Cruise or something in it.'"[27] Perhaps this explains why Pablo's ambitions, and his false rags-to-riches narrative, along with some deep thoughts about what it means to be Colombian, are voiced in Holbrook's southern drawl rather than by Wagner Moura as Pablo.[28] Ultimately, there is an irony in the fact that the sequence, which explicitly grapples with Pablo's Colombianness and the literary genre of magical realism (a subject that merits a study of its own) is better understood as a reflection of its creators' interests in framing him in distinctly US American terms.[29]

AFTER *NARCOS*: ESCOBAR AS GLOBAL BRAND

Narcos appeared at the start of an Escobar resurgence in US and global popular cultures. Following the success of the first season, writers, producers, and directors made something of a run on Medellín, producing a spate of filmic and televisual texts that focus on Escobar's Colombia.[30] Escobar himself appears as a physical presence to varying degrees in these texts, from a fleeting moment in the Bryan Cranston drama *The Infiltrator* (2016) to a menacing secondary role in *Escobar: Paradise Lost* (2014). In *Loving Pablo* (2017), based on Vallejo's best-selling memoir and loathed by critics, Javier Bardem plays Pablo as a magnetic but menacing romantic lead. Bardem was, in fact, first linked to playing Pablo in 2007, in the film adaptation of *Killing Pablo*, though that film ultimately was not made. In one of the rare instances in which Escobar has been played for laughs, Adrian Grenier, in his role as Vincent Chase, dons a fat suit and a fake mustache to play Pablo for his drama project, a movie titled *Medellín*, in the third season of HBO's *Entourage* (which predates *Narcos* by several years). The point of the storyline is that only a movie star would have the hubris to take on a role for which he was so ill suited. Whether Escobar is in the background or the forefront of these films, each depiction has contributed in its own way to the iconization of Escobar about which David Fisher writes in the foreword to *The Accountant's Story*.

Escobar has also inspired video and board games, action figures, memes, tattoos, and pop songs and albums. His image appears on T-shirts, keychains, tote bags, bumper stickers, and many other consumer goods. At times, he has appeared in surprising places: In 2017, a *Miami Herald* reporter noted that the Walmart website was selling a Christmas sweater emblazoned with Escobar wearing a Santa hat and the tongue-in-cheek message of "Let It Snow."[31] In 2018, I purchased Escobar-themed coasters from a kiosk in a tourist district in Istanbul and a "plata o plomo" T-shirt from the mall in Mishawaka, Indiana, near my workplace. (The phrase, meaning "silver or lead," is a famous Escobar catchphrase that refers to the fact that you can only work with or against the cartel.) The next year a conglomerate of game designers released an officially licensed *Narcos* board game that allows users to play as various characters from the series, including Pablo. On the box, a detailed drawing depicts Wagner Moura as Pablo seated behind a huge stack of cash. "Power is measured by the gram," it reads. I have no doubt that by the time this book is published, there will be a slew of new Escobar merchandise available for purchase online and at my local shopping center.

Like the fictional Tony Montana, Escobar has become an especially important motif in rap and hip-hop music. The title of Kanye West's 2016 album *The Life of Pablo*, released about ten months after *Narcos* appeared on Netflix, is, in part, a reference to Escobar. The list of rap and hip-hop artists who have mentioned the kingpin includes, among many others, top acts like Gucci Mane, Lil Wayne (sample lyric: "favorite subject was P.E.: Pablo Escobar"), Nas, and Migos. Soulja Boy's track titled "Pablo Escobar" typifies rappers' embrace of Escobar in its chorus:

> When you getting all this money
> These niggas they look at you funny
> These niggas thirsty bitches hungry
> All I wanna be is Pablo

Soulja Boy sounds like many of his peers when he says that he wants to be Pablo. One verse sounds strikingly like the narrative that drives the *Narcos* episode, "The Men of Always":

> They say I wouldn't make it
> Now I'm ridin' drop top 2014 Bentley all through Las Vegas
> I know that they mad that I made it, I know that they hate it
> I look at the look on they faces
> We switching the money by cases.

In Soulja Boy's song, like the *Narcos* episode, the protagonist is motivated by the odds being stacked against him. He gains his strength from being doubted and winds up at the top of his game.

Rap artists' homages to Escobar have also gone beyond their lyrics. The same year that *The Life of Pablo* was released, rapper 2Chainz and a business partner opened EscoBar, a Pablo Escobar-themed tapas restaurant and bar/hookah lounge in Atlanta's trendy Castleberry Hill neighborhood. The décor included Escobar's infamous mugshot blown up to poster size, a Medellín streetscape mural, and the front of a gold Mercedes that juts onto the dance floor, a physical representation of Latinx excess. When I visited in 2017, the place was packed with a long line waiting outside. In 2020, Escobar Inc, a holding company established by Roberto Escobar to control and commercialize Pablo's image, filed a lawsuit and injunction against the restaurant's owners for infringing on its intellectual property rights. They eventually settled out of court and the restaurant, now franchised in other locations, has been rebranded as a tapas bar called Esco.[32] As of 2022, Escobar Inc focused on Pablo Escobar-themed cryptocurrency.

A few months after EscoBar opened, Wiz Khalifa sparked controversy when he posted pictures of himself visiting Escobar's grave and Edificio Mónaco in Medellín to social media. The photos depicted the rap star smoking marijuana (Escobar was a frequent smoker) and laying flowers on the tomb. Medellín mayor Federico Gutiérrez, the person responsible for the banners that eventually covered Edificio Mónaco, was not pleased and called Khalifa a "scoundrel" for venerating Escobar through the photos. The rapper later apologized, but he and his peers have continued to celebrate Escobar in their lyrics.

Puerto Rican singers in the reggaeton genre have also produced a sizable body of work celebrating Escobar. Popular artists Farruko, J Álvarez, and Anuel AA frequently glamorize the kingpin in their lyrics. When J Álvarez arrived in Medellín to perform at the opening of the city's famous Festival of Flowers in 2016, he was wearing a colorful T-shirt with the phrase

"I'm Cartel" printed on the front and the name "Escobar" with the number 49 emblazoned on the back. He had several interviews with reporters throughout the day leading up to the concert but received a phone call from Mayor Gutiérrez in the afternoon. The mayor informed the reggaetonero that his set would be cancelled unless he changed the offending shirt, which, according to reports, the mayor described as "an offense to this city and to the nation." Gutiérrez was quoted as telling the singer, "We are thousands of victims who suffered this tragedy and we continue to suffer. Keep that in mind because that man has cost us many lives."[33] Álvarez got the message and appeared onstage in an official Flower Festival T-shirt reading "Que viva Medellín, andamos de rumba" ("Long live Medellín, we are partying"). Colombian artists Maluma and J Balvin, both of whom are from Medellín, have also publicly denounced foreign reggaeton performers for idolizing Escobar.

Despite the incidents with the Medellín mayor and other well-documented cases of frustration with Escobar's popularity with foreigners, Colombian culture industries have begun to capitalize on foreign interest in the kingpin. According to a government report, foreign tourism to Colombia increased by 9.4 percent in just one year from 2017 to 2018, with more than 22 percent of those visitors coming from the United States.[34] Pablo Escobar tours cater to US and international tourists in Medellín, so much so that his grave, his lavish self-built prison, and the rooftop where he met his demise frequently draw English-speaking crowds (including my students and me). Most of these tours are targeted at foreign tourists and offered in English. In her analysis of pop music and "global Colombianidades," María Elena Cepeda notes that "the culture industry built around Escobar constitutes a source of distress and resentment for many Colombians" but that "endless accumulation of tell-all books, films, games, and television series simultaneously provide a significant source of capital for many."[35] The sites across Medellín represent one method of profiting from the fascination that many foreigners have for Escobar (and what might be called "Escobar-adjacent") information and entertainment.

Members of Escobar's immediate family have also taken active roles in keeping the kingpin's legacy alive. As mentioned above, his brother Roberto published a popular book on his experiences working inside the cartel that was translated into English as *The Accountant's Story*. Anthropologist Patrick Naef has described Roberto posing for pictures with US tourists in front of his and his brother's "wanted" poster in the small museum that he ran in Medellín as a memorial to Pablo.[36] Pablo Escobar's son Juan Pablo, who fled Colombia with his mother and sister shortly after his father's killing in 1993 and started a new life in Argentina under the name

Sebastián Marroquín, also wrote a best-selling memoir and is featured in the documentary *Sins of My Father* (2009). In both these works, Marroquín takes a contrite posture, framing his father's excesses as a cautionary tale and his own life's work that of telling the world just how wrong he was. He also travels extensively to spread these messages in-person appearances.

Along with thirty-six other audience members from around the world, I took part in a paid conversation with Marroquín via Zoom in fall 2020. Over the course of two hours together, he hewed closely to his standard apologetic narrative and promoted himself as being on an educational mission. But Marroquín also discussed his father's growing popularity and was prickly in regard to pop culture's representations of his family. He complained that the makers of *Narcos* and *El Patrón del Mal* had no interest in working with him and claimed that both refused to tell the truth, so it fell to him to tell the "real" story of Pablo Escobar.[37] (This is a common claim across narcomedia created by insiders: that they are the holder of the story and that their narratives should take precedent.) I asked Marroquín if, given his criticisms of popular culture and the ongoing problem of glamorizing Pablo, there is any ethical way to represent his father. He told me that he was dreaming of a day when a company would come along to help him tell the "real story," a mission that is especially important because, according to him, he has received thousands of messages from kids around the world who want to be like Pablo Escobar because of how media narratives represent him. "We need to tell these stories," he said, "but we have to be very careful in the consequences of how we portray a guy like my father."[38]

Beyond the United States and Colombia and Escobar's own circle, a spate of Pablo Escobar-themed businesses have garnered attention and criticism around the world, including an ice cream parlor in Kuwait, a strip club in Russia, and bars in France, Singapore, and Argentina.[39] In 2018, Colombia's ambassador to Canada published an open letter to the owners of a new Escobar-themed restaurant in Vancouver, reminding them of the damage that Escobar had inflicted upon Colombia and asking them to reconsider the name and aesthetics of the place.[40] The next year, Pablo's Escoburgers, a pop-up hamburger joint in Melbourne, Australia, was serving its namesake sandwiches with a line of white powder and a rolled-up fake $100 bank note on top; its vegetarian counterpart came with a small baggie of white powder and a tiny spoon.

Whether they are produced in Colombia, the United States, or elsewhere, these cultural texts have a unifying concept: converting the most notorious criminal in world history into a marketable brand. Escobar has, in fact, become a branding tool connoting edginess and illicit pleasures, as the use of his image as a theme for bars and restaurants attests. The promoters of the much-derided Fyre Festival, to cite one infamous example, promised a luxury music experience in the Caribbean for moneyed millennials. Instead, it imploded due to disastrously poor planning, inspiring morbid fascination in news media, two documentaries, and several lawsuits. In videos posted on social media, organizers claimed the event would take place on a private island formerly owned by Pablo Escobar (though it had actually once been owned by Escobar co-conspirator Carlos Lehder and the owner at the time expressly forbade any association with cocaine cartels in marketing for the festival).[41] Such was the power of Escobar as a marketing tool in the aftermath of *Narcos*.

Perhaps, then, it makes sense to inquire what it might mean to call Pablo Escobar a brand. Carlo Bernard, a co-creator of *Narcos*, whom I interviewed in February 2019, describes the creation of the show as building on an existing brand. "He was already a name brand, obviously, before the show, which is part of how the show got made," he told me. "I think the show served to reinvigorate his brand awareness, maybe introduce it to a different generation of kids."[42] Bernard makes a good point in that the show proved tremendously successful at renewing popular interest in Escobar, but his characterization of Pablo Escobar as a name brand is especially revealing, considering that *Narcos* helped to turn Escobar into a global media commodity.

Netflix's marketing of *Narcos* has also drawn on edgy modes of content creation and new media platforms to generate buzz for the show. Shortly after the release of the first season, the company partnered with the *Wall Street Journal* to create an elaborate online advertorial focused on "Cocainenomics" that included timelines, interactive maps, archival photographs, and informative essays written by journalists.[43] At the top of the page, users could use their trackpads to move around a pile of cocaine. After engaging with the site's resources, they could take a quiz to determine if they had the knowledge to "stay one step ahead" like Pablo.

Shortly after "Cocainenomics" became available, a minor scandal arose when Netflix placed a giant billboard—not exactly new media—featuring actor Wagner Moura posing as Pablo and the suggestive slogan "Oh, blanca Navidad" ("Oh, White Christmas") in Madrid's Puerta del Sol public square. The billboard inspired indignation and a petition from Colombians in Spain and abroad. Even Colombia's Nobel Prize-winning president, Juan Manuel Santos, weighed in on the controversy. "The series is very good," he told an interviewer on Spanish radio, "but we Colombians lived the drama of Pablo Escobar and that suffering still hurts. Escobar should not be held up as a hero."[44] This sentiment was repeated thousands of times in op-eds, letters to the editor, and blog and social media posts.

7.4. In December 2016, a billboard in Madrid caused another skirmish in the war over Pablo Escobar's image and legacy. Alamy Photo.

These speak to the main tension I have explored in this chapter. For media makers in the United States, Escobar transformed from drug war villain to sexy, edgy filmic and televisual antihero. For many Colombians, this is an act of historical amnesia that must be corrected.

CONCLUSION

Almost one year to the day after my initial trip to Medellín, in which my students and I visited Edificio Mónaco shortly before its destruction, I returned to the city with my research assistant, Mariana, to interview Federico Gutiérrez, the mayor who had taken on the likes of J Álvarez and Wiz Khalifa. Over ice-cold lemonade on his apartment's terrace, Gutiérrez, who had recently left office, frequently mentioned his efforts regarding the Mónaco site. He took pride in having placed the banners that I saw the previous year and in presiding over the destruction of Escobar's most notorious Medellín address. Our curiosity piqued, Mariana and I headed straight to the site in the Poblado neighborhood after we wrapped up the interview. What I saw there astonished me. In just one year since its destruction, the

7.5. The city of Medellín built a parklike memorial to victims of narco violence at the former site of Edificio Mónaco. Photograph by Sara Rodriguez.

hulking building had been replaced with a meticulously planned memorial park called the Parque Conmemorativo Inflexión (Inflection Memorial Park), conceived and constructed as part of a city project that translates as "Medellín embraces its history."

The character of the block, which had been dominated by the Mónaco, has been thoroughly transformed. Now one can stand in front of where the entrance gate had been and see through to the next street, making the entire streetscape bright and airy rather than imposing and oppressive. A curvy wall etched with victims' names, reminiscent of the Vietnam Veterans Memorial in Washington, DC, takes up a good deal of the memorial's physical space. One side of the wall shows a timeline of bombings across Colombia from the 1980s to the 2000s. On the other side of the wall, thousands of small holes drilled into the granite represent individual victims. They cast a warm glow when the wall is illuminated from the inside at night. Elsewhere on the site are individual memorials to some of the highest-profile victims of narco violence, including Rodrigo Lara; quotes from each of the memorialized victims are etched into stone monoliths that resemble headstones.

7.6. Pablo Escobar–themed merchandise for sale on a Medellín street. Alamy Photo.

Like the Museo Casa de la Memoria (Memory House Museum), an interactive museum dedicated to cultural memory and armed conflict on the other side of the city, Parque Inflexión is clearly intended to reframe the historical narratives associated with Colombia's cartel era, shifting the focus from the perpetrators of violence to the victims. It is the closest thing, at the time of this writing, that Colombia has to a national memorial to the victims of narco violence. Even so, it is a tiny bit of real estate in a city and country still grappling with huge repercussions from the narco era. Gutiérrez and others cannot simply replace one narrative with another, as is reflected in the fact that even after the park was inaugurated, one could still buy stylized portraits of the Mónaco's infamous resident just a few meters from the sobering memorial.

Politicians, cultural workers, and real estate holders in Bogotá, Cali, and smaller cities have been forced to make similar decisions regarding the physical remains of 1980s and 1990s narco terrorism. In Cali, for example, Icesi University has incorporated an expropriated narco mansion into its campus, offering dance and music classes in rooms where El Caballista, a kingpin who now sits in a US federal prison, once held court. In the capital, as I write these pages, a former narco estate is being transformed into the Chinese embassy. Between Medellín and Bogotá, Escobar's sprawling estate, Hacienda Napoles, has been repurposed as a family-friendly theme park. The park's safari theme capitalizes on Escobar's fascination with exotic fauna, including the famous pet hippos, whose feral descendants now populate a growing herd that lives in the Río Magdalena. The park also incorporates the ruins of its original owner's sprawling hacienda and a replica of the entrance gate, which included a smaller-scale model of the plane used by Escobar to transport cocaine to the United States. These are only a few examples of what anthropologist Patrick Naef describes as Colombia's "Narco-heritage."[45] Surely other models will emerge for dealing with the countless former narco properties located all over Colombia, from remote *fincas* to some of the most exclusive urban addresses. The process will undoubtedly be complicated by the global fascination with Pablo Escobar and other cartel leaders who are valorized in shows like *Narcos*.

In Medellín, where Escobar's Edificio Mónaco no longer looms over its neighbors, many *paisas* have made peace with Escobar-themed tourism—or at least have shown a willingness to profit from it, as evidenced by the many Pablo Escobar-themed trinkets and T-shirts for sale on the streets of Medellín. City officials have determined that a memorial commemorating the victims of narco violence is more appropriate for the site, but time will tell whether the park becomes a regular stop on the narco tours or a space for contemplation for the locals. Even without the Mónaco, the city and the country must continue to come to terms with outsiders' fascination with Pablo's powerful legend. The building came down in mere seconds, but the interest of US popular culture in Escobar cannot be easily obliterated.

EPILOGUE

"IT'S TIME FOR A WHITE MAN TO LEAVE THE BUILDING"
Centering Latinidad in Narcomedia

Kurt Sutter created *Mayans M.C.* as a Latinx-centered spinoff of his hit series *Sons of Anarchy*, which, over the course of its 2008 to 2014 run on FX, inspired critical acclaim and a loyal fan base. When *Mayans M.C.* was wrapping up its second season and a reporter asked Sutter about the prospects for a third, he announced that he would hand over the control of the show to fellow executive producer Elgin James, who is of mixed race. "It's time for a white man to leave the building," said Sutter.[1] Although it is not uncommon for a showrunner to hand over control of a successful series after a few seasons, Sutter's answer is somewhat unique in Hollywood and the TV industry, which from its beginning to the present has been slow to hand over control to people of color.

This is especially true in the context of a mainstream show and successful franchise like *Mayans M.C.* It is also notable partly because of Elgin James, who became the showrunner, and his personal history as a gang member. James claimed to *Variety* in 2018 that his background had prepared him to helm the show and tell stories from a POC perspective. "This isn't just a TV show for Latinos. It's for everyone who feels disregarded. Who's felt invisible. Who's felt diminished," he told the industry newspaper. "The diversity starts in the writers room [sic]. What is cool is to look around the room and realize these are all people of my same complexion, to look around the set and see all these people working so hard who are mostly invisible to the world."[2] James seems to agree with Sutter that white people telling Black and brown people's stories has run its course.

Like its predecessor, *Mayans M.C.* focuses on a California motorcycle gang (the "M.C." in the title stands for "motorcycle club," which members

199

euphemistically call their gang) that deals in various illicit activities, including running drugs across the US-Mexico border. Narratively complex and hyperviolent, it exists in the diegetic world of *Sons of Anarchy* but pushes the narrative in new directions focused on the politics of identity, race, and ethnicity in the borderlands. In the first shot of the first episode, the camera focuses on a piece of graffito on the border wall: "Divided We Fall/Dividimos Caemos." This is an apt beginning for the show, which consistently grapples with the violence of the border and US culpability in perpetuating the drug wars. The second season opens with a shot of the US flag as seen from a hole in the border fence, and the show continues to underscore its border theme through not-so-subtle mise-en-scène.

In fact, *Mayans M.C.* uses many of the border tropes employed by *Weeds*. Its action involves transborder tunnels, interracial encounters, undocumented border crossers, a white American woman engaged in a criminal enterprise, a handsome and well-dressed Latinx kingpin with whom that white woman is involved, and menacing Mexican and Chicano henchmen. Also like *Weeds*, it is set largely in a fictional border town ("Santo Padre" on the US side and a sister city, "Santa Madre," on the Mexican side). The show also resembles some of the fast-paced and hyper-violent action that made *Breaking Bad* a landmark of prestige television, as I examine in chapter 5, and some of the themes prevalent in *Narcos*, such as a focus on corruption within the governmental systems that are meant to enforce the War on Drugs. In other words, there is a lot about *Mayans M.C.* that could make it standard narcomedia fare with little to add to the conversations that I staged in this book's chapters.

However, the series differs strikingly from *Weeds*, *Breaking Bad*, and *Narcos* in how it centers Latinx characters and voices. At the center of the show is main character EZ Reyes (J. D. Pardo), a Chicano member of the Mayans who had once been a promising student at Stanford but whose education stopped when he killed a cop. After his release from prison, he joins his brother in the titular motorcycle gang. EZ reads poetry and still carries a flame for his white high school sweetheart, Emily (Sarah Bolger), who now happens to be married to the head of the Galindo Cartel. EZ and more than a dozen other Latinx characters navigate the borderlands and its histories of violence and exploitation. Most have complex emotional lives and a wide range of motivations for their actions. In other words, they are fully human. Pathetically, that is a rather novel concept in the world of narcomedia.

Just a few months before FX aired the pilot of *Mayans M.C.*, President Trump ranted about undocumented migrants in a meeting at the White House that echoed his campaign rhetoric but was even more dehumanizing.

"We have people coming into the country, or trying to come in—we're stopping a lot of them," the *New York Times* reported that he said. "You wouldn't believe how bad these people are. These aren't people, *these are animals*, and we're taking them out of the country at a level and at a rate that's never happened before."[3] Rhetoric that sounded outrageous from a presidential candidate had gone fully mainstream after Trump took office, so it is all the more significant that *Mayans M.C.* would shift the white-centric perspective that is prevalent in narcomedia and tell its story from the point of view of the "bad hombres."

Opening credits that began appearing in the show's third season, after Sutter's departure, illustrate an intensified critical stance against Trump's and his followers' ideas about Mexican Americans and the American Dream. The credits begin by juxtaposing still and moving images evoking US migration myths, including Ellis Island around the turn of the twentieth century and the Statue of Liberty. But then the credits focus on Southern California, starting with a white family barbecuing in their sunny backyard but then shifting to images familiar to anyone who knows the Latinx history of the region: the Zoot Suit riots and violence against Mexican Americans; a model illustrating plans for Dodgers Stadium, which displaced an established Latinx community; César Chavez; farmworker strikes; and the like. These images then blend into War on Drugs imagery, including Nancy Reagan in a "Just Say No" button. The credits close with images of a hypermilitarized border intercut with more historical images, including one of Pancho Villa that cuts to a 1960s Chicano bike gang that cuts to the Mayans. The message is twofold and clear: Mexican Americans aren't included in the American Dream and outlaw "clubs" like the Mayans inherit a history of resistance.

The action of the series is not as historically sweeping as the opening credits, but *Mayans M.C.* does address big questions about Chicano history and identity. Most remarkably, its storylines make the aftermath of cartel violence and the trauma that reverberates for generations a central theme. EZ is compelled to take up with the Mayans partly by his grief over losing family members to cartel violence, which has affected his family for at least two generations. Even if his methods of overcoming grief are questionable, it is clear that he is traumatized by living under the specter of violence for his whole life. His father Felipe (Edward James Olmos, whose TV career stretches back to *Miami Vice*) had been a corrupt Mexican drug agent who worked for the cartel in the seventies and eighties, but went legit and assumed a new identity when he started a family. Years later, agents for the Galindo Cartel killed his wife, which sends EZ, then a college student, on a downward spiral.

This narrative of historical trauma and revenge is compounded when the Mayans surreptitiously partner with Los Olvidados, a rebel group that is made up of the children of the cartel's victims. Los Olvidados, which can be translated as "the lost ones," ruthlessly fight the cartel, sabotaging shipments of drugs and ambushing their gangs. Like EZ, they will resort to violence when necessary. Their motivations can also seem somewhat murky. When a character assumes that Adelita, the leader of Los Olvidados, is motivated by revenge, she corrects him. "Vengeance is just the match," she tells him, "Fire is much more complicated."[4] This implies that her willingness to fight is not just personal but also motivated by something bigger. This is actually a good metaphor for the series as a whole: It is plot-driven but also tackles systemic issues and problems that transcend the actions of individual characters. It is probably not a coincidence that Adelita's nom de guerre evokes women revolutionaries in Mexican history.

Mayans M.C. continuously acknowledges that the violence that comes with drug trafficking creates lasting trauma. Even Miguel Galindo (Danny Pino), the head of the cartel, deals with childhood trauma from what he has been told was the kidnapping and murder of his baby brother. If *Mayans M.C.* has an overarching theme, it is grief, as various characters grieve lost children, siblings, parents, lovers, and comrades. The series takes their grief seriously and follows their means of coping, whether positive or negative, over the course of several episodes or even seasons. In the world of narcomedia, this complex depiction of the relationship between history, violence, and trauma is strikingly atypical and, for a viewer, it can feel downright radical to follow complex Latinx characters as they heal, make mistakes, and then try to heal again.

I do not mean to imply that *Mayans M.C.* offers a fix for the representational problems evident in *Weeds* or *Traffic* or *Breaking Bad* or *Narcos* or that it is a superior or more ethical text. The show does, in fact, suffer from several problems that are typical of prestige television that I mentioned in previous chapters. For example, with the exception of Adelita, which is arguably one of the meatiest roles for a Latina in recent television history, Latinas represent only a fraction of the Latinx speaking roles in the hypermasculine world of the show. A blonde white woman is at the center of much of a romantic triangle between EZ and a Mexican crime boss, once again framing white femininity in idealized terms and giving a white woman the female lead of the series. When Latinas do appear, they are frequently victimized by the Latino men around them, including in one gruelingly violent scene in which one of the Mayans drowns his own mother in her bathtub. Furthermore, although the Mayans do business with white gangs (and a Samoan gang early in season one), the show's racial schema does not include many African Americans.

Despite these gripes, *Mayans M.C.* does represent a fitting way to conclude this study of narcomedia. It is important that the series features a Latino lead and ensemble, which, in the media climate of the late 2010s, was still a remarkable fact. According to a survey conducted by the Annenberg Inclusion Initiative at the University of Southern California, from 2007 to 2018—the year that *Mayans M.C.* aired its first season—only 3 percent of films had a Latinx lead character and only 4.5 percent of speaking characters were Latinos.[5] This gross underrepresentation does not even begin to capture the politics of misrepresentation like those that I have examined in this book, as well as the myriad stereotypes I have not mentioned that frame Latinos and Latinas as Others.

However, media activism has begun to call attention to the problem. As Mary Beltrán notes in *Latino TV*, some Latinx writers, directors, and producers organized in late 2020 around the hashtag #EndLatinXclusion and wrote a scathing letter to Hollywood, demanding an increase in Latinx representation by Latinx creators. This form of media activism shows that, finally, at least there are enough Latinos working behind the scenes to make a fuss.[6] *Mayans M.C.* demonstrates that a popular, mainstream series can center Latinx experiences at the border and, despite political rhetoric that does the opposite, can construct Latinx characters as three-dimensional human beings. It is an imperfect text, but aren't they all?

These days, I no longer sleep in front of the TV, but I do still watch a lot of it. Luckily, there are many more ways of engaging with complex and compelling Latinx storytelling than there were when I was a kid. *Mayans M.C.*, which was just renewed as I was finishing writing this book, was joined by several recent series on TV and streaming that tell Latinx stories from Latinx points of view. These include now-cancelled standouts like *Gentefied* (Netflix, 2020–2021), *On My Block* (Netflix, 2018–2021), *Vida* (Starz, 2018–2020), and *One Day at a Time* (Netflix, 2017–2019; Pop, 2020), all of which included Latinxs behind the camera as well as in front. Each of these series was short-lived but attracted critical praise and audiences loyal enough to campaign to save it from cancellation.[7] They also refused to sacrifice complexity in order to create "positive" representations of latinidad, which—as I have stressed throughout this book—is not the antidote for negative representational practices. Beyond Latinx representation, some of my favorite newer shows challenge the white-centrism that has been prevalent in narcomedia and on TV in general, such as the hilarious and heartfelt *Reservation Dogs* (FX, 2021–), which has a mostly Native and Indigenous cast and production team, and *South Side* (Comedy Central, 2019; HBO Max, 2021–2022), an excellent and slyly ambitious stoner comedy, which is made in Chicago by a mostly Black cast and crew.

None of these series focuses on the narcotics trade as its central theme, but all demonstrate how people of color can construct their own narratives outside the confines of white-centrism and the other modes of Othering that I have examined throughout *Narcomedia*. They also seem invested in speaking to people of color in their audiences rather than making white audiences comfortable, as so many of their predecessors had done. Some of these recent shows may have already wrapped, but let us hope that their creators keep dreaming up new ways of telling their stories.

ACKNOWLEDGMENTS

Many Notre Dame colleagues—past and present—helped give me the encouragement, feedback, and resources to make this book possible. There are too many to name here, but I am especially thankful to Tom Anderson, Ashlee Bird, Jaimie Bleck, Tobias Boes, Pete Cajka, Annie Gilbert Coleman, Kathleen Sprows Cummings, Laurel Daen, Erika Doss, Luis Fraga, Paloma Garcia-Lopez, Korey Garibaldi, Perin Gürel, Therese Hanlon, Jennifer Huynh, Jason Kelly, Tim Matovina, Maria McKenna, Rebecca McKenna, Margaret Meserve, Marie Lynn Miranda, Marisel Moreno, Ernest Morrell, Sarah Mustillo, Jennifer Parker, Sarah Quesada, Francisco Robles, Anne García Romero, Bob Schmuhl, Siiri Scott, Tom Tweed, and Sophie White. Among my Notre Dame crew, Katie Schlotfeldt stands apart as a particularly ardent supporter and cheerleader who helped tremendously with the logistics for writing this book. This book is made possible in part by support from the Institute for Scholarship in the Liberal Arts, College of Arts and Letters, University of Notre Dame. The Institute for Latino Studies at Notre Dame was especially supportive of this project, and I thank all those affiliated with ILS for helping me workshop parts of this book while I was living in Colombia. Thanks to its fabulous directors, Luis Fraga and Timothy Matovina, I was able to take a life-changing sabbatical in 2019–2020 that provided the time to read for, reflect on, and write this book. Earlier in the process of conceptualizing this book, Luis and Tim also kindly encouraged me to pursue this dream project over another, staider, idea. Pamela Wojcik provided a great model for keeping one's soul and humor intact while working as a department chair. Pam Butler, a friend from long before we converged at Notre Dame, continues to serve as a key sounding board and support. Kate Marshall and Ian Newman are more than colleagues; I thank them and Evie and Nesta for being my Forest Avenue family.

Although I had been to Colombia many times prior to January 2019, a very special trip from that time shaped some of the ideas in this book. Thanks to generous funding from Notre Dame International's Insider

Project, as well as from John McGreevy and the College of Arts and Letters, I was able to bring five students and two colleagues to Cali and Medellín for research and education. I thank students Irla Atanda, Bailey Kendall, Julie Mardini, Marcela Gonzalez Fajardo, and Diego Reynoso. Irla will always have a special place in my heart for returning to Cali for her thesis research and for being a remarkable student and friend. Photographer Barbara Johnston recorded it all with good humor and created many of the images that appear throughout this book and on the cover. The cover collage, designed by Taylor Packet Johnson, captures the spirit of the trip and, more broadly, the beauty of Colombia despite the ugly realities depicted in narcomedia texts. It stands as a good metaphor for the mix of beauty and pathos found in making, consuming, and analyzing narcomedia texts—and reflects my hope for a brighter future for that remarkable country. Amanda Skofstad provided thought-provoking questions every step of the way and a gorgeously written article that captured our adventures. Guest speaker David Restrepo changed my understanding of the coca leaf and its potential in a post-War-on-Drugs Colombia and, along with Ezra Axelrod, provided great friendship when I returned to Cali.

I was lucky to receive reports from two incisive reviewers for this book: María Elena Cepeda and an anonymous reader. Both reports were models of the form: thorough but kind, supportive but tough. The finished book reflects the care they put into reading and responding to the manuscript, and I am especially grateful to Dr. Cepeda, whose advice improved many aspects of the manuscript, especially its engagement with Latinx media studies. This was all facilitated by Kerry Webb, my wonderful editor, and Nicole Guidotti-Hernández and Lorgia García-Peña, the editors of the Latinx: The Future Is Now series. I am deeply grateful to Nicole for recruiting me to this phenomenal series and for guiding me at every step (and in many more matters unrelated to this book). I am also thankful to Robert Devens at the University of Texas Press for encouraging my work with great enthusiasm and to Lynne Ferguson and Sally Furgeson for editing it so carefully. I can't thank Rio Hartwell enough for helping develop and edit the manuscript before I submitted it to the press, for doing the indexing, and, most importantly, for cheering on this project with incredible patience and devotion. Rio's thoughtful eye improved my work immeasurably. Jorge Rios provided crucial assistance in procuring and selecting the images for this book. I very much appreciate his resourcefulness and support in helping me cross the finish line.

I owe huge thanks to several individuals and organizations who invited me to give talks related to this research and who, in turn, provided crucial feedback. These include Jessica Namakkal at Duke University (who also belongs in the list of friends below), the Japanese Association for American Studies, Anne Martínez and the University of Groningen, graduate students in Latin American Studies at the University of Cologne, the Spanish Department at Furman University, Joseph Rezek and the American Literature and Culture Seminar at Harvard, the School for International Studies at Peking University, and the Notre Dame Alumni group of New Haven. I am also grateful to Aldona Pobutsky for sharing her wonderful book on Pablo Escobar in Colombian pop culture with me when it was still in galleys and to my fabulous and hilarious former research assistant, Irma Rodenhuis.

This book benefitted tremendously from the generosity of several cultural workers who sat with me for interviews to discuss their work. Special thanks to Tanner Cipriano, a beloved former student who also happened to work for *Narcos* and helped to arrange for a visit to that show's writers' room. I am grateful to him and for the warm welcome from the creative staff of the show. Co-creator Dough Miro sat for not one but two candid interviews. His co-creator also welcomed me into the writers' room and then talked with me for a long while after a busy day of plotting a season of *Narcos Mexico*. Former Medellín mayor Federico Gutierrez welcomed my research assistant and me into his home for an afternoon of conversation about the city and Pablo Escobar's legacy and the city's public image. Author Mark Bowden talked with me for hours about his book *Killing Pablo* and its influence on other works.

I warmly thank the many friends who believed in this project, told me what to watch (and sometimes suffered through watching with me), and allowed me to vent over the course of producing this published work. Thanks especially to Mike Amezcua, Cornell Bar, Jenn Blair, Laura Gamboa, Lynn Hudson, Sonjia Hyon, Jonna Kosalko, Aaron Lecklider, Mireya Loza, Bethany Moritz, Anne Martínez, Naomi Paik, Yael Prizant, Jane Rhodes, Brian Solem, and the late, great Summer Coronado, who I wish could have seen this book in the world. Andrea Bersh, Juan Pablo Milanese, and Luca helped make Cali a home for me during a crucial year of writing. Mil gracias a mi amiga Milena Ospina Franco por todo el apoyo y amor. As always, Kevin Murphy served as a reminder of everything that is good in academia and in life, and I thank him for being my guide in both. Julio Capó was kind enough to send me primary sources out of the blue that led to this book's first chapter. A major thanks to the "Chicken Ranch" crew who met consistently on Friday nights through the COVID pandemic, brightening a scary world: Sandra Botero (beloved friend and endlessly patient consultant on translations and word choices for this book), Mike Talbot, and Lucía Tiscornia. Santiago Quintero, a charter member of the Chicken Ranch, is an intellectual soul sibling who generously allowed me to bounce many ideas off of him for several years of getting this manuscript together. I am grateful for our many talks and for having a friend who will buy matching *Scarface* sweatshirts with me in Bogotá. Crystal Whitlow helped nurture an idea for an article on *Breaking Bad* that grew into this book and nurtured the rest of me in every other way. I also must thank the many wonderful students over the years who have sent me information about narcos in pop culture that I never would have found in the wild.

I am grateful, as always, for the love and support from my family: Leon, Linda, Tom, Jackie, Marianna, and Cassie Ruiz. Thank you, Mom and Dad, for never restricting my TV intake. And thank you, Fran Hobson, Heather Hobson, and the Ruiz clan. My Colombian family has also found a huge place in my heart. Mil gracias a mi familia colombiana: Armando Albarracín, Laura Albarracín, Wladi Krasyuk, y la nena Emma. Thank you for counting me among your own and being so quick to offer love and advice. Lamentably, my incredible mother-in-law, Helga Dierolf, left us as this book went into production and the immense loss has left a hole in all of our hearts. Although it still feels unreal that she will never hold this book in her hands, her unrelenting support profoundly shaped it.

I include among my Colombian family Mariana Pulecio Díaz and Daniela Hernández Rizo, both of whom worked diligently as research assistants and helped make a sabbatical one of the most magical years of my life. I love our "narcomedia fam" and am sorry that I made you watch *Weeds*.

Finally, I dedicate this book to my brilliant husband, Juan Guillermo Albarracín Dierolf. Without Juan's loving guidance and generous feedback there is no possible way that I could have researched and written it. From watching certain *novelas* in an endless loop to road-tripping to a Pablo Escobar–themed restaurant to patiently answering a million questions about the history and politics of Latin America, Juangui has been the encouraging and patient collaborator on this book from the very beginning. More than that, he has ceaselessly modeled the rigorous scholar, devoted dog dad, and loving person I hope to be. His support is more valuable by the gram than any of the substances mentioned in *Narcomedia*.

NOTES

INTRODUCTION

1. Paul Eiss, "The Narcomedia: A Reader's Guide," *Latin American Perspectives* 41, no. 2 (March 2014): 78–98.

2. In this sense, I see narcomedia as a critical category like film noir and others that are defined in retrospect by critics and scholars. Scholars of film studies have shown that no filmmaker set out to explicitly create a film noir, but that critics developed the term later to describe the moods, styles, and mise-en-scène that tie together a diverse set of film texts. Similarly, narcomedia represents my attempt to categorize a body of work to which artists, writers, and filmmakers have contributed since the early 1980s and to identify the conventions that these texts have in common, even if their creators had no intention of creating what I am calling "narcomedia."

3. David Farber, ed., *The War on Drugs: A History* (New York: NYU Press, 2022), 1.

4. Diane Coyle, *Sex, Drugs, and Economics: An Unconventional Intro to Economics* (New York: Texere, 2004), 8.

5. See, for example, the 2017 report of the think tank Global Financial Integrity, which estimates that drug trafficking accounted for $426–653 billion in 2014.

6. Curtis Marez, *Drug Wars: The Political Economy of Narcotics* (Minneapolis: University of Minnesota Press, 2004), 3.

7. *The Role of the Entertainment Industry in Deglamorizing Drug Use, Hearing Before the Permanent Subcommittee on Investigations of the Committee on Governmental Affairs*, 95th Cong. (1985).

8. Daniel Hernandez, "'American Dirt' Was Supposed to Be a Publishing Triumph. What Went Wrong?" *Los Angeles Times*, January 26, 2020.

9. Tatiana Flores, "'Latinidad Is Cancelled': Confronting an Anti-Black Construct," *Latin American and Latinx Visual Culture* 3, no. 3 (2021): 60.

10. Flores, "'Latinidad Is Cancelled,'" 64.

11. Herman Gray, *Watching Race: Television and the Struggle for Blackness*, 2nd ed. (Minneapolis: University of Minnesota Press, 2004), 12.

12. Arlene Dávila, *Latinx Art: Artists, Markets, and Politics* (Durham, NC: Duke University Press, 2020), 15.

13. Esteban del Río, "Authenticity, Appropriation, Articulation: The Cultural Logic of Latinidad," in *The Routledge Companion to Latina/o Media*, ed. María Elena Cepeda and Dolores Inés Casillas (New York: Routledge, 2017), 9.

14. Ramón H. Rivera-Servera, *Performing Queer Latinidad: Dance, Sexuality, Politics* (Ann Arbor: University of Michigan, 2012), 25.

15. Brian Eugenio Herrera, *Latin Numbers: Playing Latino in Twentieth-Century U.S.*

Popular Performance (Ann Arbor: University of Michigan Press, 2015), 139. I particularly like Herrera's idea of "executing the stereotype" to describe how some Latinx creators have deployed stereotypes in order to implode them.

16. See among other works by Valdivia, "Transnational Media, Hybrid Bodies, and Culture: Borders and the Latina/o Transnation," in *Mapping Latina/o Studies: An Interdisciplinary Reader*, ed. Angharad Valdivia and Matthew Garcia (New York: Peter Lang Inc., 2012).

CHAPTER 1. "SAY GOODNIGHT TO THE BAD GUY"

1. John C. Almack, *Straight Thinking on Narcotics: Alcohol, Tobacco, Opium, Morphine, Cocaine, and Marihuana* (Mountain View, CA: Pacific Press Publishing Association, 1940).

2. Joseph Spillane, "Did Prohibition Work? Reflections on the End of the First Cocaine Experience in the United States, 1910–1945," *Journal of Drug Issues* 28, no. 2 (Spring 1998): 527; David F. Musto, *The American Disease: Origins of Narcotics Control* (New York: Oxford University Press, 1973), 6–7.

3. Cary O'Dell, "The Cokey Comedies of the Silent Screen Era," Rogerebert.com, May 4, 2015.

4. Paul Gootenberg, *Andean Cocaine: The Making of a Global Drug* (Chapel Hill: University of North Carolina Press, 2008); Marez, *Drug Wars*; and Spillane, "Did Prohibition Work?" among others, show that the cultural figure of the cocaine fiend was a product of the white imagination but one that helped shape anti-cocaine laws in the 1910s.

5. Musto, *The American Disease*, 7.

6. See Musto, *The American Disease*. There is no consensus among historians or medical professionals as to why cocaine largely disappeared from the American scene in the 1930s, but one convincing theory posits that advances in the synthesis and marketing of amphetamines in the early 1930s supplanted the demand for cocaine.

7. Among others, see Ann Crittenden and Michael Ruby, "Highs, Horns and Bugs Crawling," *New York Times* September 1, 1975, for fascinating early coverage of cocaine's resurgence in the United States. The reportage for most of the 1970s saw cocaine abuse as a personal problem rather than a social ill, and, in retrospect, many news sources appear to have glamorized casual use. Along with the *New York Times*, *Rolling Stone* produced a good number of articles in this vein.

8. Gootenberg, *Andean Cocaine*, 310.

9. "Cocaine: A Major Drug Issue of the Seventies," *Hearings before the House Select Committee on Narcotics Abuse and Control*, 96th Cong. (1979).

10. "Cocaine: A Major Drug Issue."

11. See Jimmie L. Reeves and Richard Campbell, *Cracked Coverage: Television News, the Anti-Cocaine Crusade, and the Reagan Legacy* (Durham, NC: Duke University Press, 1994).

12. The 99th Congress voted this designation into law as Public Law 99–481 on October 16, 1986.

13. David F. Allen and James F. Jekel, *Crack: The Broken Promise* (New York: St. Martin's Press, 1991), 1.

14. Pop culture has repeated these dynamics of white-user-as-victim for decades and with various modes of addiction as the centerpiece. For example, *Dopesick* (2021)

focuses on white victims who get addicted to opioids and the white business executives who develop and market Oxycodone. This obviously reflects the real history of the prescription drug crisis in the late 1990s and early 2000s, but the focus on who is victimized—in this case, a young white woman in Appalachia who represents the millions who were introduced to the drug by their doctors—contrasts with the narratives of Latinos as the progenitors and never the victims that I examine throughout this book.

15. Joan Didion, *Miami* (New York: Simon and Schuster, 1987), 26.

16. John A. Meyers, "A Letter from the Publisher," *Time*, November 23, 1981, 1.

17. Juan León, "Tropical Overexposure: Miami's 'Sophisticated Tropics' and the Balsero," in *Tropicalizations*, ed. Frances R. Aparicio and Susana Chávez-Silverman (Hanover, NH: Dartmouth University Press, 1997), 217.

18. "Florida: A Place in the Sun," *Time*, December 19, 1955, 18.

19. James Kelly, "South Florida: Trouble in Paradise," *Time*, November 23, 1981.

20. Kelly, "South Florida," 23.

21. Kelly, "South Florida," 26.

22. Kelly, "South Florida," 32.

23. Kelly, "South Florida," 26. "As in other parts of the world where the citizens shop for guerrilla discounts and bargains in semiautomatic weapons, there was in Miami an advanced interest in personal security," Didion states in *Miami*, 24. The "Cocaine Cartels" episode of ABC's *Close Up*, described in this chapter and chapter 7, also features images and descriptions of everyday Miamians learning how to shoot at gun ranges.

24. Alejandro Portes and Alex Stepick, *City on the Edge: The Transformation of Miami* (Berkeley: University of California Press, 1993).

25. Gregory Jaynes, "Miami Crime Rises as Drugs Pour In," *New York Times*, August 12, 1981. Some outlets reported the truck as a rental from Ryder, others as a loaner from Burger King.

26. "The Cocaine Cartel," *Closeup*, August 30, 1983, https://catalog.archives.gov/id/37978.

27. Robert Sherrill, "Can Miami Save Itself? A City Beset by Drugs and Violence," *New York Times*, July 19, 1987.

28. *The Golden Girls* is one of the few 1980s TV series set in a sunny, crime-free, practically all-white, retiree-friendly Miami.

29. Walter Pincus and Mary Thornton, "Reagan Will Visit South Florida to Laud Special Drug Task Force," *Washington Post*, November 16, 1982.

30. Guy D. Garcia, "Running Pot Where It's Not as Hot," *Time*, November 29, 1982.

31. These include *The Secret Six* (1931), *Bad Company* (1931), *City Streets* (1931), *Okay, America!* (1932), *The Beast of the City* (1932, on which Ben Hecht also worked as an uncredited scriptwriter), and *Gabriel Over the White House* (1933).

32. *The Sopranos*, season 3, episode 2, "Proshai, Livushka," directed by Tim Van Patten, written by David Chase, aired March 4, 2001. Tony is moved by the devotion of the main character's mother to her gangster son, something lacking in his relationship to his own mother, who died in the episode. Throughout its long run, *The Sopranos* referenced showrunner David Chase's devotion—and indebtedness—to classic gangster movies.

33. J. E. Smyth, "Revisioning Modern American History in the Age of *Scarface*," *Historical Journal of Film, Radio, and Television* 24, no. 4 (2004): 553.

34. See Gregory D. Black, *Hollywood Censored: Morality Codes, Catholics, and the Movies* (Cambridge, UK: Cambridge University Press, 1994); Chris Yogerst, "Hughes,

Hawks, and Hays: The Monumental Censorship Battle over *Scarface* (1932)," *Journal of American Culture* 40, no. 2 (June 20, 2017).

35. Yogerst, "Hughes, Hawks, and Hays," 118.

36. Yogerst, "Hughes, Hawks, and Hays," 137.

37. Yogerst, "Hughes, Hawks, and Hays," 142.

38. Bernard Weinraub, "Tony Montana's Revenge," *Tampa Bay Times*, September 1, 2005; Larry Grobel, "Al Pacino Has Something to Say: A Conversation with the Closed-mouth Star of *Scarface*," *Rolling Stone*, February 2, 1984.

39. As Portes and Stepick show in *City on the Edge*, building on previous scholarship, the *Miami Herald* played a key role in building the narrative of the Marielitos as degenerates (see chapter 2 of *City on the Edge*).

40. See Gastón Fernández, "Race, Gender, and Class in the Persistence of the Mariel Stigma Twenty Years after the Exodus from Cuba," *International Migration Review* 41, no 3 (2007): 602–622; Jillian M. Jacklin, "The Cuban Refugee Criminal: Media Reporting and the Production of a Popular Image," *International Journal of Cuban Studies* 11, no. 1 (2019): 61–83.

41. Jacklin, "The Cuban Refugee Criminal," 65–66.

42. Monette's novelization rises far above most other texts of this type, but because it was created as a tie-in for the film, I do not analyze it on its own in this chapter.

43. Oliver Stone, *Scarface: The Movie Scriptbook* (San Diego, CA: IDW Publishing), 4.

44. Quoted in Douglas Keesey, *Brian De Palma's Split-Screen: A Life in Film* (Oxford: University Press of Mississippi, 2015), 156.

45. Tony the Tiger, the cereal mascot, had also been around since the early 1950s; the big-cat-as-symbol device will appear again in *Weeds* and *Narcos*, two more narcomedia staples.

46. "Brian De Palma on *Scarface*, *Mission: Impossible*, and the Movie He Made in College," interview, *Here's the Thing with Alec Baldwin* podcast, May 5, 2020.

47. See, for example, the documentary film, *De Palma*, directed by Noah Baumbach and Jake Paltrow (2015), and *Here's the Thing* podcast.

48. Richard Corliss, "Say Goodnight to the Bad Guy," *Time*, December 5, 1983.

49. Carrie Rickey, "The Whys of Remakes and the Hows of One," *New York Times*, January 1, 1984.

50. Shula Beyer, "Leaders Worried Scarface Remake Means Slap in the Face for Cubans," *Miami Herald*, July 30, 1982.

51. "Anti-Film Furor Is Threat to Scar Image of Exiles," *Miami Herald*, August 28, 1982.

52. "Denució Demetrio Pérez Jr. los Peligros de la Producción fílmica 'Cara Cortada,'" *El Imparcial*, August 26, 1982. (Translation mine.)

53. Nicolás Ríos, "Demetrio Pérez daña imagen de la comunidad," *Réplica* 13, no. 163 (September 9, 1982). (Translation mine.)

54. Ríos, "Demetrio Pérez daña imagen de la comunidad."

55. Grobel, "Al Pacino Has Something to Say," 17.

56. Jay Ducassi, "Bad Reviews May Drive *Scarface* Filming Elsewhere," *Miami Herald*, August 20, 1982.

57. Jay Ducassi, "Rewrite or Be Banned, *Scarface* Producer Told," *Miami Herald*, August 21, 1982.

58. Michael Kranish, "Save Scarface, Governor Says," *Miami Herald*, August 22, 1982.

59. Jay Ducassi, "Scarface Finds Cuban Friends, Will Stay," *Miami Herald*, August 24, 1982.

60. "Pact on Miami Filming," *New York Times*, September 4, 1982.

61. Guillermo Martinez, "Film Referendum Being Considered," *Miami Herald*, August 27, 1982.

62. Guillermo Martinez, "Filming of 'Scarface' Harms Cuban Image," *Miami Herald*, August 27, 1982.

63. Roberto Fabricio, "Anti-Film Furor Is Threat to Scar Image of Exiles," *Miami Herald*, August 28, 1982.

64. Jay Ducassi, "Film-Feud Sequel: *Scarface* Crew to Stage Pullout," *Miami Herald*, August 31, 1982.

65. "Filmmakers Welcome, Beach Says," *Miami Herald*, September 2, 1982.

66. Minutes of Regular Meeting, City Commission of Miami, Florida, prepared by the Office of the City Clerk, September 9, 1982. Although Mayor Maurice Ferré spent most of the allotted time discussing whether the Commission should discuss the topic at all, the civic leaders present did address the need for a film commission for Miami and surrounding communities. Today the City of Miami has a full-service film office, and a unit called FilMiami serves Dade County.

67. "'Scarface' Does Quiet Reshooting in Miami," *Variety*, April 27, 1983.

68. At the time of this writing in 2022, the location of the chainsaw scene with the Colombians had recently been converted to a CVS drugstore.

69. Linda Ruth Williams, *The Erotic Thriller in Contemporary Cinema* (Bloomington: Indiana University Press, 2005), 138.

70. Fredric Tasker, "At Gusman, A Hot Time Was Had," *Miami Herald*, December 14, 1983.

71. Chon A. Noriega, *Shot in America: Television, the State, and the Rise of Chicano Cinema* (Minneapolis: University of Minnesota Press). See also Herrera, *Latin Numbers*, 132–134.

72. See Arcelia Gutiérrez, "Situating Representation as a Form of Erasure: #OscarsSoWhite, Black Twitter, and Latinx Twitter," *Television and New Media* 33, no. 1 (2020): 100–118." Media scholars in other branches of ethnic studies have also shown the power of organizing in other communities. See, for example, Lori Kido Lopez's *Asian American Media Activism: Fighting for Cultural Citizenship* (New York: NYU Press, 2016).

73. The case of *Cruising* provides an interesting parallel. Not only was Pacino also the star of that film, but gay rights activists tried to get the New York City government to ban the film's production on location. When they were not successful, they actively tried to interfere with filming by shining lights and blasting noise. Like *Scarface*, *Cruising* initially received an X rating from the MPAA, but Friedkin made enough cuts for the movie to eventually receive an R. *Cruising*, however, has not been embraced by cultural workers, artists, or audiences to have a long afterlife like *Scarface*.

74. facecuba.org.

75. Oliver Stone, *Chasing the Light: Writing, Directing, and Surviving* Platoon, Midnight Express, Scarface, Salvador, *and the Movie Game* (Boston and New York: Houghton Mifflin Harcourt, 2020), 177.

76. Stone, *Scarface: The Movie Scriptbook*, 37.

77. "Brian De Palma on *Scarface*," *Here's the Thing with Alec Baldwin*.

78. Angharad N. Valdivia, *Latina/os and the Media* (Cambridge, UK and Malden, MA: Polity Press, 2010), 80.

79. Grobel, "Al Pacino Has Something to Say," 18.

80. Pauline Kael, *State of the Art* (New York: Dutton, 1985), 105.

81. Armitrage Trail, *Scarface* (UK: Dean Street Press, 2019). Kindle version, locs. 173–174.

82. See "On Saddam's Money Trail," *Newsweek*, April 7, 1991.

83. *Narcos: Mexico*, season 2, episode 2, "Alea Iacta Est," directed by Amat Escalante, written by Eric Newman and Eva Aridjis, aired February 13, 2020.

84. Carlo Bernard, personal interview with Jason Ruiz, February 15, 2019.

85. See, for example, Gilligan's interview with Terry Gross on NPR's *Fresh Air*, September 19, 2011.

86. *Breaking Bad*, season 5, episode 3, "Hazard Pay," directed by Adam Bernstein, written by Peter Gould, aired July 29, 2012.

87. Dimitri A. Bogazianos, *5 Grams: Crack Cocaine, Rap Music, and the War on Drugs* (New York: NYU Press, 2012), 1.

88. "Scarface Bust Found in Real-Life Mobster's Home," *The World*, March 30, 2012.

89. "Scarface Statue Theft Costs Cops their Careers," *Toronto Sun*, August 13, 2019.

90. Mia Galuppo, "Antoine Fuqua in Talks to Direct 'Scarface' for Universal," *Hollywood Reporter*, August 10, 2016.

91. Michael Cieply, "Escobar, a Gangster Now Hot in Hollywood," *New York Times*, October 30, 2007. Luna did go on to portray a real-life Mexican kingpin with oblique ties to Escobar in *Narcos: Mexico* on Netflix.

CHAPTER 2. MIAMI VICES

1. The Smithsonian National Portrait Gallery now holds the original Richard Bernstein painting that *Time* used for the cover image. Richard Bernstein, *Cool Cops, Hot Show*, 1985, object no. NPG.88.TC96, National Portrait Gallery, Smithsonian Institution. Bernstein's original work places Johnson and Thomas against a yellow background.

2. Richard Zoglin, "Cool Cops, Hot Show," *Time*, September 16, 1985. Another article in the issue focuses on NBC's newfound dominance over the other big three networks and includes a photo of Brandon Tartikoff, then president of NBC Entertainment, sporting a *Miami Vice* T-shirt.

3. Ironically, the top right corner of the issue includes a teaser for another article on cocaine use among major league baseball players. The accompanying image depicts powder cocaine oozing out of a baseball's seams. This secondary lead story suggests that the main article could focus on the show's glamor, but cocaine was never far away.

4. At the time of *Miami Vice*'s premiere, NBC chair and veteran producer Grant Tinker did not see the show in these terms. Despite having green-lighted the show, he lamented to a *New York Times* reporter that the series was just another violent show intended to make inroads with male viewers (Peter W. Kaplan, "NBC Head Says Viewers Spurn Quality Shows," *New York Times*, September 30, 1984). Tinker identified *The Cosby Show* as the type of quality programming that he wanted more of. A few months later, *Times* writer Sally Bedell Smith described the show as "aggressively modern" and praised its cinematography and use of music (Sally Bedell Smith, "'Miami Vice': Action TV with Some New Twists," *New York Times*, January 3, 1985).

5. Counting the number of *Miami Vice* episodes depends on how one tallies the episodes, which were repackaged over the years for syndication, and whether this count

includes unaired "lost" episodes from season five. Other series examined in this study were similarly long-lived, but when *Miami Vice* aired, television seasons were much longer than, say, those of twenty years later when *Breaking Bad* aired on basic cable. Both series lasted five seasons, but *Miami Vice* aired almost twice as many episodes as *Breaking Bad*: 112 versus 62.

6. Communications scholar Cathy Schwichtenberg made an interesting case for the deeper meanings behind the show's seemingly breezy artificiality back, arguing that critics had fundamentally misunderstood the series as all style and no substance. Cathy Schwichtenberg, "Sensual Surfaces and Stylistic Excess: The Pleasure and Politics of *Miami Vice*," *Journal of Communication Inquiry* 10, no. 3 (1986): 45–65.

7. Douglas Kellner, "Critical Perspectives on Television from the Frankfurt School to Postmodernism," in *A Companion to Television*, 1st ed., ed. Janet Wasko (Malden MA: Blackwell Publishing, 2005), 41.

8. See Jason Mittell, *Complex TV: The Poetics of Contemporary Television Storytelling* (New York: NYU Press, 2015). Mittell sees this narrative mode as starting in the nineties, but it is easy to see how TV texts like those I analyze in subsequent chapters—for example, *Breaking Bad*—connect to *Miami Vice*, which is both episodic and serialized in the vein in which Mittell writes.

9. See Todd Gitlin, *Watching Television: A Pantheon Guide to Popular Culture* (New York: Pantheon Books, 1986); Lawrence Grossberg, "The In-Difference of Television," *Screen* 28, no. 2 (1987) 28–46; and Douglas Kellner, *Media Culture : Cultural Studies, Identity and Politics Between the Modern and the Postmodern* (London and New York: Routledge, 1995), 238–248.

10. James Lyons, *Miami Vice* (London: Wiley-Blackwell, 2010), 16. See also Howard Cohen, "How 'Miami Vice' Changed TV," *Miami Herald*, September 28, 2014.

11. Mann and Yerkovich skirmished in the press over who deserved credit for creating the show several times in the 1980s, but eventually reunited to co-produce the 2006 film. It is fair to describe Mann as what we would now call a "showrunner" until season three, when Dick Wolf took over the show's operations.

12. Lyons, *Miami Vice*. In a short critical interpretation of the series, Lyons points out that *Miami Vice* also obviously riffs on shows like *Starsky and Hutch*, movies like *48 Hours*, and John D. MacDonald's 1964 novel *The Deep Blue Good-by* (not "Goodbye," as Lyon writes).

13. León, "Tropical Overexposure," 216.

14. León, "Tropical Overexposure," 215.

15. Jesse Serwer, "'The Sky Started Raining Panties': Don Johnson on 30 Years of 'Miami Vice,'" *Rolling Stone*, October 9, 2014.

16. *Miami Vice*, season 4, episode 18, "Badge of Dishonor," directed by Richard Compton, written by Michael Duggan, Peter Lance, and Dick Wolf, aired March 18, 1988.

17. Zoglin, "Cool Cops, Hot Show."

18. Piñero wrote the first season's fifteenth episode, "Smuggler's Blues," and in the second season returned as another drug lord, Esteban Revilla. Two decades later, "Smuggler's Blues" would serve as the rough plot for Mann's *Miami Vice* movie.

19. *Miami Vice*, season 1, episode 5, "Calderone's Return (Part II)," directed by Paul Michael Glaser, written by Joel Surnow and Alfonse Ruggiero Jr, aired October 26, 1984. The daughter, named Angelina, reenters Tubbs's life in a later episode (season 2, episode 22, "Sons and Lovers"), this time with Tubbs's son, whom she bore without

the father's knowledge. In that episode, she is killed by her half-brother, yet another instance of Latinx violence. Incidentally, this takes place in the episode immediately following the "Trust Fund Pirates" episode described below.

20. *Miami Vice*, season 2, episode 21, "Trust Fund Pirates," directed by Jim Johnston, written by Daniel Pyne, aired May 2, 1986.

21. On hyperfertility, see Elena R. Gutiérrez, *Fertile Matters: The Politics of Mexican-Origin Women's Reproduction* (Austin: University of Texas Press, 2008).

22. Jesus Rangel, "Producers Soothe Miami's Sensitivity About TV Filming," *New York Times*, August 2, 1984.

23. In 2005, Florida passed the nation's first "stand your ground" law, which permits the use of deadly force when someone believes that they are at risk of great bodily harm in a confrontation. Given the depictions of Floridians needing to arm themselves in both the *Time* article and *Miami Vice*, this seems traceable to the discourse that Florida was under siege since the early 1980s. In 2012 and 2013, George Zimmerman's attorneys used a stand your ground defense in the aftermath of his killing Black teenager Trayvon Martin in an altercation. At the time of this writing, thirty-eight states have stand your ground or similar self-defense laws.

24. *Miami Vice*, season 4, episode 10, "Love at First Sight," directed by Don Johnson, written by Peter McCabe, aired January 15, 1988.

25. On the de-sexing of Black partners in buddy cop films, see Christopher Ames, "Restoring the Black Man's Lethal Weapon: Race and Sexuality in Contemporary Cop Films," *Journal of Popular Film and Television* 20, no. 3 (Fall 1992): 52–60.

26. *Miami Vice*, season 4, episode 17, "Hell Hath No Fury," directed by Virgil W. Vogel, written by David Black and Michael Duggan, aired March 11, 1988. In this case, the (non-consensual) sex took place several years prior to the diegetic present and the rapist had recently been released from prison.

27. *Miami Vice*, season 1, episode 9, "Glades," directed by Stan Latham, written by Rex Weiner and Allan Weisberger, aired November 30, 1984.

28. *Miami Vice*, season 3, episode 20, "By Hooker By Crook," directed by Don Johnson, written by Dick Wolf and John Schulian, aired March 20, 1987.

29. *Miami Vice*, season 3, episode 17, "The Afternoon Plane," written and directed by David Jackson, aired February 20, 1987. Though it was actually Crockett who killed Calderone, Tubbs says in the episode that it was him—and it is Tubbs against whom Orlando seeks revenge. This narrative inconsistency, not exactly rare for *Vice*, is unexplained in "The Afternoon Plane" and elsewhere.

30. This setting is probably modeled after islands in the Caribbean like Norman's Cay in the Bahamas, which had been used by drug lord Carlos Lehder as a headquarters for his cocaine smuggling operations in the late 1970s and early 1980s.

31. See María Elena Cepeda, "'A Cartel Built for Love': 'Medellín,' Pablo Escobar, and the Scripts of Global Colombianiada," in *Critical Dialogues in Latinx Studies*, ed. Ana Y. Ramos-Zayas and Mérida M. Rua (New York: NYU Press, 2021), 39. Cepeda prefers the term US-Colombian studies for reasons outlined in her book *Musical ImagiNation* and elsewhere.

32. Lina Rincón, Johana Londoño, Jennifer Harford Vargas, and María Elena Cepeda, "Reimagining US Colombianidades: Transnational Subjectivities, Cultural Expressions, and Political Contestations," *Latino Studies* 18, no. 3 (2020): 301–325.

33. *Miami Vice*, season 4, episode 15, "Indian Wars," directed by Leon Ichaso, written by Frank Coffey and Carl Waldman, aired February 26, 1988. This is one of the

few episodes in which interracial solidarity is a theme. Undercover as a PhD student researching a dissertation, Tubbs attempts to make inroads with militaristic young Native men by stating that he, too, knows what it feels like to be marginalized. "You think you're the only people of color who have to crawl on their knees in this country?" Tubbs asks. "Give me a little Trail of Tears and I'll give you a Little Rock. For every Indian massacred, I'll give you a lynching. You had Custer, we have the Klan. What's the difference?"

34. This is the case in both the "Indian Wars" episode and another episode later in the season. In "Badge of Dishonor," Tubbs teams up with a Black female detective from South Beach who, he later discovers, is on the take. In the episode's climax, she is killed by the Cuban Americans with whom she is colluding.

35. *Miami Vice*, season 5, episode 10, "To Have and to Hold," directed by Eugene Corr, written by William Conway, aired February 10, 1989. Once again, Tubbs romances a member of the family, a woman who, like Angelina, is murdered in the episode climax.

36. *Miami Vice*, season 3, episode 24, "Heroes of the Revolution," directed by Gabrielle Beaumont, written by Dick Wolf, aired May 8, 1987.

37. *Miami Vice*, season 2, episode 8, "Bushido," directed by Edward James Olmos, written by John Leekley, aired November 22, 1985. He did not go on to helm more *Miami Vice* episodes, but he did direct several episodes of a later series, *Battlestar Galactica*.

38. Like people of color, women were seriously underrepresented behind the camera, aside from roles such as hair and wardrobe. Although those roles are important, especially in the creation of a show as fashion-conscious as *Miami Vice*, only three women—all white women—ever directed for the series.

39. Kellner, *Media Culture*, 244.

40. Both Johnson and Thomas released albums during the *Miami Vice* run. Johnson's reached the *Billboard* Top 20 and was certified platinum. It included a Top 5 single, "Heartbeat."

41. Kellner, *Media Culture*, 244.

42. See Serwer, "The Sky Started Raining Panties." In a 1988 *Barbara Walters Special*, Johnson cited the birth of his son in 1982 as his inspiration for quitting drugs and alcohol.

43. Kai Ito, "The Anti-Drug Message Will Get a Rock Beat," *Los Angeles Times*, July 16, 1986.

44. https://www.youtube.com/watch?v=wwUFovpkhMc.

45. *Blues* and *Vice* share an interrelated history of producers and writers behind the scenes and actors onscreen. Many character actors from *Blues* made their way onto *Vice*, suggesting that casting agents saw *Blues* as something of an audition for *Vice*. (Both shows cast guest actors in multiple roles over their runs. Edward James Olmos played two separate characters over the run of *Blues* and Tony Plana played four roles across the two shows). Other intertextual Easter eggs are to be found as well, such as the fact that a *Blues* villain in the show's third season is named Sonny Crockett.

46. In the case of Asian characters, I am struck by the frequent presence of an Asian woman who plays a cop in the background for much of the series. Despite being an almost constant presence, she never utters a line.

47. *Miami Vice*, season 4, episode 5, "Child's Play," directed by Vern Gillum, written by Priscilla Turner and Michael Piller, aired October 30, 1987.

48. *Miami Vice* is not a true anthology series, which would consist entirely of disconnected episodes. Stories do sometimes overlap over the show's run, and it does reference previous storylines from time to time. Even so, an essential aspect of the show's style is that the episodes function as stand-alone mini-movies with clear beginnings, middles, and endings that do not pick up where the previous episode left off.

49. Herrera, *Latin Numbers*, chapters 2 and 3.

50. I must admit here that some of the guest performances over the course of the series are mind-boggling from the perspective of "How did they do that?" I have already mentioned Piñero, but season two, when the series hit its stride, included performances by Pam Grier (who reprises a role she played in the first season), Little Richard, Phil Collins, Willie Nelson, and no less than Eartha Kitt as a Santeria priestess. This and other seasons include before-they-were-famous appearances by Bob Balaban, Steve Buscemi, Helena Bonham Carter, Liam Neeson, and John Leguizamo. Despite my delight in some of the guest performances, it is also dispiriting to watch promising young actors in roles that do not move the needle in terms of stereotypical representations.

51. When I asked Moreno about the experience in a 2019 interview, she remembered little about it except to recall that *Vice* was "such a hot show at the time." See Jason Ruiz, "Vivencias: Rita Moreno," *Latino Studies* 17, no. 3 (2019): 390–400.

52. *Miami Vice*, season 5, episode 19, "Miracle Man," directed by Alan Myerson, written by Robert Ward and Gillian Horvath (teleplay by Rob Bragin), aired June 21, 1989.

53. *Miami Vice*, season 2, episode 20, "Free Verse," directed by John Nicolella, written by Shel Willens and Jim Trombetta, aired April 4, 1986.

54. Piven's son Jeremy would eventually star in HBO's *Entourage*, a series that, by odd coincidence, included a plotline involving a white actor (played by Adrian Grenier) attempting to convincingly portray another iconic Colombian, Pablo Escobar.

55. Jack Zink, "Casablanca Image Now Suits Miami as Tourist Biz Booms," *Variety*, June 4, 1986.

56. Steven Rybin, *Michael Mann: Crime Auteur* (Lanham, MD: Scarecrow Press, 2013), 74.

57. Kim Masters, "Fleeing the Scene," *Slate*, July 13, 2006, https://slate.com/news-and-politics/2006/07/how-jamie-foxx-forced-a-different-ending-of-miami-vice.html.

58. Emma Coronel Aispuro, the wife of Guzmán, also began to appear on *Cartel Crew* late in its second season. Like Blanco, she has taken an entrepreneurial approach to her husband's notoriety: During his trial in 2019, she trademarked the El Chapo name and began working on a fashion line featuring his name and likeness. Around the same time, one of Guzmán's daughters started a competing fashion line.

59. Serwer, "'The Sky Started Raining Panties.'"

60. Joe Otterson, "'Miami Vice' Reboot in Works at NBC from Vin Diesel," *Variety*, August 2, 2017.

61. Charles Rabin, "Miami Used to Be a Murder Capital. Now, Not So Much, as Crime Rates Hit Historic Low," *Miami Herald*, January 8, 2019.

62. Valerie Conners, "The Show that Redefined Miami," *BBC Travel*, December 11, 2014, http://www.bbc.com/travel/story/20141205-the-show-that-redefined-miami.

63. Although I reference the "girls' weekend" trope with my tongue in cheek here, that is the actual premise of several episodes in the *Real Housewives* reality TV franchise

(which also included a short-lived *Real Housewives of Miami*) as well as several movies in the "chick flick" genre, such as the 2017 ensemble comedy *Rough Night*, that have filmed in this fun and pleasurable new Miami.

CHAPTER 3. "THE MOST ALIVE DEAD MAN IN THE WORLD"

1. Juan Pablo Escobar, *Pablo Escobar: My Father* (New York: St. Martin's Press, 2017), 286–297. Alonso Salazar J. quotes Pablo Escobar's brother Roberto making almost identical claims in *La Parábola de Pablo: Auge y Caída de un Gran Capo de Narcotráfico* (Bogota, Colombia: Planeta, 2001), 13. (Translation mine.) Juan Pablo Escobar repeats this claim in many of his public appearances, including one that I attended in fall 2020.

2. James Brooke, "A Drug Lord Is Buried as a Folk Hero," *New York Times*, December 4, 1993.

3. Bryan Andrés González, "El cambio extremo de la casa donde cayó Pablo Escobar," *El Tiempo*, December 3, 2018.

4. I find Alonso Salazar J's *La Parábola de Pablo* and Mark Bowden's exhaustively researched *Killing Pablo: The Hunt for the World's Greatest Outlaw* (New York: Grove Press, 2015) to be the most reliable. I use these sources, along with documentary footage, in my assessment of the facts of Escobar's death. Incidentally, these books also serve as the source material for *El Patrón del Mal* and *Narcos* (according to author Mark Bowden in a personal interview with me).

5. Estimated by Colombian news magazine *La Semana*.

6. Bruce Bagley, "Colombia and the War on Drugs," *Foreign Affairs* 67, no. 1 (Fall 1988): 70.

7. Peter Andreas, *Smuggler Nation: How Illicit Trade Made America* (New York: Oxford University Press, 2013), 278.

8. John Corry, "TV Weekend; Cocaine in Colombia: Dad-Daughter Sleuths," *New York Times*, August 19, 1983. Much of the documentary focuses on money laundering, which the *Times* reviewer found less compelling than stories of Colombian crime families.

9. "The Future of the Andean War on Drugs After the Escape of Pablo Escobar," Joint Hearing before the Subcommittee on Western Hemisphere Affairs and Task Force on International Narcotics Control, 102nd Cong. (1992).

10. Alma Guillermoprieto, "Exit El Patrón," *New Yorker* (October 25, 1993): 78.

11. Andreas, *Smuggler Nation*, 288.

12. Guillermoprieto, "Exit El Patrón," 83.

13. Elaine Shannon, "The Cali Cartel: New Kings of Coke," *Time*, July 1, 1991.

14. "Message From President Clinton to Colombian President Gaviria on Pablo Escobar," *U.S. Newswire*, December 3, 1993.

15. Douglas Farah, "Escobar Killed in Medellín," *Washington Post*, December 3, 1993.

16. Bowden, *Killing Pablo*, 260–261.

17. Cepeda, "A Cartel Built for Love," 42.

18. Aldona Bialowas Pobutsky, "Peddling Pablo: Escobar's Cultural Renaissance," *Hispanic Studies* 96, no. 4 (December 2013): 695 and 684, respectively.

19. *El Faro*, quoted in Patrick Naef, 'Narco-heritage' and the Touristification of the Drug Lord Pablo Escobar in Medellin, Colombia," *Journal of Anthropological Research* 74, no. 4 (Winter 2018): 497.

20. *El Patrón del Mal*, season 1, episode 1, directed by Carlos Moreno, written by Camilo Cano and Juan Camilo Ferrand. Here and throughout I reference the episodes as they were numbered for international distribution (seventy-four forty-three-minute episodes) rather than how they were numbered for their original airings on Colombian television (113 twenty-five-minute episodes). (Translations mine.)

21. Gabriela Sáenz Laverde, "Yury Buenaventura es el autor de la música de El Patrón," *Revista Diners*, June 13, 2012, https://revistadiners.com.co/cultura/2682_yury-buenaventura-es-el-autor-de-la-musica-de-el-patron/.

22. The real Murphy has been a popular speaker on the subject of Escobar's killing over the past three decades, and he has successfully fashioned himself as a veteran of the War on Drugs. At the time of this writing, both Murphy and his former partner Javier Peña continue to make illustrated presentations across the country.

23. *Narcos*, season 2, episode 10, "Al Fin Cayo!" directed by Andrés Baiz, written by Carlo Bernard and Doug Miro, aired September 2, 2016. Shooting script provided by production staff. Emphasis is in the original text, which differs slightly from the dialogue in the finished episode.

24. See Barbie Zelizer, *About to Die: How News Images Move the Public* (New York: Oxford University Press, 2010), chapter 6.

25. Juan Pablo Escobar claims the photo of his father dressed as Al Capone was made in Las Vegas. Escobar, Pablo Escobar, photo insert, English edition (no page number).

26. Margaret Schwartz, *Dead Matter: The Meaning of Iconic Corpses* (Minneapolis: University of Minnesota Press, 2015), 1.

27. *El Tiempo*, "¡Al Fin Cayo!" December 4, 1993.

28. A 2017 online anniversary celebration of the newspaper's 130th year in publication included this cover as one of its thirteen most iconic important editions.

29. *Revista Semana*, no. 605, December 7–14, 1993.

30. Jay Ruby, *Secure the Shadow: Death and Photography in America* (Cambridge: MIT University Press, 1995), 16.

31. Bowden, *Killing Pablo*, 257.

32. Bowden, *Killing Pablo*, 258.

33. Jackie Strause, "The Real DEA Agents of 'Narcos' Break Down What Season 2 Got Right," *Hollywood Reporter*, September 15, 2016.

34. Bowden, *Killing Pablo*, 258.

35. See especially Ruby, *Secure the Shadow*, 15–16.

36. Salazar J., *La Parábola de Pablo*, 285.

37. Jeannette Catsoulis, "'Escobar, Paradise Lost' Stars Benicio Del Toro as Drug Lord," *New York Times*, June 25, 2015. Catsoulis is being somewhat generous here, since some of the artistic license taken by writer-director Andrea di Stefano is galling: For example, he sets Medellín near a beach, and he has Escobar communicate with Nick in English. Di Stefano, an Italian actor making his directorial debut, filmed in Panama using very few Colombian actors or technicians, so perhaps these choices are predictable. Either way, the film stands out as one of the texts examined in this chapter with one of the least tenable relationships to its legendary subject. (NB: The *New York Times* uses a comma to separate "Escobar" from the rest of the title. Since the film's titles do not use any punctuation marks, various sources use either a comma or a colon.)

38. See, for example, Daniel Cooper Alarcón, *The Aztec Palimpsest: Mexico in the Modern Imagination* (Tucson: University of Arizona Press, 1997); Jason Ruiz, *Americans in the Treasure House: Travel to Porfirian Mexico and the Cultural Politics of Empire* (Austin: University of Texas Press, 2014).

CHAPTER 4. DANCING TOWARD REVENGE

1. Alan L. Gansberg, *Little Caesar: A Biography of Edward G. Robinson* (New York: Scarecrow Press, 2004), 48. More recently, Javier Bardem, as a queer-coded villain named Raoul Silva in the 2012 James Bond movie *Skyfall*, also played a variation on this theme. Silva looks especially similar to the character Javier Ospina in *The Infiltrator*, down to the light linen suit and silk scarves. In a particularly infamous scene, Silva interrogates Bond with such sexual aggression that it barely qualifies as "coded."

2. *Miami Vice*, season 1, episode 1, "Brother's Keeper," directed by Thomas Carter, written by Anthony Yerkovich, aired September 16, 1984.

3. Later in the series, in a much more sympathetic portrayal of a queer character, Esai Morales portrays the gay son of a kingpin whose ex-lover dies of AIDS in his arms (*Miami Vice*, season 4, episode 6, "God's Work," directed by Jan Eliasberg, written by Edward Tivnan, aired November 6, 1987). In the show's final season, four years later, a flamboyant queer gangster nicknamed "El Gato" (played by out gay actor John Polito) grows increasingly unhinged over a two-episode story arc and is eventually killed by a trained puma.

4. The association between cross-dressing and criminality is a well-established film and TV trope and often hinges on the idea that cross-dressers harbor dark secrets or otherwise have something to hide. This is the conceit of *Psycho* (1960), which many thrillers have emulated. The 1980s saw a number of films that used the device, including, perhaps most infamously, Brian De Palma's *Dressed to Kill* (1980). Most of these characters end up dead by the end credits.

5. In the book on which the movie is based, Ospina's interest in Bob grows over the course of a few days and reaches a climax when Ospina gropes him in the back of a taxi. "All this time I thought he had been looking for a wire when he was actually hitting on me!" writes Mazur. "A million thoughts from kicking his ass to politely asking him to stop flashed through my head. He was, after all, the key to the cartel. A simple yes or no from him and our fate was fixed in Medellín. But there was no way that I was going to put up with this—not even for my country." Robert Mazur, *The Infiltrator: The True Story of One Man Against the Biggest Drug Cartel in History* (New York: Back Bay Books, 2009), 142.

6. Mazur, *The Infiltrator*, 193.

7. Fernando Vallejo, *Our Lady of the Assassins* (London: Serpent's Tail, 2001), 82. All references here are to the English translation by Paul Hammond.

8. See Russo's watershed and encyclopedic *The Celluloid Closet: Homosexuality in the Movies* (Harper & Row, 1981) and Dyer's *Now You See It: Studies on Lesbian and Gay Film* (London: Routledge, 1990), among other works.

9. Carlos Ulises Decena's *Tacit Subjects* provides a good starting point for understanding how silence and speaking around sexuality works in Latinx communities. Decena's work helps challenge the binaries between "closeted" and "out" through ethnographic research with Dominican migrant men. Carlos Ulises Decena, *Tacit Subjects: Belonging and Same-Sex Desire Among Dominican Immigrant Men* (Durham, NC: Duke University Press, 2011).

10. See, for example, James Brooke, "Crackdown Has Cali Cartel on the Run," *New York Times*, June 27, 1995, which begins with the following provocative sentence: "Until last month, Helmer Herrera Buitrago could relax in his penthouse bathtub while monitoring on closed circuit television who was coming and going from his private 14-story office and residential tower here." To be fair, the article and countless others published in the *Times* and other leading papers do not tend to address the sexual proclivities of

the cartel members. My point is that it is not through journalistic reportage that ideas about real-life queer narcos circulate, but through the pulpier (and commercially successful) long-form works of nonfiction.

11. William C. Rempel, *At the Devil's Table: The Untold Story of the Insider Who Brought Down the Cali Cartel* (New York: Random House, 2011), 9–10.

12. See, for example, Iván Gallo, "Pacho Herrera: El capo gay del cartel Cali al que Pablo Escobar le tenia miedo," *Las 2 Orillas*, September 17, 2017. The release of the third season of *Narcos* occasioned many Colombian newspapers and magazines to posthumously profile Herrera, about whom they were much more open than in the coverage from the 1990s. Most, like Gallo, repeated a gay-but-brutal narrative that is evident in Rempel's book and in *Narcos*.

13. Jackson Diehl, "East of the Andes; Economy Booms in Cocaine Country," *Washington Post*, November 11, 1982.

14. Ryan Gilbey, "From Sean Connery to Harrison Ford: Actors Who Secretly Played Roles Gay," *Guardian*, February 2, 2017.

15. Brett Martin, *Difficult Men: Behind the Scenes of a Creative Revolution: From* The Sopranos *and* The Wire *to* Mad Men *and* Breaking Bad (New York: Penguin, 2013). Martin's analysis merits some criticism here since it celebrates its subjects' irascible manliness, paying scant attention to the toxic potential of the macho workplace. Fortunately, prestige television diversified somewhat since the original runs of *The Sopranos*, *Mad Men*, and *Breaking Bad*, due in no small part to online media activism and the considerable efforts of women in the industry.

16. I am reluctant to suggest that their use of antiheroic leads make these series subversive since prestige television has relied on lead characters who operate outside the law since Tony Soprano. Antiheroes have remained the norm rather than the exception on prestige television since that time, so this is one way in which neither *Narcos* nor *Breaking Bad* is innovative.

17. After consulting with friends on three continents, I am assured that the scene takes place in what is called a "balneario" in Colombia. I am grateful to Cali nightlife expert Mauricio Guerrero for issuing the final verdict on the correct terminology.

18. This translation, like others in this book, is based on the English subtitles provided by Netflix. A more direct translation of what he says here would be "to let the past stay in the past," but that is a minor detail.

19. *Narcos*, season 3, episode 1, "The Kingpin Strategy," directed by Andi Baiz, written by Carlo Bernard, Doug Miro, and Eric Newman, aired September 1, 2017.

20. Following this shot, a brief scene shows the disposal of Claudio's and his friend's bodies in the Cauca River. The voice-over from Pedro Pascal's character contrasts the methods of the Cali Cartel (discreet, brutal but businesslike) with those of Escobar (bold, ostentatious, public), repeating the oft-told story of how the Gentlemen of Cali got their ironic name.

21. The Salazar family is based on the Montoya family, the real-life competitors to the Cali Cartel who, like their fictionalized counterparts, were based in the north of Valle de Cauca.

22. Carillo Fuentes is the subject of yet another example of narcomedia, Telemundo's "El Señor de Los Cielos," which changes his name and fictionalizes his story. He also appears in Univision/Netflix's *El Chapo* series. In the United States, Carillo Fuentes is most infamous as the kingpin who tried to hide his identity through plastic surgery and who died on a plastic surgeon's operating table in 1997.

23. *Narcos*, season 3, episode 5, "MRO," directed by Josef Kubota Wladyka, written by Chris Brancato, Doug Miro, and Carlo Bernard, aired September 1, 2017.

24. *Breaking Bad*, season 4, episode 8, "Hermanos," directed by Johan Renck, written by Sam Catlin and George Mastras, aired September 4, 2011.

25. The episode's title is "Hermanos," which means "brothers," and works on multiple levels in the plot. The chicken chain is named Los Pollos Hermanos but Max poignantly refers to Gus as his brother while he begs for Gus's life.

26. *Breaking Bad*, season 4, episode 10, "Salud," directed by Michelle MacLaren, written by Peter Gould and Gennifer Hutchison, aired September 18, 2011.

27. *Breaking Bad*, season 4, episode 11, "Crawl Space," directed by Scott Winant, written by George Mastras and Sam Catlin, aired September 25, 2011.

28. *Better Call Saul*, season 3, episode 4, "Sabrosito," directed by Thomas Schnauz, written by Jonathan Glatzer, aired May 1, 2017.

29. *Better Call Saul*, season 5, episode 5, "Dedicado a Max," directed by Jim McKay, written by Heather Marion, aired March 16, 2020.

30. *Better Call Saul*, season 3, episode 3, "Sunk Costs," directed by John Shiban, written by Gennifer Hutchison, aired April 24, 2017.

31. *Better Call Saul*, season 4, episode 5, "Piñata," directed by Andrew Stanton, written by Gennifer Hutchison, aired September 10, 2018.

32. *Breaking Bad*, season 4, episode 13, "Face Off," written and directed by Vince Gilligan, aired October 9, 2011. The episode is considered one of the best of the series and received seven nominations at the Sixty-Fourth Primetime Emmy Awards.

33. According to several industry news sources as of January 2023, *Griselda* is not officially a spinoff of *Narcos* but shares many of the same producers and creative staff, including some of the actors.

34. Aldona Bialowas Pobutsky, *Pablo Escobar and Colombian Narcoculture* (Gainesville: University Press of Florida, 2020), 133–134.

35. Mónica Cruz, "Catherine Zeta-Jones y el blanqueamiento de una narca colombiana en Hollywood," *El Pais*, January 27, 2018.

36. One exception was *IndieWire*, which did review the movie, panning it and giving it a "D" grade (Hanh Nguyen, "Brownface Casting Is Just One of Many Insults in this Schlocky 'Narcos' Knockoff," *IndieWire*, January 20, 2018). Like many online sources, author Nguyen critiques the casting and accuses the filmmakers of brownface.

37. Dana Schwartz, "Catherine Zeta-Jones Defends Playing Latina Character in *Cocaine Godmother*," *Entertainment Weekly*, January 18, 2018.

38. See Lina Ximena Aguirre, "Sin Tetas No Hay Paraíso: Normalization of Feminine Body in Drug-traffic World," *Taller de Letras* 48 (2011): 121–128; Stacey Hunt, "Twenty-first Century Cyborgs: Cosmetic Surgery and Aesthetic Nationalism in Colombia," *New Political Science* 37, no. 4 (2015): 543–561; Jesús Antonio Pardo León, "Aesthetic Transformations: Narco-Culture, the Production of Cultural Values and the Validation of the Narco Phenomenon," *Calle 14* 13, no. 24 (2018): 400–409.

39. Pobutsky, *Pablo Escobar and Colombian Narcoculture*, 163.

CHAPTER 5. DARK MATTERS

1. Will Kriegshauser, "Five Things *Breaking Bad* Has Taught Us About the Drug Trade," *Playboy*, August 2011.

2. See Mary Beltrán, *Latina/o Stars in U.S. Eyes: The Makings and Meanings of Film

and TV Stardom (Urbana: University of Illinois Press, 2009); Rosa Linda Fregoso, *The Bronze Screen: Chicana and Chicano Film Culture* (Minneapolis: University of Minnesota Press, 1993); Charles Ramirez Berg, *Latino Images in Film: Stereotypes, Subversion, Resistance* (Austin: University of Texas Press, 2002); Clara Rodriguez, *Latin Looks: Images of Latinas and Latinos in U.S. Media* (Boulder CO: Westview Press, 1997).

3. *Breaking Bad*, season 4, episode 6, "Cornered," directed by Michael Slovis, written by Vince Gilligan and Gennifer Hutchison, aired August 21, 2011.

4. Chuck Klosterman, "Bad Decisions: Why AMC's *Breaking Bad* Beats *Mad Men*, *The Sopranos*, and *The Wire*," *Grantland* (August 2, 2011).

5. Emily Nussbaum, "Child's Play," *New Yorker* (August 27, 2012): 82.

6. Importantly, Latino representation on prime-time television was at an egregious low point when *The Sopranos* debuted in the late 1990s, so much so that the National Council of La Raza would call for a television "Brown Out" in July 2009. See Dana E. Mastro and Elizabeth Behm-Morawitz, "Latino Representation on Primetime Television," *Journalism and Mass Communication Quarterly* 82, no. 1 (Spring 2005): 110–130.

7. The popularity of high-quality series on basic cable networks, such as AMC and FX, is a more recent phenomenon that deserves critical attention of its own. For the purposes of this book, I have lumped together series that appear on basic cable (as *Breaking Bad* does) with those broadcast on premium networks, such as HBO and Showtime.

8. Dana Polan, "Cable Watching: HBO, *The Sopranos*, and Discourses of Distinction," in *Cable Visions: Television Beyond Broadcasting*, ed. Sarah Banet-Weiser, Cynthia Chris, and Anthony Freitas (New York: New York University Press, 2007). For Polan, who is interested in the politics of taste, the capital "Q" in "Quality" emphasizes the aspirational nature of *The Sopranos*, other series following it, and the critics and fans who champion it. In her contribution to *Cable Visions*, Polan rather grumpily posits that HBO has pioneered and cornered the market producing Quality television that appeals to intellectuals, critics, and Emmy voters. Polan identifies the first period of Quality television in the 1950s, with the work of Rod Serling and other writers, directors, and performers who innovated the use of television as a venue for social critique. The anthology *The Sopranos and Philosophy* particularly irritates Polan; interestingly but unsurprisingly, *Breaking Bad and Philosophy* was released following Polan's essay. Richard Greene and Peter Vernezze, eds., *The Sopranos and Philosophy: I Kill Therefore I Am* (Chicago: Open Court, 2004); Robert Arp and David R. Koepsell, eds., *Breaking Bad and Philosophy* (Chicago: Open Court Press, 2012).

9. By turning to *Breaking Bad* as a representative text regarding drugs, crime, and ethnicity in prestige television, I am leapfrogging over one of the most influential televisual texts of the twenty-first century: *The Wire* (HBO, 2002–2008), David Simon's sixty-episode police epic set in Baltimore. *The Wire* explores the systemic failures that lead to drug economies that devastate Black communities and thoughtfully examines the ways that racism both creates and is created by those failures. The series has inspired dozens of academic considerations and a good number of college classes as well, all of which consider the politics of race in the series. David Simon won the respected MacArthur Genius Grant in 2010. But *The Wire* largely tells the story of selling and policing drugs in black-white terms, so it does not work well as an object of study for narcomedia. Even so, I am indebted to the ample scholarship on the series, which helped to spark (and legitimize) academic interest in cable and then streaming TV narratives.

10. Even a series like Lena Dunham's controversial *Girls* (HBO, 2012–2017) owes a debt to *The Sopranos*. Though *Girls* does not deal with crime or criminality as a key theme, it self-consciously plays up its main characters' whiteness. This fact has garnered more than its share of criticism from audiences and media critics, the standing joke being that the series should be called *White Girls*. Dunham stages herself as the show's explicit antihero, another thing she has in common with Tony Soprano.

11. *Weeds*, season 3, episode 3, "The Brick Dance," directed by Lev L. Shapiro, written by Roberto Benabib, aired August 27, 2007.

12. With this said, *The Sopranos* did not shy away from exposing its antihero's racism, such as when Tony harangued his daughter's mixed-race Black boyfriend.

13. *Ozark*, season 1, episode 10, "The Toll," directed by Jason Bateman, written by Chris Mundy, aired July 21, 2017. Darlene, played with gritty conviction by Lisa Emery, is one of several white characters constructed as Ozarks "rednecks" in the series. The Byrd family, white and middle class, encounters their cultural difference alongside the Latino threat. The show's rednecks, however, are positioned as threatening *and* salt-of-the-earth, humble, and proud. In other words, they are complex and contradictory, whereas Latinx characters are foreign and dangerous.

14. *Ozark*, season 2, episode 9, "The Badger," directed by Ben Semanoff, written by Paul Kolsby and Martin Zimmerman, aired August 31, 2018.

15. According to the 2020 US Census, Albuquerque is 49.2 percent Hispanic and 38.3 percent white, making it somewhat egregious that only one recurring non-criminal Latino character is played by a Latino actor over the five seasons of the series.

16. Josh Gajewski, "'Breaking Bad' Crosses into Narcocorrido Territory," *Los Angeles Times*, April 20, 2009. In this brief article, Gajewski points out that Gilligan chose Garza's rewritten corrido, which ends on an ominous note, with Heisenberg facing the all-powerful cartels: "The fury of the cartel / Ain't no one escaped yet / But that homie's dead / He just doesn't know it yet." He opted for Garza's version over one penned by Gilligan himself, which had made Heisenberg victorious in the end. Here is a rare example of a Latino voice taking precedence in the series.

17. Leo R. Chavez, *The Latino Threat: Constructing Immigrants, Citizens, and the Nation* (Stanford, CA: Stanford University Press, 2008), 2.

18. Chavez, *The Latino Threat*, 3.

19. Before Krazy 8's death, we, along with Walt, hear a bit of his biography—that, not unlike Jesse (as we will learn), he is the rebellious son of a disappointed father. This humanizes the character, suggesting again that Gilligan intends to contest the dominant discourses that construct Latinos as inherently criminal. Still, as I argue below, this glimmer of critique is undone by the subsequent treatment in the series of its Latino characters, who become increasingly, even monstrously, dehumanized as the series continues.

20. *Breaking Bad*, season 2, episode 2, "Grilled," directed by Charles Haid, written by George Mastras, aired March 15, 2009.

21. Again, since I am interested in intertextuality between *Breaking Bad* and other crime dramas, it should be noted that Walt and Jesse attempt to poison Tuco's burrito with the ricin that they smuggled into the shack. This is a potential poisoned cannoli in *The Godfather Part III* (1990).

22. In the two films, both of which have been read by media critics as "white savior" narratives, Latino thugs appear only briefly in the story to serve as impediments to the white hero (or, in the case of *Falling Down*, antihero). In contrast, *Breaking Bad* and *Scarface* imbue their Latino thugs with three-dimensional characteristics.

23. Jillian Hernandez, *Aesthetics of Excess: The Art and Politics of Black and Latina Embodiment* (Durham, NC: Duke University Press, 2020), 10.

24. As Hernandez explains, "chonga" refers to working-class young women who embrace a shamelessly brazen, sexually liberated stance and style.

25. At this point in the series, at least five significant Latino characters have been killed, but no non-Latinos have met their ends. This trend will continue through the final season and is notable for a series in which the main (white) character is diagnosed with terminal cancer in the pilot. (I consider any character with a name to be a significant one.) While I do not want to reduce Latino signification in *Breaking Bad* to a mere matter of numbers, it is nonetheless telling that Gilligan and his writers are willing to kill off Latino characters while white ones, who also engage in risky behavior in a supremely dangerous industry, survive.

26. The show leaves unexplained why Mexican migrants would be swimming the river in Albuquerque. Perhaps the Río Grande is powerful enough as a symbol of Mexican Americanism that audiences will accept that a crossing in Albuquerque, which lies hundreds of miles north of the border, is logical.

27. It is not an overstatement to refer to *Breaking Bad* as a universe, considering that the series spurred both a successful spinoff, *Better Call Saul*, and a Netflix original film, *El Camino: A Breaking Bad Movie* (2019). The former serves as a prequel and the latter as an epilogue for the series. The *Breaking Bad* universe also includes *Metástasis*, its Colombian adaptation; *Talking Bad*, an aftershow that aired in 2013; and *The Road to El Camino* (2019), a short documentary about the making of the film.

28. *Better Call Saul*, season 1, episode 1, "Uno," directed by Vince Gilligan, written by Vince Gilligan and Peter Gould, aired February 8, 2015.

29. *Better Call Saul*, season 1, episode 2, "Mijo," directed by Michelle MacLaren, written by Peter Gould, aired February 9, 2015.

30. In line with what I have argued about whiteness being at the center of suburban crime dramas is that a key plotline in the first season of *Better Call Saul* features the story of an innocent-seeming white couple, a county treasurer and his sunny wife, who are actually embezzling county funds.

31. In terms of Gus's good citizenship, the show stretches a bit against its audience's disbelief by making Gus, of all things, a donor to the DEA, which puts him face-to-face with Hank on a number of occasions.

32. *Breaking Bad*, season 5, episode 16, "Felina," directed and written by Vince Gilligan, aired September 29, 2013.

33. See, for example, Emily Nussbaum in the *New Yorker*'s blog ("The Closure-Happy *Breaking Bad* Finale," September 30, 2013) and Alessandra Stanley in the *New York Times* ("A Clear Ending to a Mysterious Beginning," September 30, 2013).

34. James Poniewozik, "Review: 'El Camino,' a 'Breaking Bad' Sequel, Is Suspenseful and Superfluous," *New York Times*, October 11, 2019.

35. Quoted in Jonathan Gray and Amanda Lotz, *Television Studies* (Cambridge UK: Polity Press, 2019), 150.

CHAPTER 6. BAD HOMBRES

1. Janell Ross, "From Mexican Rapists to Bad Hombres: The Trump Campaign in Two Moments," *Washington Post*, October 20, 2016.

2. The US-Canada border has inspired only a few such depictions, such as *Frozen*

River (2008), in which a white woman partners with a native woman to smuggle people across the border in northern New York. Putting a white woman at the center of the text echoes many of the narratives examined throughout this chapter and elsewhere in this book. For the sake of clarity, I use the word "border" in the pages that follow to refer specifically to the US-Mexico border, with the caveat that it is not the only border that shapes North American identities and cultures. Brégent-Heald addresses the US-Canadian border in her article, referenced in this chapter. Dominique Brégent-Heald, "Dark Limbo: *Film Noir* and the North American Borders," *Journal of American Culture* 29, no. 2 (June 2006): 125–138.

3. See Mark Edberg, *El Traficante: Narcocorridos and the Construction of a Cultural Persona on the U.S.-Mexico Border* (Austin: University of Texas Press, 2004); Díaz Santana, *Historia de la música norteña Mexicana: Desdes los grupos precursors al auge del narcocorrido* (Mexico City: Valdés Editores, 2015); Elijah Wald, *Narcocorrido: A Journey into the Music of Guns, Drugs, and Guerrillas* (New York: Rayo, 2001), among others. The documentary *Narco Cultura* (2013) also provides an interesting entry point for thinking about the form and significance of the *narcocorrido*.

4. Ryan Rashotte, *Narco Cinema: Sex, Drugs, and Banda Music in Mexico's B-Filmography* (New York: Palgrave Macmillan, 2015), 1.

5. See Deborah L. Jaramillo, "Narcocorridos and Newbie Drug Dealers: The Changing Image of the Mexican Narco on US Television," *Ethnic and Racial Studies* 37 no. 9 (2014): 1587–1604.

6. Camilla Fojas, *Border Bandits: Hollywood on the Southern Frontier* (Austin: University of Texas, 2008), 2.

7. An even earlier movie with "greaser" in the title is D. W. Griffith's *The Greaser's Gauntlet* (1908). The fact that Griffith intended the greaser to be a sympathetic character speaks to the mainstream prevalence of the term. For further reading on the image of American Indians in film history, see Philip Joseph Deloria, *Playing Indian* (New Haven, CT: Yale University Press, 2008) and the documentary *Reel Injun: On the Trail of the Hollywood Indian*, directed by Neil Diamond, Catherine Bainbridge, and Jeremiah Hayes (2010).

8. On the history and meaning of the bandit, see Valdivia, *Latina/os and the Media*, 85–92.

9. Monica Muñoz Martinez, *The Injustice Never Leaves You: Anti-Mexican Violence in Texas* (Cambridge, MA: Harvard University Press, 2018).

10. See especially Ramirez Berg, *Latino Images in Film*.

11. On the Bracero Program, see Mireya Loza's *Defiant Braceros: How Migrant Workers Fought for Racial, Sexual, and Political Freedom* (Chapel Hill: University of North Carolina Press, 2016); Deborah Cohen's *Braceros: Migrant Citizens and Transnational Subjects in the Postwar United States and Mexico* (Chapel Hill: University of North Carolina Press, 2011); and Nicole M. Guidotti-Hernández's *Archiving Mexican Masculinities in Diaspora* (Durham, NC: Duke University Press, 2021).

12. Brégent-Heald, "Dark Limbo," 126.

13. Howard Thompson, "Screen: *Touch of Evil*; Orson Welles Is Triple Threat in Thriller," May 22, 1958.

14. The religious symbolism of naming the family members María, José, and Chucho (a nickname for Jesús) is not exactly subtle, but it underscores Nava's attempt to construct the family as archetypically Mexican American, a sort of Chicanx ur-family.

15. See, if you must, *Borderland* (2007) and *On the Border* (1998).

16. Mary Beltrán, *Latino TV: A History* (New York: NYU Press, 2021).

17. Reece Jones, "Border Wars: Narratives and Images of the US-Mexico Border on TV," in *Placing the Border in Everyday Life*, ed. Reece Jones and Corey Johnson (London: Routledge, 2014), 188.

18. The DEA has compiled highlights of its history from 1973 to the present in memo form. They can be accessed here: https://www.dea.gov/history.

19. Alex M. Saragoza, "The Border in American and Mexican Cinema," *Aztlan: A Journal of Chicano Studies* 21, nos. 1–2 (1992): 159.

20. Fojas, *Border Bandits*, chapter 3.

21. This speech is identical in the script and the completed film.

22. Robert finally finds Caroline a few scenes later by following Seth back to the hotel that had been their base in the inner city. He has to chase away a john, since Caroline is now prostituting herself. He weeps over her barely conscious body.

23. Anthony Quinn won in 1953 for *Viva Zapata!* and in 1957 for *Lust for Life*. At the time of del Toro's win, only José Ferrer had ever won for best actor and no Latina had ever won in the best actress category. Ferrer's son Miguel plays Eduardo Ruiz in *Traffic*. Del Toro has been playing parts in narcomedia since 1990, when he appeared in *Drug Wars: The Camarena Story*, a TV movie detailing the death of DEA agent Kiki Camarena (who is also the subject of *Narcos: Mexico*). The fact that, in the years following his Oscar win, del Toro has had to settle for parts in inferior narcomedia texts speaks to Hollywood's inability to provide roles that match Latino actors' talents.

24. *Weeds* predates *Breaking Bad* by three years, but receives very little credit from critics for creating the suburban crime template that the later show and others would follow. Emily Nussbaum has argued that woman-created and woman-centered series have garnered much less praise for creating the prestige television movement than those created by men. Nussbaum has suggested, for example, that *Sex and the City* (created by a man but focused on women and based on a book written by Candace Bushnell) is more of a point of origin for prestige television than *The Sopranos* but that critics and television scholars have often dismissed it as fluff and focused instead on the gravitas and cinematic qualities of the mob drama.

25. Emily Nussbaum, "Riot Girl," *New Yorker* (September 4, 2017): 38.

26. The centrality of Piper, the white protagonist of *Orange Is the New Black*, was the subject of harsh criticism from some audience members and critics when the show premiered. As the show continued past its first couple of seasons and it became clear that Piper's story was just one of many explored in *Orange*, the show—and reactions to it—grew more complex. See Joy Press, *Stealing the Show: How Women Are Revolutionizing Television* (New York: Simon and Schuster, 2018), chapter 8.

27. Heylia reappears for a four-episode arc in season seven and Conrad appears in one season eight episode.

28. *Weeds*, season 4, episode 5, "No Man is Pudding," directed by Craig Zisk, written by Rolin Jones, aired July 4, 2008.

29. *Weeds*, season 4, episode 11, "Head Cheese," directed by Craig Zisk, written by Roberto Benabib, Rolin Jones, and Matthew Salsberg, aired August 25, 2008. Obviously, there is much more that could be written about this plotline and the racial logics of the border, but since it doesn't involve the drug trade, I mention it only briefly here.

30. Neil MacFarquhar, "What's a Soccer Mom, Anyway?," *New York Times*, October 20, 1996. For a scholarly perspective, see Lisa Swanson's ethnographic work in

"Complicating the 'Soccer Mom': The Cultural Politics of Forming Class-Based Identity, Distinction, and Necessity," *Research Quarterly for Exercise and Sport* 80, no. 2 (June 2009): 345–354.

31. *Weeds*, season 4, episode 8, "I Am the Table," directed by Adam Bernstein, written by David Holstein and Brendan Kelly, aired August 4, 2008.

32. The third season of *Good Girls*, a network suburban crime drama, features a similar storyline, with suburban mom Beth faking a pregnancy in an attempt to convince Latino kingpin Rio not to kill her. In both cases, the racial-ethnic formula is the same: A white woman who has already had sex with a Latino kingpin must weaponize her reproductivity to stay alive.

33. *Weeds*, season 5, episode 2, "Machetes Up Top," directed by Michael Pressman, written by Victoria Morrow, aired June 15, 2009.

34. Press, *Stealing the Show*, 235–236.

CHAPTER 7. FROM PUBLIC ENEMY TO GLOBAL MEDIA COMMODITY

1. Escobar, *Pablo Escobar, My Father*, 81.
2. Cepeda, "A Cartel Built for Love," 46.
3. Rincón, et al., "Reimagining US Colombianidades," 308.
4. Aldona Bialowas Pobutsky, "Going Down Narco Memory Lane: Pablo Escobar in the Visual Media," in *Territories of Conflict: Traversing Colombia Through Cultural Studies*, ed. Andrea Fanta Castro, Alejandro Herrero-Olaizola, and Chloe Rutter-Jensen, (Rochester: University of Rochester Press, 2017), 287.
5. Bagley, "Colombia and the War on Drugs," 70.
6. The episode is part of the Drug Enforcement Agency collection at the National Archives under the title "The Cocaine Cartel" and is accessible through the following URL: https://catalog.archives.gov/id/37978.
7. Corry, "TV Weekend; Cocaine in Colombia."
8. "The Future of the Andean War on Drugs."
9. *La Niña* aired on Caracol from April 26 to September 16, 2016.
10. Jim Wyss, "Colombia's Escobar Resurrected in New Telenovela," *Miami Herald*, June 10, 2012.
11. A good example of the transferability of texts from Colombian to US popular culture is the fact that Netflix eventually picked up *El Patrón del Mal* and packaged it as original programming.
12. Roberto Escobar and David Fisher, *The Accountant's Story; Inside the Violent World of the Medellín Cartel* (New York: Grand Central Publishing, 2009), vii.
13. Doug Miro, personal interview with Jason Ruiz, April 19, 2017.
14. Miro, personal interview with Jason Ruiz, April 19, 2017.
15. Miro is credited as a co-writer of the episode. The other writers are Chris Broncato and Carlo Bernard.
16. *Narcos*, season 1, episode 3, "The Men of Always," directed by Guillermo Navarro, written by Dana Calvo, Doug Miro, Chris Broncato, and Carlo Bernard, aired August 28, 2015. This is the first of several instances in the first two seasons of the series that Murphy's narration mentions magical realism.
17. *Narcos* credits its main characters with these revelations, but most scholars, as well as other media such as *El Patrón del Mal*, point to the role of the press in exposing

Escobar's cartel connections (see, for example, Bagley, "Colombia and the War on Drugs"). This is another instance of the series taking artistic license and transferring the agency of Colombians to the US DEA agents.

18. In real life, it took months for Escobar to be ousted from Congress. In *Narcos*, the rejection is very quick and instigated by DEA agents Murphy and Peña, who track down the mugshot and provide it to Lara. The idea that the DEA was behind Lara's actions enraged many Colombian viewers and critics.

19. Emily Nussbaum, "The Great Divide: Norman Lear, Archie Bunker, and the Rise of the Bad Fan," *New Yorker*, March 31, 2014.

20. Wyss, "Colombia's Escobar"; other sources place the total number of people killed directly or indirectly by Escobar much higher.

21. The version of *El Patrón del Mal* distributed internationally was condensed to seventy-four episodes.

22. Eric Hobsbawm, *Bandits* (New York: Pantheon Books, 1991), 20.

23. Mark Bowden, personal interview with Jason Ruiz, August 1, 2019.

24. For some reason, *Narcos* uses the real headline from *Semana* but places it on the cover of *El Espectador*, which is a real newspaper in Bogotá, considered to be the newspaper of record for Colombia. This is curious because the headline became infamous as Escobar's criminal misdeeds became undeniable even to apologists in the media. Editors of *Semana* have apologized and revisited the headline and its implications several times over the years.

25. *Fargo*, season 4, episode 5, "The Birthplace of Civilization," directed by Dana Gonzales, written by Noah Hawley and Francesca Sloane, aired October 18, 2020.

26. Late in season two, the series again delves into Pablo's motivations, but does so through plot rather than through voice-over narration. In a total departure from historical events, as his endgame nears its conclusion, Pablo and one of his closest *sicarios* hide out at Pablo's father's farm, where it becomes clear that Pablo remains a disappointment to his father despite his successes in his criminal enterprises.

27. Bowden, personal interview with Jason Ruiz, August 1, 2019.

28. The third season of the series, focused on the Cali Cartel, is narrated by Pedro Pascal as Mexican American DEA agent Javier Peña. Although this shift in perspective compellingly diversifies the narrative voice, *Narcos*' point of view remains US-centric and police-centric.

29. There is much more to be written about magical realism as part of mythologizing Escobar. The editors of a recent special issue of *Latino Studies*, "US Colombianidades," point out that "the discursive stylings of a heavily commodified magical realism" have been central to selling the Escobar mystique and, by extension, Colombianness. See Rincón, et al., "Reimagining US Colombianidades," 308.

30. Chris Lee, "Why Can't Hollywood Get Enough of Pablo Escobar?" *Vanity Fair*, July 14, 2016.

31. Catalina Ruiz Parra, "Pablo Escobar: From Narco-Terrorist to Marketing Success," *Miami Herald*, September 26, 2017.

32. Preezy Brown, "2 Chainz To Expand Business After Settling With Pablo Escobar's Family," *Vibe*, August 15, 2022.

33. *El Espectador*, July 29, 2016. (Translation mine.)

34. "Resultados para el turismo para el año 2018," Ministerio de Comercio, Industria y Turismo.

35. Cepeda, "A Cartel Built for Love," 42.

36. Naef, "Narco-heritage," 494–495.
37. On *El Patrón del Mal*, he claimed that the series "made comedy out of a tragedy" and that *Narcos* "had no respect for the facts."
38. "Pablo Escobar: A Story to Learn from It!" live Zoom event, hosted by Shaun Atwood, September 13, 2020. I cannot account for the odd syntax of the event's title.
39. See Ruiz Parra, "Pablo Escobar: From Narco-Terrorist to Marketing Success."
40. Spencer Harwood, "Vancouver's New Escobar Restaurant Taking Heat over Perceived Insensitive Name," *National Post*, May 2, 2018.
41. The island is also the subject of *The Legend of Cocaine Island* (2018), one of several Netflix original documentaries focused on Colombian cartels that appeared after 2015 to capitalize on the popularity of *Narcos*. Several true crime podcasts also emerged around this time to satisfy intense interest in cartels and kingpins.
42. Bernard, personal interview with Jason Ruiz, February 15, 2019.
43. https://www.wsj.com/ad/cocainenomics.
44. Pamela Rolfe, "Colombia Calls on Madrid to Remove Enormous 'Narcos' Poster," *Hollywood Reporter*, December 16, 2016.
45. Naef, "'Narco-Heritage,'" 486.

EPILOGUE. "IT'S TIME FOR A WHITE MAN TO LEAVE THE BUILDING"

1. Lynette Rice, "Kurt Sutter Will Step Down from *Mayans M.C.* If Show Goes to Third Season," *Entertainment Weekly*, August 28, 2019, https://ew.com/tv/2019/08/28/kurt-sutter-will-step-down-mayans-mc-third-season/.
2. Elgin James, "How a Former Gang Member Lent Authenticity to 'Mayans M.C.,'" *Variety*, September 4, 2018, https://variety.com/2018/tv/news/mayans-mc-elgin-james-sons-of-anarchy-1202924110/.
3. Julia Hirschfield Davis, "Trump Calls Some Unauthorized Immigrants 'Animals' in Rant," *New York Times*, May 16, 2018. Emphasis mine.
4. *Mayans M.C.*, season 1, episode 7, "Cucaracha/K'uruch," directed by Rachel Goldberg, written by Elgin James, aired October 16, 2018. In one shocking scene, Adelita orders one child to kill another child who has betrayed Los Olvidados by pushing him off a high roof. The scene underscores the fact that, although Adelita and the group are defined by their victimhood, they also hurt people. This intersects with EZ's narrative and helps to illustrate the murky ethics conveyed in the series.
5. Stacy L. Smith, Marc Choueiti, Ariana Case, Katherine Pieper, Hannah Clark, Karla Hernandez, Jacqueline Martinez, Benjamin Lopez, and Mauricio Mota, "Latinos in Film: Erasure on Screen and Behind the Camera Across 1,200 Popular Movies," USC Annenberg Initiative, August 2019, http://assets.uscannenberg.org/docs/aii-study-latinos-in-film-2019.pdf. The report points out that, in these years, Latinos made up more than 18 percent of the US population.
6. Beltrán, *Latino TV*, 194–195.
7. Christina Morales, "End of 'One Day at a Time' Removes One of TV's Few Latino Families," *New York Times*, December 10, 2020.

SELECT FILMOGRAPHY

A Better Life. Dir. Chris Weitz. Summit Entertainment, 2011.
Alias JJ. Caracol Television Series (released in the United States on Netflix as *Surviving Escobar*), 2017.
American Made. Dir. Doug Liman. Universal Pictures, 2017.
Blow. Dir. Ted Demme. New Line, 2001.
Born in East LA. Dir. Cheech Marin. Universal Pictures, 1987.
The Bridge. Developed by Elwood Reid and Meredith Stiehm, based on the *The Bridge* by Måns Mårlind, Hans Rosenfeldt, and Björn Stein. FX Television Series, 2013–2014.
Capone. Dir. Josh Trank. Vertical Entertainment, 2020.
Clear and Present Danger. Dir. Phillip Noyce. Paramount Pictures, 1994.
Cocaine: One Man's Seduction. Dir. Paul Wendkos. NBC Made-for-TV Movie, 1983.
Colombiana. Dir. Olivier Megaton. Stage 6 Films, 2011.
Cruising. Dir. William Friedkin. United Artists, 1980.
Delta Force 2: The Colombian Connection. Dir. Aaron Norris. Metro-Goldwyn-Mayer, 1990.
De Palma. Dirs. Noah Baumbach and Jake Paltrow. Empire Ward Pictures, 2015.
Drug Wars: The Camarena Story. NBC Television Miniseries, 1990.
Drug Wars: The Cocaine Cartel. NBC Television Miniseries, 1990.
El Camino: A Breaking Bad Movie. Dir. Vince Gilligan. Netflix, 2019.
El Norte. Dir. Gregory Nava. Cinecom International/PBS, 1983.
Escobar: El Patrón del Mal. Caracol Television Series, 2012.
Escobar: Paradise Lost. Dir. Andrea Di Stefano. Pathé/Entertainment One, 2014.
Friday. Dir. F. Gary Gray. New Line Cinema, 1995.
The Infiltrator. Dir. Brad Furman. Good Films, 2016.
Jane the Virgin. Developed by Jennie Snyder Urman, based on *Juana La Virgen*, created by Perla Farías. CW Television Series, 2014–2019.
Little Caesar. Dir. Mervyn LeRoy. Warner Brothers Pictures, 1931.
Loving Pablo. Dir. Fernando León de Aranoa. Millennium Films, 2017.
Maria Full of Grace. Dir. Joshua Marston. HBO Films/Fine Line Features, 2004.
Mayans M.C. FX Television Series. 2018 to present.
Miami Vice. NBC Television Series. 1984–1989.
Miami Vice (feature film). Dir. Michael Mann. Universal Pictures, 2006. Unrated Director's Cut referenced in this book.
Mr. & Mrs. Smith. Dir. Doug Liman. Twentieth Century Fox, 2005.
My Family/Mi Familia. Dir. Gregory Nava. New Line Cinema, 1995.
The Mystery of the Leaping Fish. Dirs. John Emerson and Christy Cabanne. Triangle Film Corporation, 1916.
Narco Cultura. Dir. Shaul Schwartz. Ocean Size Pictures, 2013.

Narcos. Netflix Television Series. 2015–2017.
Our Lady of the Assassins. Dir. Barbet Schroeder. Paramount Classics, 2000.
Queen of the South. USA Network Television Series. 2016–2021.
The Road to El Camino: A Breaking Bad Movie. Dir. Vince Gilligan. Netflix, 2019.
Scarface. Dir. Brian De Palma. Universal Pictures, 1983.
Scarface. Dir. Howard Hawks. United Artists, 1932.
Sicario. Dir. Denis Villeneuve. Lion's Gate, 2015.
Sins of My Father. Dir. Nicolas Entel. 2009.
Skyfall. Dir. Sam Mendes. Sony Pictures, 2012.
The Untouchables. Dir. Brian De Palma. Paramount Pictures, 1987.

BIBLIOGRAPHY

Aguirre, Lina Ximena. "Sin Tetas No Hay Paraíso: Normalization of Feminine Body in Drug-traffic World." *Taller de Letras* 48 (2011): 121–128.

Alarcón, Daniel Cooper. *The Aztec Palimpsest: Mexico in the Modern Imagination*. Tucson: University of Arizona Press, 1997.

Albrecht, Michael Mario. *Masculinity in Contemporary Quality Television*. Surry, UK: Ashgate Press, 2015.

Allen, David F., and James F. Jekel. *Crack: The Broken Promise*. New York: St. Martin's Press, 1991.

Almack, John C. *Straight Thinking on Narcotics: Alcohol, Tobacco, Opium, Morphine, Cocaine, and Marihuana*. Mountain View, CA: Pacific Press Publishing Association, 1940.

Amaya, Hector. *Citizenship Excess: Latino/as, Media, and the State*. New York: NYU Press, 2013.

Ames, Christopher. "Restoring the Black Man's Lethal Weapon: Race and Sexuality in Contemporary Cop Films." *Journal of Popular Film and Television* 20, no. 3 (Fall 1992): 52–60.

Andreas, Peter. *Smuggler Nation: How Illicit Trade Made America*. New York: Oxford University Press, 2013.

Aparicio, Frances R. "Jennifer as Selena: Rethinking Latinidad through Popular Culture and Media," *Latino Studies* 1 (2003): 90–105.

Aparicio, Frances R., and Susana Chávez-Silverman, eds. *Tropicalizations: Transcultural Representations of Latinidad*. Hanover, NH: Dartmouth University Press, 1997.

Arp, Robert, and David R. Koepsell, eds. *Breaking Bad and Philosophy*. Chicago: Open Court Press, 2012.

Bagley, Bruce. "Colombia and the War on Drugs." *Foreign Affairs* 67, no. 1 (Fall 1988): 70–92.

Beltrán, Mary. *Latina/o Stars in U.S. Eyes: The Makings and Meanings of Film and TV Stardom*. Urbana: University of Illinois Press, 2009.

Beltrán, Mary. *Latino TV: A History*. New York: NYU Press, 2021.

Benavides, O. Hugo. *Drugs, Thugs, and Divas: Telenovelas and Narco-Dramas in Latin America*. Austin: University of Texas Press, 2008.

Berg, Charles Ramirez. *Latino Images in Film: Stereotypes, Subversion, and Resistance*. Austin: University of Texas Press, 2002.

Bernhardt, Mark. "'I'm in the Empire Business': Markets, Myth, Race, and the Conquest of the American West in *Breaking Bad*." *Journal of Popular Culture* 51, no. 5 (2018): 1256–1278.

Black, Gregory D. *Hollywood Censored: Morality Codes, Catholics, and the Movies*. Cambridge, UK: Cambridge University Press, 1994.

Bogazianos, Dimitri A. *5 Grams: Crack Cocaine, Rap Music, and the War on Drugs*. New York: NYU Press, 2012.

Bowden, Mark. *Killing Pablo: The Hunt for the World's Greatest Outlaw*. New York: Grove Press, 2015 (Reprint Edition, originally published 2001).

Bowden, Mark. Personal interview with the author. August 1, 2019.

Brégent-Heald, Dominique. "Dark Limbo: *Film Noir* and the North American Borders." *Journal of American Culture* 29, no. 2 (June 2006): 125–138.

Cepeda, María Elena. "'A Cartel Built for Love': 'Medellín,' Pablo Escobar, and the Scripts of Global Colombianiada." In *Critical Dialogues in Latinx Studies*, edited by Ana Y. Ramos-Zayas and Mérida M. Rua. New York: NYU Press, 2021.

Cepeda, María Elena, and Dolores Inés Casillas, eds. *The Routledge Companion to Latina/o Media*. New York: Routledge, 2017.

Chavez, Leo R. *The Latino Threat: Constructing Immigrants, Citizens, and the Nation*. Stanford, CA: Stanford University Press, 2008.

Ciafone, Amanda. *Counter-Cola: A Multinational History of the Global Corporation*. Berkeley: University of California Press, 2019.

Cohen, Deborah. *Braceros: Migrant Citizens and Transnational Subjects in the Postwar United States and Mexico*. Chapel Hill: University of North Carolina Press, 2011.

Coyle, Diane. *Sex, Drugs, and Economics*. New York: Texere, 2004.

Davenport-Hines, Richard. *The Pursuit of Oblivion: A Global History of Narcotics 1500–2000*. London: Weidenfeld and Nicholson, 2001.

Dávila, Arlene. *Latinx Art: Artists, Markets, and Politics*. Durham, NC: Duke University Press, 2020.

Decena, Carlos Ulises. *Tacit Subjects: Belonging and Same-Sex Desire Among Dominican Immigrant Men*. Durham, NC: Duke University Press, 2011.

Deloria, Philip Joseph. *Playing Indian*. New Haven: Yale University Press, 1998.

del Río, Esteban. "Authenticity, Appropriation, Articulation: The Cultural Logic of Latinidad." In *The Routledge Companion to Latina/o Media*, edited by María Elena Cepeda and Dolores Inés Casillas. New York: Routledge, 2017.

Díaz-Santana, Luis. *Historia de la música norteña Mexicana: Desdes los grupos precursores al auge del narcocorrido*. Mexico City: Valdés Editores, 2015.

Didion, Joan. *Miami*. New York: Simon and Schuster, 1987 (1998 Vintage International Edition cited here).

Dueñas, Gabriela Polit. *Narrating Narcos: Culiacán and Medellín*. Pittsburgh, PA: University of Pittsburgh Press, 2013.

Duncan, Gustavo. "Una lectura política de Pablo Escobar." *Co-herencia* 10, no. 9 (July–December 2013): 235–262.

Dyer, Richard. *Now You See It: Studies on Lesbian and Gay Film*. London and New York: Routledge, 1990.

Dyer, Richard. *White*. London and New York: Routledge, 1997.

Edberg, Mark Cameron. *El Trafficante: Narcocorridos and the Construction of a Cultural Persona on the U.S.-Mexico Border*. Austin: University of Texas Press, 2004.

Eiss, Paul. "The Narcomedia: A Reader's Guide." *Latin American Perspectives* 41, no. 2 (March 2014): 78–98.

Escobar, Juan Pablo. *Pablo Escobar: My Father*. New York: St. Martin's Press, 2017.

Escobar, Roberto, with David Fisher. *The Accountant's Story: Inside the Violent World of the Medellín Cartel*. New York: Grand Central Publishing, 2009.

Esquivel-Suárez, Fernando. "The Global War on Drugs." *Global South Studies: A Collective Publication with The Global South* 23 (August 23, 2018).

Farber, David, ed. *The War on Drugs: A History*. New York: NYU Press, 2022.
Farzad, Roben. *Hotel Scarface: Where Cocaine Cowboys Partied and Plotted to Control Miami*. New York: Berkeley (Penguin) Press, 2017.
Fernández, Gastón A. "Race, Gender, and Class in the Persistence of the Mariel Stigma Twenty Years after the Exodus from Cuba." *International Migration Review* 41, no. 3 (2007): 602–622.
Flores, Tatiana. "'Latinidad Is Cancelled': Confronting an Anti-Black Construct." *Latin American and Latinx Visual Culture* 3, no. 3 (2021): 58–79.
Fojas, Camilla. *Border Bandits: Hollywood on the Southern Frontier*. Austin: University of Texas Press, 2008.
Fregoso, Rosa Linda. *The Bronze Screen: Chicana and Chicano Film Culture*. Minneapolis: University of Minnesota Press, 1993.
Fregoso, Rosa Linda. *MeXicana Encounters: The Making of Social Identities on the Borderlands*. Berkeley: University of California Press, 2003.
Fuller, Stephanie. *The US-Mexico Border in Cold War Film: Romance, Revolution, and Regulation*. New York: Palgrave Macmillan, 2015.
Gansberg, Alan L. *Little Caesar: A Biography of Edward G. Robinson*. New York: Scarecrow Press, 2004.
García Márquez, Gabriel. *News of a Kidnapping*. Trans. Edith Grossman. New York: Knopf, 1997.
Gitlin, Todd. *Watching Television: A Pantheon Guide to Popular Culture*. New York: Pantheon Books, 1986.
Gray, Herman. *Watching Race: Television and the Struggle for Blackness*, 2nd ed. Minneapolis: University of Minnesota Press, 2004.
Gray, Jonathan, and Amanda Lotz. *Television Studies*. Cambridge UK: Polity Press, 2019.
Gootenberg, Paul. *Andean Cocaine: The Making of a Global Drug*. Chapel Hill: University of North Carolina Press, 2008.
Gootenberg, Paul. "The 'Pre-Colombian' Era of Drug Trafficking in the Americas: Cocaine, 1945–1965." *The Americas* 64, no. 2 (October 2007): 133–176.
Greene, Richard, and Peter Vernezze, eds. *The Sopranos and Philosophy: I Kill Therefore I Am*. Chicago: Open Court, 2004.
Grossberg, Lawrence. "The In-Difference of Television." *Screen* 28, no. 2 (1987): 28–46.
Guidotti-Hernández, Nicole M. *Archiving Mexican Masculinities in Diaspora*. Durham, NC: Duke University Press, 2021.
Guillermoprieto, Alma. "Exit El Patrón." *New Yorker*, October 25, 1993, 72–85.
Gutiérrez, Arcelia. "Situating Representation as a Form of Erasure: #OscarsSoWhite, Black Twitter, and Latinx Twitter," *Television and New Media* 23, no. 1 (2020): 100–118.
Gutiérrez, Elena R. *Fertile Matters: The Politics of Mexican-Origin Women's Reproduction*. Austin: University of Texas Press, 2008.
Hernandez, Jillian. *Aesthetics of Excess: The Art and Politics of Black and Latina Embodiment*. Durham, NC: Duke University Press, 2020.
Herrera, Brian Eugenio. *Latin Numbers: Playing Latino in Twentieth-Century U.S. Popular Performance*. Ann Arbor: University of Michigan Press, 2015.
Hobsbawm, Eric. *Bandits*. New York: Pantheon Books, 1991.
Hoyos, Héctor. *Beyond Bolaño: The Global Latin American Novel*. New York: Columbia University Press, 2015.
Hunt, Stacey. "Twenty-First Century Cyborgs: Cosmetic Surgery and Aesthetic Nationalism in Colombia." *New Political Science* 37, no. 4 (2015): 543–561.

Jacklin, Jillian M. "The Cuban Refugee Criminal: Media Reporting and the Production of a Popular Image." *International Journal of Cuban Studies* 11, no. 1 (2019): 61–83.

Jacobs, Jason, and Steven Peacock, eds. *Television Aesthetics and Style*. London: Bloomsbury, 2013.

Jaramillo, Deborah L. "Narcocorridos and Newbie Drug Dealers: The Changing Image of the Mexican Narco on US Television." *Ethnic and Racial Studies* 37 no. 9 (2014): 1587–1604.

Jones, Reece. "Border Wars: Narratives and Images of the US-Mexico Border on TV." In *Placing the Border in Everyday Life*, edited by Reece Jones and Corey Johnson. Surrey, England: Ashgate Publishing, 2014.

Kael, Pauline. *State of the Art*. New York: Dutton, 1985.

Keesey, Douglas. *Brian De Palma's Split-Screen: A Life in Film*. Oxford: University Press of Mississippi, 2015.

Kellner, Douglas. "Critical Perspectives on Television from the Frankfurt School to Postmodernism." In *A Companion to Television*, 1st ed., edited by Janet Wasko. Malden MA: Blackwell Publishing, 2005, 29–50.

Kellner, Douglas. *Media Culture: Cultural Studies, Identity and Politics Between the Modern and the Postmodern*. London and New York: Routledge, 1995.

Kenney, Michael. *From Pablo to Osama: Trafficking and Terrorist Networks, Government Bureaucracies, and Competitive Adaptation*. University Park: Pennsylvania State University Press, 2007.

Klosterman, Chuck. "Bad Decisions: Why AMC's *Breaking Bad* Beats *Mad Men*, *The Sopranos*, and *The Wire*." *Grantland* (August 2, 2011).

Konnikova, Maria. "Why Do We Admire Mobsters?" *New Yorker*, September 16, 2015.

Lee, Chris. "Why Can't Hollywood Get Enough of Pablo Escobar?" *Vanity Fair*, July 14, 2016.

Lee, Robert G. *Orientals: Asian Americans in Popular Culture*. Philadelphia: Temple University Press, 1999.

León, Juan. "Tropical Overexposure: Miami's 'Sophisticated Tropics' and the Balsero." In *Tropicalizations*, edited by Frances R. Aparicio and Susana Chávez-Silverman. Hanover, NH: Dartmouth University Press, 1997.

List, Chris. "*El Norte*: Ideology and Immigration." *Jump Cut*, no. 34 (March 1989): 27–31.

Lopez, Lori Kido. *Asian American Media Activism: Fighting for Cultural Citizenship*. New York: NYU Press, 2016.

Loza, Mireya. *Defiant Braceros: How Migrant Workers Fought for Racial, Sexual, and Political Freedom*. Chapel Hill: University of North Carolina Press, 2016.

Lyman, Michael D., and Gary W. Potter. *Organized Crime*, 4th ed. New York: Prentice Hall, 2007.

Lyons, James. *Miami Vice*. Wiley-Blackwell Studies in Film and Television. London: Wiley-Blackwell, 2010.

MacQuarrie, Kim. *Life and Death in the Andes: On the Trail of Bandits, Heroes, and Revolutionaries*. New York: Simon and Schuster, 2015.

Manderson, Desmond. "Symbolism and Racism in Drug History and Policy," *Drug and Alcohol Review* 18, no. 2 (June 1999): 179–186.

Manning, Paul, ed. *Drugs and Popular Culture: Drugs, Media and Identity in Contemporary Society*. London: Willan Publishing, 2007.

Marez, Curtis. *Drug Wars: The Political Economy of Narcotics*. Minneapolis: University of Minnesota Press, 2004.

Markert, John. *Hooked in Film: Substance Abuse on the Big Screen.* Plymouth, UK: Scarecrow Press, 2013.

Marshall, Kate. "Atlas of a Concave World: *Game of Thrones* and the Historical Novel." *Critical Quarterly* 57, no. 1 (April 2015): 61–70.

Marshall, P. David. *Celebrity and Power: Fame in Contemporary Culture.* Minneapolis: University of Minnesota Press, 1997.

Martin, Brett. *Difficult Men: Behind the Scenes of a Creative Revolution: From* The Sopranos *and* The Wire *to* Mad Men *and* Breaking Bad. New York: Penguin, 2013.

Martinez, Monica Muñoz. *The Injustice Never Leaves You: Anti-Mexican Violence in Texas.* Cambridge, MA: Harvard University Press, 2018.

Martinez, Ramiro Jr., Amie Nelson, and Matthew Lee. "Revisiting the Scarface Legacy: The Victim/Offender Relationship and Mariel Homicides in Miami." *Hispanic Journal of Behavioral Sciences* 23 (2001): 38–39.

Mastro, Dana E., and Elizabeth Behm-Morawitz. "Latino Representation on Primetime Television." *Journalism and Mass Communication Quarterly* 82.1 (Spring 2005): 110–130.

Mazur, Robert. *The Infiltrator: The True Story of One Man Against the Biggest Drug Cartel in History.* New York: Back Bay Books, 2009.

Miro, Doug. Personal interview with Jason Ruiz. April 19, 2017.

Mittell, Jason. *Complex TV: The Poetics of Contemporary Television Storytelling.* New York: NYU Press, 2015.

Mittell, Jason. "Narrative Complexity in Contemporary American Television." *Velvet Light Trap*, no. 58 (2006): 29–40.

Morales, Natalia, and Santiago La Rotta. *Los Pepes: Desde Pablo Escobar hasta Don Berna, Macaco y Don Mario.* Bogotá, Colombia: Planeta, 2009.

Murphy, Kevin P., Jason Ruiz, and David Serlin, eds. *The Routledge History of American Sexualities.* New York and London: Routledge Press, 2023.

Musto, David F. *The American Disease: Origins of Narcotics Control.* New York: Oxford University Press, 1973.

Naef, Patrick. "'Narco-heritage' and the Touristification of the Drug Lord Pablo Escobar in Medellin, Colombia." *Journal of Anthropological Research* 74 no. 4 (Winter 2018): 485–502.

Noriega, Chon A. *Shot in America: Television, the State, and the Rise of Chicano Cinema.* Minneapolis: University of Minnesota Press, 2000.

Nussbaum, Emily. "Child's Play." *New Yorker,* August 27, 2012.

Nussbaum, Emily. "The Great Divide: Norman Lear, Archie Bunker, and the Rise of the Bad Fan." *New Yorker,* March 31, 2014.

Nussbaum, Emily. *I Like to Watch: Arguing My Way Through the TV Revolution.* New York: Random House, 2019.

Nussbaum, Emily. "Riot Girl." *New Yorker,* September 4, 2017.

Palmer, R. Barton, and Steven M. Sanders, eds. *The Philosophy of Steven Soderbergh.* Lexington: University of Kentucky Press, 2011.

Pardo León, Jesús Antonio. "Aesthetic Transformations: Narco-Culture, the Production of Cultural Values and the Validation of the Narco Phenomenon." *Calle 14* 13, no. 24 (2018): 400–409.

Paredes, Deborah. *Selenidad: Selena, Latinos, and the Performance of Memory.* Durham, NC: Duke University Press, 2009.

Pobutsky, Aldona Bialowas. "Going Down Narco Memory Lane: Pablo Escobar in the

Visual Media." In *Territories of Conflict: Traversing Colombia Through Cultural Studies*, edited by Andrea Fanta Castro, Alejandro Herrero-Olaizola, and Chloe Rutter-Jensen. Rochester, NY: University of Rochester Press, 2017.

Pobutsky, Aldona Bialowas. *Pablo Escobar and Colombian Narcoculture*. Gainesville: University Press of Florida, 2020.

Pobutsky, Aldona Bialowas. "Peddling Pablo: Escobar's Cultural Renaissance." *Hispanic Studies* 96, no. 4 (December 2013): 684–699.

Polan, Dana. "Cable Watching: HBO, *The Sopranos*, and Discourses of Distinction." In *Cable Visions: Television Beyond Broadcasting*, edited by Sarah Banet-Weiser, Cynthia Chris, and Anthony Freitas. New York: New York University Press, 2007.

Portes, Alejandro, and Alex Stepick. *City on the Edge: The Transformation of Miami*. Berkeley: University of California Press, 1993.

Posner, Gerald. *Miami Babylon: Crime, Wealth, and Power—A Dispatch from the Beach*. New York: Simon and Schuster, 2009.

Press, Joy. *Stealing the Show: How Women Are Revolutionizing Television*. New York: Simon and Schuster, 2018.

Ramirez Berg, Charles. *Latino Images in Film: Stereotypes, Subversion, Resistance*. Austin: University of Texas Press, 2002.

Rashotte, Ryan. *Narco Cinema: Sex, Drugs, and Banda Music in Mexico's B-Filmography*. New York: Palgrave Macmillan, 2015.

Reeves, Jimmie L., and Richard Campbell. *Cracked Coverage: Television News, the Anti-Cocaine Crusade, and the Reagan Legacy*. Durham, NC: Duke University Press, 1994.

Rempel, William C. *At the Devil's Table: The Untold Story of the Insider Who Brought Down the Cali Cartel*. New York: Random House, 2011.

Restivo, Angelo. *Breaking Bad and Cinematic Television*. Durham, NC: Duke University Press, 2019.

Riding, Alan. "Cocaine Billionaires; The Men Who Hold Colombia Hostage." *New York Times Magazine*, March 8, 1987.

Rincón, Lina, Johana Londoño, Jennifer Harford Vargas, and María Elena Cepeda. "Reimagining US Colombianidades: Transnational Subjectivities, Cultural Expressions, and Political Contestations." *Latino Studies* 18, no. 3 (2020): 301–325.

Rivera-Servera, Ramón H. *Performing Queer Latinidad: Dance, Sexuality, Politics*. Ann Arbor: University of Michigan Press, 2012.

Rodriguez, Clara. *Latin Looks: Images of Latinas and Latinos in U.S. Media*. Boulder: Westview Press, 1997.

Rojas-Sotelo, Miguel L. "Narcoaesthetics in Colombia, Mexico, and the United States: Death Narco, Narco Nations, Border States, Narcochingadazo?" *Latin American Perspectives* 41, no. 2 (2014): 215–231.

Rose, Gillian. *Visual Methodologies: An Introduction to Researching with Visual Materials*, 3rd ed. London: Sage Publications, 2012.

Rosen, Jonathan D. *The Losing War: Plan Colombia and Beyond*. Albany: SUNY Press, 2014.

Rotella, Sebastian. "*Sicario*'s Dirty War on Mexican Cartels Is Not Yet Reality." *ProPublica*, October 23, 2015.

Ruby, Jay. *Secure the Shadow: Death and Photography in America*. Cambridge: MIT University Press, 1995.

Ruiz, Jason. *Americans in the Treasure House: Travel to Porfirian Mexico and the Cultural Politics of Empire*. Austin: University of Texas Press, 2014.

Ruiz, Jason. "Dark Matters: Vince Gilligan's *Breaking Bad*, Suburban Crime Dramas, and *Latinidad* in the Golden Age of Cable Television." *Aztlán: A Journal of Chicano Studies* 40, no. 1 (Spring 2015): 37–62.

Ruiz, Jason. "Vivencias: Rita Moreno." *Latino Studies* 17, no. 3 (2019): 390–400.

Russo, Vito. *The Celluloid Closet: Homosexuality in the Movies*, revised ed. New York: Harper and Row, 1987.

Rybin, Steven. *Michael Mann: Crime Auteur*. Lanham, MD: Scarecrow Press, 2013.

Sáenz Laverde, Gabriela. "Yury Buenaventura es el autor de la música de El Patrón." *Revista Diners*, June 13, 2012.

Salazar J., Alonso. *La Parábola de Pablo: Auge y Caída de un Gran Capo del Narcotráfico*. Bogotá, Colombia: Planeta, 2001.

Santa Anna, Otto. *Juan in a Hundred: The Representation of Latinos on the Network News*. Austin: University of Texas Press, 2013.

Saragoza, Alex M. "The Border in American and Mexican Cinema." *Aztlan: A Journal of Chicano Studies* 21, nos. 1–2 (1992): 155–190.

Schwartz, Margaret. *Dead Matter: The Meaning of Iconic Corpses*. Minneapolis: University of Minnesota Press, 2015.

Schwichtenberg, Cathy. "Sensual Surfaces and Stylistic Excess: The Pleasure and Politics of *Miami Vice*." *Journal of Communication Inquiry* 10, no. 3 (1986): 45–65.

Shannon, Elaine. "The Cali Cartel: New Kings of Coke." *Time*, July 1, 1991.

Shaw, Deborah. "'You are Alright But . . .': Individual and Collective Representations of Mexicans, Latinos, Anglo-Americans and African-Americans in Steven Soderbergh's *Traffic*." *Quarterly Review of Film and Video* 22 (2005): 211–223.

Silva, Tom. "The Golden Age of Cable." *Huffington Post*, August 6, 2012.

Smith, Stacy L., Marc Choueiti, Ariana Case, Katherine Pieper, Hannah Clark, Karla Hernandez, Jacqueline Martinez, Benjamin Lopez, and Mauricio Mota. "Latinos in Film: Erasure on Screen and Behind the Camera Across 1,200 Popular Movies." USC Annenberg Initiative, August 2019.

Smyth, J. E. "Revisioning Modern American History in the Age of *Scarface*." *Historical Journal of Film, Radio, and Television* (2004): 535–563.

Sontag, Susan. "Notes on Camp." In *Camp: Queer Aesthetics and the Performing Subject: A Reader*, edited by Fabio Cleto. Ann Arbor: University of Michigan Press, 1999.

Spillane, Joseph. "Did Prohibition Work? Reflections on the End of the First Cocaine Experience in the United States, 1910–1945." *Journal of Drug Issues* 28, no. 2 (Spring 1998): 517–538.

Stone, Oliver. *Chasing the Light: Writing, Directing, and Surviving* Platoon, Midnight Express, Scarface, Salvador, *and the Movie Game*. Boston and New York: Houghton Mifflin Harcourt, 2020.

Stone, Oliver. Scarface: *The Movie Scriptbook*. San Diego, CA: IDW Publishing.

Swanson, Lisa. "Complicating the 'Soccer Mom': The Cultural Politics of Forming Class-Based Identity, Distinction, and Necessity." *Research Quarterly for Exercise and Sport* 80 no. 2: 345–354.

This American Life. Episode 469. "Hiding in Plain Sight." July 13, 2012.

Triay, Victor Andres. *Fleeing Castro: Operation Pedro Pan and the Cuban Children's Program*. Gainesville: University Press of Florida, 1998.

Trutnau, John-Paul. *A One Man Show? The Construction and Deconstruction of a Patriarchal Image in the Reagan Era: Reading the Audio-Visual Poetics of* Miami Vice. Bloomington, IN: Trafford Publishing, 2006.

Tucker, Ken. *Scarface Nation: The Ultimate Gangster Movie and How it Changed America.* New York: St. Martin's Griffin, 2008.

United States House of Representatives Joint Hearing Before the Subcommittee on Western Hemisphere Affairs and Task Force on International Narcotics Control of the Committee on Foreign Affairs. *The Future of the Andean War on Drugs After the Escape of Pablo Escobar.* 102nd Congress, July 29, 1992.

Valdivia, Angharad N. *Latina/os and the Media.* Cambridge, UK and Malden, MA: Polity Press, 2010.

Valdivia, Angharad N. "Transnational Media, Hybrid Bodies, and Culture: Borders and the Latina/o Transnation." In *Mapping Latina/o Studies An Interdisciplinary Reader,* edited by Angharad Valdivia and Matthew Garcia. New York: Peter Lang Inc., 2012.

Valencia, Sayak. *Gore Capitalism.* South Pasadena, CA: Semiotext(e), 2018.

Vallejo, Fernando. *La Virgen de los Sicarios.* Bogotá: Alfaguara, 1994.

Vallejo, Fernando. *Our Lady of the Assassins.* London: Serpent's Tail, 2001.

Vallejo, Virginia. *Amando a Pablo, Odiando a Escobar.* Bogotá, Colombia: Giralbo Press, 2007.

Vallejo, Virginia. *Loving Pablo, Hating Escobar.* New York: Vintage, 2018.

Wald, Elijah. *Narcocorrido: A Journey into the Music of Guns, Drugs, and Guerillas.* New York: Rayo, 2001.

Wanat, Matt, and Leonard Engel. *Breaking Down Breaking Bad: Critical Perspectives.* Albuquerque: University of New Mexico Press, 2016.

Williams, Linda. *On the Wire.* Durham, NC: Duke University Press, 2014.

Williams, Linda Ruth. *The Erotic Thriller in Contemporary Cinema.* Bloomington: Indiana University Press, 2005.

Williams, Raymond. *Television: Technology and Cultural Form.* 3rd ed. New York and London: Routledge, 2003.

Wollen, Peter. "Foreign Relations: Welles and *Touch of Evil,*" *Sight and Sound,* October 1, 1996, 6–10.

Yogerst, Chris. "Hughes, Hawks, and Hays: The Monumental Censorship Battle Over *Scarface* (1932)." *Journal of American Culture* 40 (2): 134–144.

Zelizer, Barbie. *About to Die: How News Images Move the Public.* New York: Oxford University Press, 2010.

INDEX

about-to-die photographs, 87
Accountant's Story, The, 178, 188, 191
addiction, 20, 24, 65; depictions of victims of, 161–163, 210n14; in film history, 18–19
After School Specials, 1, 162
African Americans. *See* Black people
Albuquerque, population dynamics of, 225n15
Al Capone (1959), 25
All in the Family, 184
Aloha, 117
Álvarez, J, 190–191, 194
American Dirt, 6–7
American Dream: in depictions of Escobar, 179, 187; and histories of exclusion, 201; in narcomedia, 28, 39, 137; as narrative device and Tony Montana, 28, 39
American Made, 99, 187
Anuel AA, 190
Anzaldúa, Gloria, 159
Avianca flight, 82, 85, 203

Baiz, Andi, 110
Baldwin, Alec, 36
Balvin, J, 190
Bauer, Steven, 69, 114; as Manny, 27–28, 30, 36–37, 40, 42
Bernard, Carlo, 113, 193
Better Call Saul, 113, 115, 137–139, 144
Better Life, A, 154, 166
Blackness, 8, 140, 148, 159–161, 163
Black people: depictions of in narcomedia, 15, 129–130, 160–161, 165, 224n9; and drug vilification, 18–20, 59, 156; and excess, 135; and *latinidad*, 7; in

Miami Vice, 52, 54–56, 59–62, 66–68, 217n34
Blanco, Griselda, 5, 11, 73–74; grave of, 99; in narcomedia, 117–122; origins of, 107–108
Blow, 69, 73, 177, 187
Border Incident, 151–152
Bordertown, 154
Border Wars, 155
Born in East L.A., 154
Bowden, Mark, 6, 81, 91–94, 185–188
Breaking Bad, 6–7, 125–128, 145; "bad fans" and, 184; border depictions in, 151, 158; and Gus Fring's complexity, 139–141; and *latinidad* connection, 48, 113; Latinx criminality and excess in, 58, 132–139, 226n25; queer depictions in, 108, 115–116; *Scarface* influence on, 41–42; suburban crime drama aspect of, 128–131; television run of, 214n5; universe of, 226n27; white centrality in, 64, 141–144, 170
Bregman, Martin, 26, 29–33
Bridge, The, 155, 166
Bright Lights, Big City, 59
Broncho Billy and the Greaser, 127, 135, 149–152, 170
Brown, Georg Stanford, 65
Brown, Olivia, 54, 63–64
brownface, 69–70, 117–118, 152–153
Buenaventura, Yuri, 83
Bush, George H. W., 1, 24

Cagney, James, 25
Cagney & Lacey, 47
Cali, Colombia, 12, 196
Cali Cartel, 80, 105–109, 158, 173

Canadian border, 226n2
Capone, Al, 25, 87, 185
Caracol television network, 82, 177
Caribbean, 16, 21; as setting, 192, 216n30
Carlito's Way, 69
Cartel Crew, 108, 122, 218n58
censorship. *See* Hays Office
Chicago, 25–26, 29, 38, 204
Chico and the Man, 144
chonga, 135, 226n24
Clear and Present Danger, 81
Clinton, Bill, 80
Clinton, Hillary, 147
Closeup, 24, 78, 176
Coca-Cola, 17
cocaine: and antidrug efforts, 65; Griselda Blanco connection to, 107–108; *Cocaine Godmother*, 117–122; Escobar's connection to, 77–81, 87, 175–177; Pacho Herrera connection to, 106, 109; history of, 17–20, 24, 158, 210n6; and Miami legacy, 73; in *Miami Vice*, 69; reportage on, 210n7, 214n3; in *Scarface*, 28, 40, 61; user depictions of, 59, 162–163
Cocaine Cowboys, 5, 65, 74, 108, 119, 121
Cocaine Fiends, The, 18
Cocaine Godmother, 69, 117–122
Cocaine: One Man's Seduction, 20, 59, 162–163
coca plant, 17
Coconut Grove, 23
Collins, LeRoy, 21
Colombia: and Colombians as villains, 33, 36–37, 52–53, 58, 61, 104, 131; and commodification of narcohistory, 191–194; Edificio Mónaco, 173, 197; Escobar's connection to, 77–88; and Escobar's death, 89–95, 107; and grievability, 95–99; narcohistory of through white perspectives, 64; narcomedia production in, 9–10, 108; Plan Colombia, 4, 20, 176; and views on US-made narcomedia, 118, 183; War on Drugs involvement of, 4, 20; and War on Drugs symbolism, 176–179
Corner, The, 163
Cosby Show, The, 54

crack, 1; history of, 19–20; in narcomedia, 40, 42, 159–160
Cranston, Bryan, 102–103, 145, 188
Crash, 157
Crockett, Sonny (character), 47, 49, 52–53, 55–60; in advertisements, 72; white centrism of, 62–65
Cruising, 213n73
Cruz, Raymond, 134, 141
Cuates de Sinaloa, Los, 132, 149
Cubans: and brownface, 37; Cuban Americans and *Scarface*, 30–32, 34–36, 71; as "Good Latinos," 77; as refugees, 22, 26–27

Dade County, Florida, 31, 50
DEA. *See* Drug Enforcement Agency
Deliverance, 57
Delta Force 2: The Colombian Connection, 187
De Palma (2015 documentary), 43
De Palma, Brian, 27, 37–43; and MPAA battle, 29, 34; and *Scarface* shoot challenges, 35–36
Desperate Housewives, 167
Didion, Joan, 20–21
Dora the Explorer, 144
"Dos Gardenias" (Ángel Canales cover), 110
Dos Hombres mezcal, 145
Do the Right Thing, 140
Dressed to Kill, 221n4
Drug Enforcement Agency (DEA), 23, 92, 95, 158, 229n17, 230n18; in *Breaking Bad*, 126, 133–134; in *Cocaine Godmother*, 119; and Escobar's death, 91–95; in *Narcos*, 112, 179, 187; and *Traffic* consultation, 157; in *Weeds*, 166
Drug Wars: The Camarena Story, 228n23

Edificio Mónaco, 107, 173–174, 190, 193–197
El Caballista, 196
El Camino: A Breaking Bad Movie, 141, 143–144, 226n27
El Chapo, 11, 59n58, 73, 115–116
#EndLatinXclusion, 203
Entourage, 189

EscoBar, 190
Escobar, Juan Pablo (Sebastián Marroquín), 75–76, 84, 88–89
Escobar, Pablo, 75–77, 173, 194–197; death of, 80–81; death of in narcomedia, 82–87, 95–99, 109, 178–184; and Edificio Mónaco bombing, 107; on *Forbes* billionaire list, 177; as global commodity, 175–176, 188–194; in law enforcement memoirs, 187; postmortem images of, 87–95; and rags-to-riches narratives, 184–186; rise to power of, 78–79; and tours, 99, 174
Escobar, Roberto, 190
Escobar: Paradise Lost, 9, 95–99

Fabricio, Roberto, 32–33
Facts About Cuban Exiles (FACE), 35
Falcon Crest, 49
Falling Down, 135
Fargo (FX series), 129, 186
Farrell, Colin, 72
Farruko, 190
Ferré, Maurice, 32, 45
Festival of the Flowers, Medellín, 190–191
Florida, 15–17, 145, 216n23; Cuban American political influence in, 77; and *Miami Vice*, 45–46, 48–50, 67, 74; and *Scarface*, 27–30, 32–34; in *Time* magazine, 21–23, 45–46, 65. *See also* Miami
Forbes billionaire list, 79
Foxx, Jamie, 72
Fring, Gus (character), 113–116, 139–141, 143
Frito Bandito (character), 35
Frozen River, 226n2
Fruit of the Drunken Tree, 6
Fuqua, Anthony, 43
Fyre Festival, 192–193

Gaghan, Stephen, 164
gangster genre, 101, 120, 211n32
García Márquez, Gabriel, 70
Gaviria, César, 80, 84–85
Gaviria, Hermilda, 85, 89
Genet, Jean, 104

Gentified, 203
Ghost in the Shell, 117
Gilligan, Vince, 41–42; and latinidad, 127, 132–133, 136, 140, 144
Girls, 225n10
Godfather, The, 35, 41
Goodfellas, 41
Good Girls, 129, 229n32
Grand Theft Auto: Vice City, 71–72
Gran Torino, 135
Gray, Herman, 8
Greaser's Gauntlet, The, 227n7
greaser trope, 127, 135, 149–151
Great Train Robbery, The, 149
Griselda (forthcoming), 117
Guillermoprieto, Alma, 79–80
Gutiérrez, Federico, 190–191
Guzmán, Joaquín. *See* El Chapo

Hacienda Napoles, 19, 197
Haggis, Paul, 157
Haitians, 15, 23
Havana, 62
Hawks, Howard, 25–26, 38
Hayek, Salma, 127, 168
Hays Office, 26, 38
Hecht, Ben, 25, 38
Herrera, Pancho, 11, 105–108, 112–116
Heston, Charlton, 117, 152–153
High Noon, 60
Hill Street Blues, 56, 66–67
hip-hop, 40, 83; influence of Escobar in, 189–190; influence of *Scarface* in, 42–43
Hughes, Howard, 25–26
Hung, 129
Hussein, Saddam, 40

ICE, 170–171
Icesi University, 196
Infiltrator, The, 102–104
Italian Americans, 35, 37, 70, 72; stereotypes and tropes of, 25, 38, 73, 130

Jane the Virgin, 155
Jardines Montesacro cemetery, 76, 99
Jay Z, 42
Johansson, Scarlett, 117–118

244 | Index

Jones-Miller Act, 18
Juarez Cartel, 111, 164
"Just Say No," 1, 66, 201

Kael, Pauline, 37
Kelly, James, 22–23
Khalifa, Wiz, 190, 194
Killing Pablo, 6, 81, 91, 93, 173, 179, 185, 187–188
Kohan, Jenji, 165, 170–171

Lara, Rodrigo, 82, 181, 184, 195
Latin America: audiences in, 177; depiction of in US media, 16, 21; in media studies, 9–10; and narco as signifier, 3; relations of with US, 20, 77–81, 148; terminology about, 8
Latinas, 28, 62, 120, 128, 135, 202
latinidad, 144–145; and Blackness, 148; and brownface, 68–69; and Gus Fring, 140–141; and greaser trope, 127, 135, 149–151; media representations of, 4; and Miami Vice, 48; narcomedia depictions of, 7–9, 12, 167, 199–204; and the performance of excess, 104, 137; on prestige television, 127–128; and queer narratives, 102, 113, 126; and *Scarface*, 36–37, 45, 47; and South Florida, 17; as threat to white body politic, 125, 131–134; and the War on Drugs, 179
Latinization, 15, 49, 144
Latino Threat Narrative, 132, 134–135, 137
Latinx: activism, 35, 203; brownface, 69–70, 117–118, 152–153; domestic worker trope, 168; excess as trope, 40, 49, 104, 127, 131, 135–137, 190, 192; fiery trope, 38; generational trauma as theme, 201–203; greaser trope, 127, 135, 149–151; hypersexuality trope, 120; kingpin trope, 6–7, 104, 200; "Latino Threat Narrative," 132–135, 137; naming conventions, 11; politics of "coming out," 106; queer double-stereotyping, 102; roles and representation on *Miami Vice*, 53–56, 61–64, 67–70; stereotypes in *Breaking Bad*, 58, 132–139, 226n25; studies, 8–9, 36–37, 48, 61, 120, 175, 206; terminology, 8, 11
Law & Order, 49
Leguizamo, John, 59
Lehder, Carlos, 11, 192, 216n30
Leigh, Janet, 152
Less than Zero, 59
Lil Wayne, 189
Little Caesar, 25, 101
Living Undocumented, 156
Lone Star, 155
Lopez, Jennifer, 153
Loving Pablo, 11, 99, 177, 181, 188
Luna, Diego, 43

Mad Men, 128
magical realism, 29, 180–181, 229n16
Maluma, 191
Mann, Michael, 72, 215n11
Mann, Thomas, 104
Manny. See Bauer, Steven
Mariel Boatlift, 26–27, 49
Marielitos, 26–27, 30–32, 35–37
marijuana, 19, 129–130, 165–167, 187, 190
Marin, Cheech, 154
Mastrantonio, Mary Elizabeth, 38
Mayans M.C., 199–203
Mazur, Robert, 102–104
McDuffie, Arthur, 50
Medellín, Colombia: coverage of, 24, 176; and Escobar, 78–80; in literature, 6; narco history of, 173, 184–185, 188, 190, 191–194; in narcomedia, 84, 104–107, 118, 120, 180; narco-tourism in, 98–99; Olivos neighborhood in, 75
Medellín Cartel, 86, 97, 109, 173
Miami: Beach, 23, 33, 54; and crisis narratives, 19–24, 55; and *Miami Vice*, 45, 47, 49, 54, 71; *Scarface* shooting in, 24, 26–27, 29–34; War on Drugs in, 5, 15
Miami Herald, 31–34, 55, 188, 212n39
Miami Vice, 45, 47, 49–52; "The Afternoon Plane" episode, 59–62; and border narratives, 148; Colombians as villains in, 61; Latinx representations in, 61–64, 68–70; legacy of, 71–74;

Miami depicted in, 54; as object of study, 48; queer characters in, 102; white-centered narratives in, 54–60, 66–68
Migos, 189
Mi Hermano Pablo, 178–180
Minaj, Nicki, 135
Minutemen, 156
Miro, Doug, 113, 179
Miss Bala, 154
Mob Wives, 72–74
Moncada, Dolly, 109
Montana, Tony (character), 28, 36; death of, 38; influence of, 40–43, 77, 135; as Marielito, 26–27; in 1932 version of *Scarface*, 25; Pacino as, 37
Montoya Cartel, 222n21
Moreno, Rita, 218n51
Motion Picture Association of America (MPAA), 29, 213n73
Moura, Wagner, 177, 188–189, 193
MTV, 50
Murphy, Steve: depiction of in *Narcos*, 151, 179–180, 184, 186–187; photograph of Escobar's death by, 91–93
Museo Casa de la Memoria (Memory House Museum), 196
My Family/Mi Familia, 153–154, 163
Mystery of the Leaping Fish, The, 18

NAFTA, 158–159
narco as prefix, 3
narcocorridos, 83, 143, 148–149
narco-heritage, 197
narco mansions, 12, 196–197
narcomedia: Blackness and, 15, 129–130, 160–161, 165; *latinidad* and, 7–9, 12, 167, 199–204; methodologies, 10–11; in the 1980s, 36; queerness in, 101–107; *Scarface* influence on, 6, 39–43; television narratives, 5–7; and the War on Drugs, 47–48, 67; whiteness and, 57, 187–188
Narcos, 7–10; and Escobar, 179–184; Escobar death in, 82–89; and mythologizing narcohistory, 186; narrative perspective of, 187–188; queer revenge narratives in, 108–112; role of

in spreading global Escobar imagery, 188–190, 193; *Scarface* references in, 41; source material for, 93
narco tours, 99, 173, 199
Nas, 189
Nash Bridges, 65
National Institute on Drug Abuse (NIDA), 67
Nava, Gregory, 157, 227n14
Nielsen ratings, 49
Niña, La, 177
Norte, El, 153
Nussbaum, Emily, 183–184, 228n24

Odenkirk, Bob, 137
Olmos, Edward James, 54, 56, 62, 64, 201, 217n45
One Day at a Time, 155
On My Block, 203
Operation Pedro Pan, 30
Orange Is the New Black, 165, 170
Overtown, 50, 68
Ozark, 6–7, 14, 225n13

Pablo Escobar: El Patrón del Mal, 9–10, 177; depiction of Escobar death in, 82–87; reaction of Escobar's family to, 191–192; source material for, 219n4
Pacino, Al, 26; brownface and, 37–38, 69; in *Scarface* remake, 71
Parker, Mary Louise, 129, 165, 169
Parque Conmemorativo Inflexión (Inflection Memorial Park), 194–196
Partnership for a Drug-Free America, 1
Paul, Aaron, 114, 143, 145
Peña, Javier, 83–85; as character in *Narcos*, 151, 179; role of in Escobar's death, 91–95
Pepes, Los, 79, 95, 109
Pérez, Demetrio, 30–35
Pfeiffer, Michelle, 28, 41, 49
Piñero, Miguel, 52
Piven, Byrne, 70
Plan Colombia, 4, 20
Playboy, 125
Plemons, Jesse, 142
prestige television, 2, 5, 108, 202; antiheroes and, 184; Latinos and, 128; quality

programming as precursor for, 47; whiteness and, 179; women and, 169, 222nn15–16, 224n9, 228n24
Psycho, 221n4
Public Enemy, The, 25
Puro Blanco clothing line, 73

Quavos, 40
Queen of the South, 7
queerness: and activism against *Cruising*, 34–35; in *Breaking Bad*, 108, 115–116; and Gus Fring's complexity, 139–141; in *Miami Vice*, 63, 221n3; in narcohistory, 105–107; in narcomedia, 101–107; and revenge narratives, 108–123; in villains, victims, and clowns, 101–103, 125n1
Quinn, Anthony, 228n23

Rabe, David, 26
raggaeton, 190–191
rags-to-riches narrative, 185–187
rap. *See* hip-hop
Ray, 72
Reagan, Nancy, 1, 19, 201
reality television, 72–73, 122, 145, 155, 218n63
Reina del Sur, La, 112–114
Reservation Dogs, 203
Reservoir Dogs, 50
Robin Hood, 185
Robinson, Edward G., 101
"Rock Against Drugs," 65
Rolling Stone, 37, 50, 210n7
Romancing the Stone, 61

SALAD. *See* Spanish American League Against Discrimination
Salamanca, Hector (character), 113–116, 134, 137, 139–140
Salamanca, Tuco (character), 134–143
Salazar J., Alonzo, 95
Salcedo, Jorge, 106
Santiago, Saundra, 54–56, 62–64, 71–74
Santos, Juan Manuel, 193
Savages, 58, 127, 154, 160, 168
Scarface (1932), 25–27, 29, 38–39, 179
Scarface (1983): and the American Dream, 180; comparison of with *Miami Vice*, 54, 69, 71; comparison of with other versions, 38–39; and filming controversies in Miami, 30–35, 54; influence of on *Breaking Bad*, 135, 137; Latinx representations in, 36–37, 61; Latinx stereotypes in, 53; violence and, 26
Search Bloc, 75–76, 95; coverage of, 79, 89–90, 92; in narcomedia, 83–87
Semana, 89, 185
Sex and the City, 228n24
Short Eyes, 64
Sicario, 10, 154
Sicario: Day of the Soldado, 154
Simon & Simon, 4
Skyfall, 221
Soderbergh, Steven, 156–158, 160–161
Sons of Anarchy, 199–200
Sopranos, The, 142, 211n32, 222n15, 224n6, 224n8, 225n10, 225n12, 228n24
South Florida Task Force, 24
South Side, 203
Spanish American League Against Discrimination (SALAD), 30, 34
St. Elsewhere, 47
Stoller, Lou, 29
Stone, Emma, 117
Stone, Oliver, 24; and *Savages*, 127, 154; and *Scarface*, 27–29, 35–38, 179
"Streetwise" (song by Don Johnson), 65
suburban crime drama genre, 11, 128–131, 143–144, 165, 226n30
Superstore, 155
Sutter, Kurt, 199, 201

Taylor, Elizabeth, 21
Telemundo, 168
television industry, transnational dimensions of, 9–10
"Tell Me" (song), 47–48
30 Days, 156
Thomas, Philip Michael, 51–52, 54, 71, 214n1, 217n40
Tijuana Cartel, 164, 166
Time magazine, 15–16, 21, 24, 29, 45, 96
"tobacco" filter, 157
Toro, Benicio del, 164

Touch of Evil, 151–153, 164, 170
Traffic (2000), 169, 228n23
Traffik (1989), 156, 161–162
Trail, Armitage (Maurice R. Coons), 25, 38–39
true crime, 6
Trump, Donald, 147, 186, 200
Tubbs, Ricardo (character), 52, 56, 216n33, 217n34; and "The Afternoon Plane" episode, 59–62, 216n29

Untouchables, The, 25

Vallejo, Virginia, 81, 185, 188
VH1, 72, 122
video games, 40, 71–72, 189
Vietnam Veterans' Memorial, 195
Vietnam War, 19
Villa, Pancho, 87, 185, 201
Virgen de los Sicarios, La, 104–105

War on Drugs: 2–3; and the border, 148, 156–159, 164; Colombia and, 20, 77–81; Escobar as symbol of, 175–176; Latinos as villains of, 37, 59, 61, 179; in media coverage, 15; and Miami, 5, 15, 45; in narcomedia, 47–48, 67; in popular culture, 3–5; US history of, 20; and white innocence, 62, 97, 99, 163
Weeds, 165–170
welfare queen stereotype, 67
West, Kanye, 189
whiteness, 8; in Miami Vice, 54–60; in narcomedia narratives, 49, 57, 226n30; in Weeds, 129–130, 159–160, 167, 228n29
white people: centrality of in narcomedia, 11, 49, 56–57, 62, 97, 203, 226n30; and complexity vs. nonwhite stereotypes, 59; innocence of as narcomedia theme, 56–62, 144, 176; and male narrative authority, 120, 187; as victims of drug trade, 20, 59, 79, 162–163, 176, 210n14; and womanhood, 165–170
Wire, The, 2, 5
Wolf, Dick, 215n11

Yerkovich, Anthony, 47, 49

Zeta-Jones, Catherine, 5, 69, 117–121